LINCOLN CHRISTIAN COLLEGE

W9-BVI-018

SOCIOLOGY
AND THE HUMAN IMAGE

David Lyon

INTER-VARSITY PRESS
Leicester, England
Downers Grove, Illinois, USA

Inter-Varsity Press
38 De Montfort Street, Leicester LE1 7GP, England

© David Lyon, 1983

All rights reserved. No part of this publication may be reproduced, stored in a retrieval system, or transmitted, in any form or by any means, electronic, mechanical, photocopying, recording or otherwise, without the prior permission of Inter-Varsity Press.

Quotations from the Bible are from the New International Version, © 1978 by the New York International Bible Society, published in Great Britain by Hodder and Stoughton Ltd.

First published 1983

British Library Cataloguing in Publication Data
Lyon, David
    Sociology and the human image
    1. Sociology, Christian
    I. Title
    261   BT738

UK ISBN 0–85110–709–5
USA ISBN 0-87784-843-2

Set in 10/12 Melior
Photoset in Great Britain by
Parker Typesetting Service, Leicester
Printed in Great Britain by
Richard Clay (The Chaucer Press) Ltd, Bungay, Suffolk

Inter-Varsity Press, England, is the publishing division of the Universities and Colleges Christian Fellowship (formerly the Inter-Varsity Fellowship), a student movement linking Christian Unions in universities and colleges throughout the British Isles, and a member movement of the International Fellowship of Evangelical Students. For information about local and national activities in Great Britain write to UCCF, 38 De Montfort Street, Leicester LE1 7GP.

InterVarsity Press, U.S.A., is the book-publishing division of Inter-Varsity Christian Fellowship, a student movement active on campus at hundreds of universities, colleges and schools of nursing. For information about local and regional activities, write to IVCF, 233 Langdon St, Madison, WI 53703.

Distributed in Canada through InterVarsity Press, 1875 Leslie St, Unit 10, Don Mills, Ontario M3B 2M5, Canada.

To my mother and father,
for their patience and wisdom

gratis

74077

CONTENTS

Note: in order to reduce footnotes to a minimum all references are given in abbreviated form indicating author, year of publication and page number (e.g. Harris 1980: 190). Full details may be found in the Bibliography on pages 209–221.

PREFACE

You may be the exception, of course, but this book is intended for those who already have at least a smattering of sociology. It is a book about issues in sociology, some of which may appear a little baffling to the novice. What makes it different from most other books in this field is that it is written from a Christian perspective. Even among the rare books which comment on the connections between sociology and religion, this one has a relatively novel emphasis. For while I firmly believe that Christian commitment may be illuminated by social science, I also want to show how such faith may throw light on sociology, and thus also on our knowledge of the social world.

In particular the book is aimed at students, teachers and researchers in sociology, who are either keen to develop a Christian perspective, or who are simply curious about the possible links between religion and sociology. But there is also plenty here for others with a more general interest in how society 'works' (especially perhaps our closest kin, the historians). Today, Third World 'liberation theologies' and Western Christian social concern have sparked off renewed quests for social scientific tools suitable for grappling with the complexities of the modern world. A more rarefied sociology/theology dialogue is also gaining momentum, partly via the sociology of religion. I hope that what I say is relevant to all such enterprises.

There are many ways of approaching these themes. I have chosen to look at the 'human image' as a bridge between sociology and Christian commitment. Sociology is one way of uncovering aspects of human life and of helping us all to understand what it means to be human. But ideas about human existence may also be derived from Christian faith. To what extent do these overlap, contradict or have a cross-fertilizing effect? This is the subject of our exploration.

A common objection, which may have occurred to you, or which perhaps you share, is that in a secular society religion is irrelevant to doing social science. God-talk is certainly not common in the halls of Academe! But as we shall see, social scientists are becoming increasingly aware of the deeper meanings and value-loaded bases of their craft. So while Hungarian-born sociologist Karl Mannheim was probably right to describe sociology as the 'most secularized approach to the problems of human life' (Mannheim 1943: 115), the limits of this secularization are more apparent today.

Secularization is also an obstacle to *Christian* reflection in this area. The 'surrender to secularism' bemoaned by Harry Blamires (Blamires 1963) has yet to be reversed. 'Christian minds', characterized by a coherent Christian outlook on the world, are still all too rare. In fact an investigation of 'secularization' is another way into the whole sociology/Christian faith debate. Focusing as it does on religion-and-society relationships, it forms an alternative 'bridging' idea. I hope to follow this book with further writing on the secularization theme.

I must express my debt to several groups and individuals who have helped bring this book to birth. My membership of the London-based 'Ilkley Group of Christians in Sociology' is a significant source of encouragement. My colleagues in the Calvin Center for Christian Scholarship, where I held a fellowship in 1981-2, also gave me some constructive criticisms. They are Clifton Orlebeke, Mary Stewart Van Leeuwen, Mary Vander Goot and Henk Woldring. I am grateful to Calvin College, Grand Rapids, Michigan, for the unique opportunity for research and writing provided by the fellowship. Part of an early draft was produced there (though our primary joint research was on 'reflexivity'). Other friends and colleagues have commented helpfully on part or all of one draft or another: Sue Brown, Lois Chadwick, John Eldridge, Anne Goldthorpe, Doug Kennard, David Moberg, Rodger Rice, Mark Sawyer, Judy Worsnop and especially Howard Davis. Thanks to Joy Hattam for excellent typing, and to Sue, Tim, Abigail and Joshua for always calling me back to the real world, enjoyably.

David Lyon

INTRODUCTION

Today's world is in a state of crisis. Unemployment is seen as a major blight in the West; urban overcrowding and poverty the curse of developing societies. And beyond the war-racked Middle East is the growing sinister threat of nuclear self-destruction on a global level. This is the world created by industrialism, capitalism and 'communism' and by increasingly powerful states of varying political hues. It is also made by people living everyday life in hunger or affluence and fear, in frantic toil or resigned and involuntary inactivity, in a complex web of social relationships based variously on power, love, tradition and necessity.

The urban industrial expansion of the past century has stimulated increasing efforts to understand this modern world; efforts which were begun by the pioneer sociologists of the nineteenth and early twentieth centuries. But if the analyses of those classical sociologists, above all Karl Marx, Max Weber and Emile Durkheim, varied in emphasis and explanation, the sociological situation today is no less riddled with controversy. Although for a time (in the mid-twentieth century) it was assumed that certain social scientific issues had been settled, those halycon days are now well past. It is no exaggeration to say that the most developed means we possess for understanding the modern world – sociology – is itself in disarray, if not crisis.

The causes of this crisis are various (and are not unrelated to the social crisis), but have a lot to do with the breakdown of two important approaches, functionalism and empiricism. Functionalism regards 'society' as a self-maintaining system in which any routine activity functions to 'keep it going'. Functionalism is usually linked with empiricism, which, crudely put, is the view that knowledge is produced by collecting 'facts', sorting them in terms of observed regularities, and interpreting them by some theory. If there was ever a sociological 'consensus', it was around these important but now widely discredited themes. The attack on functionalism and empiricism has come from various quarters, political as well as social scientific, but the net effect has been beneficial. It pushes sociologists back to basics, to question what exactly does constitute a viable sociological explanation of a given phenomenon.

An example: the development debate

A conspicuous and interesting example of this is provided by what has come to be known as 'development'. This term was widely used to describe the experience of post-colonial societies which gained their independence after the Second World War, the so-called 'developing nations', mainly in the Third World. It was supposed that they would wish to abandon their traditions, which were an obstacle to economic development, and thus attempt to achieve a place in the modern world. Sociologists believed that such nations would travel a similar road as the 'advanced' societies such that, once the 'seed' of modernization had been sown, the organism would 'unfold' like a flower. Old kinship, community and religious patterns would be displaced by the characteristic features of modernization; bureaucratic, production-oriented, urban society. The modernization theory of development represents a variation on an old sociological theme, the shift from traditional to industrial society, from *Gemeinschaft* to *Gesellschaft* (community to association), and from religion to secularity. It focuses on internal changes in a given society, and especially on the *functional* relationships between, for example, levels of technology and styles of government, or economic change and literacy.

It became quite clear, however, that such modernization theories are deficient in several respects. When applied to actual nations in Africa, Asia or Latin America, they are simply inadequate to explain the persistence of widespread poverty, and the 'failure' of such societies to achieve growth rates comparable with the 'advanced societies'. Other factors, outside that supposedly self-subsistent system, apparently impinge on its development. A form of neo-colonialism was seen still to be present, exerting a considerable influence on changes in the allegedly independent new nations. A fresh form of analysis began to emerge which stressed the international nature of the world economy seen particularly in the capitalist enterprise, particularly via the huge trans-national corporations. Soon the notion of 'dependency' was introduced to describe not only the continuing influential presence of neo-colonial powers in Third World countries, but to indicate the interlocking relationships between power groups within dependent societies and the international dominant classes.

It comes as little surprise, then, that the main alternative to modernization theory has been Marxism and its derivatives. The neglect of power relations and class struggle is redressed in new versions of Marxist theory, bringing fresh illumination to the position of the Third World nations.

This example is interesting for several reasons. First, it shows the way in which Marxian ideas may be developed in a context quite unforeseen by Marx himself. It is also symptomatic of a more general trend towards Marx-influenced theories in social science, theories which are often replacing the older functionalist ones. Second, it illustrates the way in which time-honoured boundaries between the social sciences are breaking down, especially those between economics, political science and sociology. Social relationships in a Third World – or any – society cannot be understood in an economic or political vacuum. Third, with reference to empiricism, this example demonstrates the crucial significance of *which* concepts and theoretical frameworks are chosen to explain a given social situation. The interpretation of such 'facts' as urban poverty in Third World societies – or even what counts as 'fact' – never depends merely on observation. 'Modernization' theory in part betrays a perspective of Western social science. Dependency theory, on the other hand, regards the economic and political exploits of advanced societies in the Third World as at best a mixed blessing.

The example of dependency versus modernization theory cannot, of course, tell all. It does, however, get us into some of this book's key themes, especially Marxism and 'post-empiricism'. With the demise of functionalism and empiricism, sociology is in a state of flux. Of course some excellent individual studies have recently been produced. But the discipline as a whole is fragmented, uncertain, vague and lacking direction. Nor is there a simple switch from functionalist to Marxist orthodoxy. Neither exists in a pure form, and anyway, some contemporary Marxisms exhibit distinctly functionalist traits. As Richard Fenn notes, to a considerable extent,

> . . . sociology lacks a paradigm for knowing what is central as opposed to what is peripheral, what is superficial as opposed to what is latent, and what is material as opposed to a matter of appearance alone (Fenn 1982: 124).

Students in particular find this frustrating and tend either to abandon the discussion of meta-sociological or even theoretical issues simply to concentrate on some narrowly descriptive analysis, or alternatively to embrace the only position which *does* seem to yield some definite direction; namely Marxism.

A Christian contribution?

So what can Christianity offer here? I argue in the following pages that a Christian perspective, while it can 'solve' none of these problems, far less offer sociological 'certainty', does have potential to yield a sense of direction and priority in research and criteria for helping decide between rival theories. Of course, Christianity encompasses all earthly existence, of which social life is but one aspect. It is above all a way of life in which the unnatural severance of relationship between Creator and creature is healed by the reconciliation provided by Jesus of Nazareth. The eye-opening discovery of all who find life through his death is that Christianity offers, among many other things, a relevant and dynamic world-view which makes sense of reality and motivates appropriate action.

A Christian social perspective provides a coherent outlook with which to approach sociology, one which both takes account of the human social condition as seen through biblical lenses, and also relates this to the central sociological task of interpreting actual social processes such as urbanization and mobility. My aim, therefore, is to demonstrate how Christian commitment, not frequently associated with social scientific practice, can actually make a constructive contribution to that practice, and thus also to the concern with understanding and coping with the crises of our modern world.

Naturally, this may seem to be a presumptuous claim, and I only make it with two important qualifications. One is that Christian commitment cannot make a contribution to sociology without itself being sociologically self-critical. Biblical writers repeatedly alert their readers to the dangers of unwittingly being squeezed into social moulds. So Christians have constantly to be on guard against making mere human tradition equivalent to divine demands, and thus reflecting social context more than scriptural illumination. The second qualification is that Christian commitment is interpreted differently according to time and place. We have no fixed and timeless perspective on the social world. But what we do have is the Bible, and its own principles for interpretation, and to this alone may appeal be made for any coherence and consistency in formulating and developing a Christian perspective. At the same time, the Bible is always interpreted in a social context. This admission in no way diminishes its authority. In short, quite the reverse. I argue that it enhances the relevance and potency of the biblical message.

The social and the sociological crisis has thrown up old questions in a new form, and permitted the discussion of issues which may readily be related to a Christian perspective. Our secular context is a handicap, both because of the doubtful receptivity of the potential audience and because of the atrophying of the Christian mind. But channels of communication are opening up. Sociology has entered a novel and exciting period of change. The time is ripe for the shaping of some authentic alternatives to the confusion and apparent aimlessness of current social science.

Working it out

The plan of the rest of this book is as follows; we begin with the question, why do sociology? In a day when social sciences have a worsening public image it is well to consider the justifications for engaging in the sociological enterprise at all. So we look at some possible motivations, surveying the alternatives and commenting on their strengths and weaknesses. A Christian defence of sociology, I suggest, is that it serves a dual purpose of furthering social understanding related to a concern for justice and welfare. This does not mean, however, that Christians in social science naïvely accept all prevailing orthodoxies. The unhappy result of such naïvety is being hopelessly blown about by every wind of sociological doctrine. So I offer a mode of bringing Christian commitment and social science together, called 'critical integration'. This calls for two-way traffic, in which Christianity benefits from social science and vice versa. It also acknowledges different levels of discussion in relating sociology to humanness. But it is a *critical* integration, in two senses; one, that biblical revelation is accepted as the ultimate criterion, at crucial points, in the formulation of a Christian social perspective; two, that the product of integration is both self- and socially-critical, in an ongoing and open-ended manner.

Chapter two proposes a 'human framework' for social analysis and theory, based on a Christian perspective. It is via this framework that critical integration operates. While the latter has to do with the general mode of bringing social science and Christian commitment together, the former, the human framework, relates more specifically to the disciplinary aims of sociology. The question of humanness has a bearing both on the micro-level issue of *persons* in sociological accounts – does sociology do justice to human uniqueness? – and also on the macro-level issue of *purposes*. Christian commitment entails certain beliefs about justice and welfare, the direction of human history, and so on, which are related to sociological purposes.

The second part of the book surveys pioneer efforts to make a science of society (chapter three) and also the numerous perspectives available today (chapter four), commenting on these in the light of our human framework. This is followed by two chapters which look in a little more depth at two important issues: the role of beliefs and valuing in social science, and the question of 'action' and 'structure'. The first vexed issue is often raised by students worried that their sociology teacher is trying to ram some hot political porridge down their throats. But the issue deserves careful consideration in the light of significant contemporary debate over the whole matter of the impact of beliefs and values in social science. Christian thinking can play a part here.

The second issue, of social action and social structure, is currently in the sociological melting-pot. Some seem to say we are almost forced by strong social forces to act in particular ways. Others stress the opposite, how we may choose the way we live regardless of the supposed effect of social structure. But how are we to explain certain phenomena, like widespread unemployment, or changing family patterns, without some notion of structure? This is also a topic of concern in the Christian community, which is at last becoming more socially sensitive. But 'social structure' tends to be bandied about as a cheerword (or rather, swearword; it is generally assumed to have a malignant effect), without much critical Christian reflection on its meaning.

The perspective which has been developed thus far is little use if it does not speak to the major areas of analysis and theory on which sociological discussions currently centre. So in the third part we take a look at Marxism and feminism. They are, as Philip Abrams said, the two most important interventions in contemporary sociology (Abrams 1981: 8). Each repeats the old challenge to sociology to bring together theory and empirical study of what is really happening 'outside'. Given the above outlook, the thrust of this challenge will not be missed by Christian scholars in social science. But once again the aim is to apply the critical integration approach to these areas and to search for Christian modes of evaluation and research strategy.

Throughout this book the intention is to show how a Christian perspective on social science might be developed. The penultimate chapter is a critical discussion of attempts to make a 'Christian sociology'. I defend them against certain misplaced charges from various quarters, but finally reject the idea mainly because the label is counter-productive. The last chapter briefly spells out what I see as the constructive alternative: critical Christian social thinking in constant dialogue and interaction with contemporary sociology. Often the appropriate Christian response will be acceptance of some study or finding (even if it is then placed mentally in a different overall framework). Sometime, however, radical critique may be required, and perhaps the humble proposal of some alternative explanatory scheme.

15

Throughout, reference is made to concrete examples, without which any social perspective is arid and redundant. For the benefit of this effort at re-thinking social science is ultimately practical. Our aim should be no less than to make a contribution to understanding our times. Action without responsible reflection is folly. The last decades of the twentieth century are likely to be extremely volatile. Dreams of post-industrial paradise based on information technology are punctured by nightmares of mass joblessness, discontentment among ethnic minorities and fears of political violence or war. There are times for re-assessing priorities and testing of hopes. Christian commitment must meet the challenge of such days. Part of that responsibility is fulfilled in the development of Christian minds for social science. Marx once complained about the 'utopian socialists'' 'fanatical and superstitious belief in the miraculous effects of their social science' (Marx in McLellan 1977: 245). Christian faith is centred in God, not science. But social science does have a place in relation to faith, and is an entirely proper expression of the highest Christian aspiration: to love and serve God and neighbour.

Part 1

Setting the scene

1

WHY DO SOCIOLOGY?

*There are two kinds of sociologists. One kind is
always buried under computer print-outs,
the other kind writes about dead Germans.*

The popular image of the sociologist differs according to place
and time. In the USA some sociologists tend to be pictured as
Boy Scout type do-gooders, trying to 'help people'. For various
reasons, quite the opposite impression was held in Britain in the
1970s. Sociologists were seen as social parasites, planning the
disruption of stable civilization from revolutionary cells. In
both societies, of course, another popular view was the
sociologist as a head-counter, reducing supposed preferences
for political parties or propensities to post-natal depression to
statistical averages on computer print-outs.

This chapter is about different reasons for doing sociology.
They may or may not be linked with popular images of what
sociology is and what sociologists do. We explore three different
justifications for doing sociology – to integrate, liberate or
demystify society – critically examining them to expose their
strengths and weaknesses from a Christian viewpoint. Inevitably
the question of what sociology is is also raised, and some
pointers are given here. The popular images of the sociological
enterprise may in fact turn out to be quite misleading.

Of course, there are also elements of truth in all these images
(and they, of course, do not exhaust the possibilities!). Much

sociology has been devoted to the study of 'social problems' and used for their amelioration. Early British studies of poverty in the industrial cities of London and York paved the way for a continuing tradition of social surveys, yoked with legal reforms. But some studies of poverty indicate that reformism is inadequate. Michael Harrington's book, *The Other America*, puts it like this: 'To be impoverished is to be an internal alien, to grow up in a culture that is radically different from the one that dominates the society' (Harrington 1962: 23–24). When it is suggested that the dominant culture of a society requires dethroning, it is hardly surprising that some sociologists acquire the agitator-activist label.

These images of what sociologists do also suggest why sociology is done. Some may study sociology with the intention to change society, other perhaps to control it, and yet others simply to make sense of it, to comprehend what is going on. But besides the popular images, one may also look to the uses made of sociology today in order to see why people consider it worth studying.

All sorts of people are required to study sociology, with a view to enhancing their social awareness and ability to deal with specific circumstances in the course of their employment. Nurses, planners, social and community workers, personnel managers, journalists, clergy, teachers and many others are all obliged to have at least a nodding acquaintance with some sociological ideas. Indeed, from time to time work related to one or another of these occupations has generated significant studies and debates within sociology. During the 1960s and 1970s, for example, British sociology of education was virtually all on one track, the relationship between class and educational achievement. It was a prominent political issue. And in the later 1970s and early 80s increasing attention is paid to the struggle for space within cities. This follows the controversial analyses of Manuel Castells and others, which present a Marxist interpretation of urban life. To many planners and community workers it is a convincing alternative to more elderly theories.

But sociologists tend not to operate with conceptions of their task which are narrowly related to occupation. Of course, it is no accident that much sociological work is associated with some occupational area. Research money is more likely to be available for some studies (for example into educational inequality) than others (such as the bias of TV news). But most sociologists would, I believe, be happy with more general justifications for what they are trying to do.

Coping with change

We inhabit a world characterized by increasing complexity and rapidity of change. At least that is how it appears to many people today. Much modern life seems well beyond our comprehension let alone our control. The era of microchips and, more broadly, information technology, is upon us. Profound effects upon personal and public life (such as computer diagnosis of illness and massive and rapid propaganda dissemination) are experienced as things which happen to our society rather than processes we understand. Sociologists attempt to document changes and perhaps to predict the possible outcomes of particular policies or to warn of their consequences.

An illustration would be the so-called race riots in Bristol, Brixton and Liverpool, England, in the early 1980s. Whenever such events occur, the air is immediately thick with explanations, many of which portray the blacks as culpable. Others, less unsympathetic to the ethnic groups involved, blame police provocation. Unfortunately, because right-wing governments tend to pay less attention to social science, little informed sociological comment was made available at the time. But sociologists studying the situation back in the 1970s predicted such happenings on the basis of a much longer-term explanation. An old colonialist paternalism still lurks in policy-making corridors of power. Even with the best will in the world, many British policies sound 'anti-immigrant'. As John Rex wrote, several years before Bristol and Brixton: 'The choice is really between effective political organization on their own behalf and mindless violence and despair' (Rex and Tomlinson 1980: 295).

Most sociologists would subscribe to the view that sociology enables us to understand a little more about complexity and change in society. In the nineteenth century one of the great themes was loss of community. Many believed that industrialization and capitalism had broken up the precious intimacy and long-term nature of traditional social groups. Sociologists such as Ferdinand Tönnies seemed to share Benjamin Disraeli's regret that 'modern society acknowledges no neighbour'.

Today's issues are different. The revival of community is, for some at least, much lower on the sociological agenda (though Christians may wish to keep *some* understanding of community there). But in the last decades of the twentieth century themes such as the place of women in society, and the nature of work are attracting considerable sociological attention. Since the second war a large number of women have entered the labour market. The time-honoured notion that the woman's place is in the home is called in question as never before. Male dominance in law and language, in work and welfare, is exposed and attacked. Sociology is itself contributing to women's consciousness of their 'double-bind' (see chapter eight) and their dependence.

As for work, its definition is also up for grabs. Since the mid-nineteenth century the idea of work as a necessary (and potentially noble) duty has been part of the official outlook of employers. But everyone knew that available work – for most this meant paid employment on terms set by the employer – was not all it was cracked up to be. But work was the road to making a living and ensuring social recognition and worth. In the late 1970s however, opportunities for paid employment began diminishing at an alarming rate. Not only was there a slump, but doomwatchers predicted increased structural unemployment as new technologies replace human brain power in the very sector which had so recently been soaking up displaced workers – the service industries. Thus the major source of livelihood *and* of social acceptance is simultaneously threatened. Who knows what 'work' will mean in the year 2000?

The magnitude and rapidity of such changes as these have profound ramifications. Once we thought we knew what was meant by work. Once we assumed that domestic labour was women's special sphere. Now we are not so sure. This leads us to consider deeper reasons for doing sociology. Sociology may have a technical role in contributing to the breadth of understanding in certain occupations (and we suggested that this is not really a valid justification for doing sociology). But sociology also enables us to stand back and view wider social changes in their historical context. And as we do that, we realize that fundamental matters are at stake. We are really talking about the human condition.

What is sociology?

Before moving to that wider context, however, it is important to note this: by suggesting that the historical emergence of sociology may be seen as an intellectual attempt to cope with rapid social change, we come close to saying what the discipline is. Needless to say this constitutes a huge bone of contention among those who see sociology as having very different disciplinary aims. But if we continue with our example of work and unemployment, we may show what *sociologists* are interested in. For instance, sociologists may be keen to understand the social situation we call 'unemployment', at a given time. Unlike novelists or psychologists, however, we do not only want to document for example what it is like to be unemployed, but to show the relationship between the institutions of the workplace and people's actions on the one hand, and the outcome of that social situation on the other. Unlike economists, who might tend to see things in terms of supply, demand, production and so on, sociologists are concerned with social action in the social context.

Christopher Harris has produced an elegant phrase which sums up this sociological concern not *only* with situations or *only* with action or *only* with institutions, but with change involving all three. I shall lean on this as a working definition: 'The aim of sociology as an intellectual practice is, through the study of social situations, to exhibit the relation between social situations and their outcomes' (Harris 1980: 22). It is because sociology constitutes an attempt to understand a combination of distinguishable items that it is so complex (sometimes unnervingly so!). A mere description of 'the modern nuclear family', for instance, is not sociology. Neither is a collection of individuals' accounts of what life is like for them in their families. Sociology is more than that. As we see in chapter eight, sociologists are concerned to explain why particular forms of family life have developed in industrial societies, and what this means for men, women and children today in terms of their aspirations and anxieties.

This is a problem to which we are obliged to return later. But for the present purposes, I must make it clear that sociology cannot simply be defined in terms of its subject matter, or, as we shall see, a distinctive perspective, or even, as Berger would like, a distinctive method (Berger and Kellner 1981: 16). In fact, as Harris reminds us at the beginning of his book, school children may get some (rather biased!) idea of the subject matter of two disciplines from the saying, 'geography is about maps, history about chaps'; but they would be baffled by sociology. 'Society', as we shall see, raises more problems than it solves as a candidate for sociology's object of study.

Nevertheless, there remains a 'social reality' with which sociology grapples, even if 'society' is rejected as a description of what sociologists study. Certainly it is intangible and complex, but the reality of the social world, and the fact that it requires interpretation, may readily be illustrated. In fact, illustration is made possible because sociologists always begin with the everyday, commonsense understandings of social life upon which we all depend for our social existence. We all know, for example, that the most common meaning of the word 'work' is paid employment. But we would be hard pressed to say *why* work is predominantly understood as paid employment. No one decreed it, and as it happens, many people would, say, on Christian or feminist grounds, question the rightness of such a state of affairs. The definition of work is a *social* phenomenon, and one whose origins and consequences require explanation. And from there we return to where we were a few moments ago: seeing sociology in its wider context.

La condition humaine

When we speak of 'work' or 'woman's place' we address issues of perennial concern. They touch our very humanity. Robert Nisbet sees 1830-1900 as a golden age in sociology. Why? Because then the perceived tension between communal traditional ties and the more modern secular, rationalist and individualist outlook stimulated an unmatched creative burst of sociological thinking. And were those great classical sociologists content to document the growth of cities or the development of capitalism? By no means. They bequeathed to us the terms by which many still perceive the social world today; community, authority, status, the sacred, alienation, class, power, ideology and so on. Such evocative terms enlarge our vision, set the terms for debate and indicate the profoundly human focus of the sociological enterprise.

Sociology does not forget its past. While other sciences may progress without direct reference to Newton or Galileo, sociology frequently returns to its forebears for insight and inspiration. As a British Open University publication puts it: sociology 'is an attempt to grapple in a systematic way with fundamental problems of human social life'. Their list of such problems includes 'individuality, order, tradition, inequality, power and change' (Bocock *et al.* 1980: 7). Of course, politicians and philosophers, novelists and social workers could also be said to grapple with social problems. The systematic work of sociologists, on the other hand, is to try to explain, understand and interpret the social world using concepts and categories which illuminate the actual processes of persistence or change.

Such problems and concepts often have strong links with Christian understandings of the social world. An idea of community is at the heart of Old and New Testament teaching. Practical evidence for it exists in the initial settlement of the previously nomadic Hebrews in Canaan or in the early church in Jerusalem where 'All the believers were together and had everything in common' (Acts 2: 44). This does not mean, however, that 'community' is, or ought to be, a central sociological concept. To qualify as such its appropriateness to sociology's disciplinary aims must be demonstrated. Inequality is another key biblical theme, again engaging the attention of both prophets and apostles. Jesus himself made a searing indictment on the wealthy and luxurious lifestyle which ignored the poor and disadvantaged in the story of the rich man and Lazarus (Luke 16: 19–31). As it happens, all the problems and themes mentioned above do in fact find their counterparts or analogues in a Christian world view rooted in a biblical framework. So two problems invite further discussion. To what extent should Christians accept the sociological agenda, and learn from it? And at which point would people working from a biblical perspective wish to raise priorities or make a conceptual or moral critique of sociological categories and explanations? Such issues are what this book is all about. First, however, we must examine the justifications for doing sociology at all.

Justifying sociological involvement

In a sense, sociology needs no justification. We all do a kind of commonsense social theorizing in everyday life, interpreting events in categories with which we are familiar. When vandalism in the local high street is blamed on 'bad homes' or 'unemployment', then some theoretical link is being made between cause and effect. Such commonsense interpretations are made as routine responses to the world in which God has placed us. He expects us to try to comprehend what is happening around us, and to 'discern the signs of the times'.

Here, then, is a starting point for sociological reflection: the desire to understand our social environment. But this quickly spills over into another kind of justification. We want to understand *in order that* our social practices might be more just or humane. And at this point more than commonsense sociologizing is required. The treatment accorded to our high street vandals, assuming they are caught, may be more or less just according to what sort of theory about their behaviour is proposed. It may well be the case that the 'bad homes' thesis, if believed by those passing sentence, could make things worse for the offender (Walter 1979). A careful sociological interpretation could throw different light on the matter which would mean fairer treatment of offenders. Of course this is a relatively trivial example. Others appear elsewhere in the book which indicate the potential scope of social benefit attending sociological investigation.

Social science has a bad name in the media of western societies in the 1980s. This is partly because in the 1960s some sociologists were excessively sanguine about sociology's problem-solving potential, and made inflated claims for it. It is also because of the real and imagined subversive tendencies of social science. This has sometimes been related to an exaggerated demand for 'relevance' in which 'History itself is devalued and replace by sociology' (Martin 1978a: 67). While the 'bad name' was thus earned, there is also a danger that the sociological baby will gurgle down the drain along with the dirty bathwater.

A vigorous defence of social science is required from those who value democracy in our day. It provides a unique source of information and analysis which is not (directly, at least) government-controlled. Those who do not attack or abandon sociology tend to appropriate it for their own ends. In the Soviet Union, for instance, this is exactly what has happened. Far from being an aid to democracy, it is its enemy. Soviet sociology investigates the felt needs and opinions of the Russian population in order to tighten state control.

In order to consider further the question of justifying sociological involvement, let us consider the kinds of rationale offered by three prominent American sociologists. They are Talcott Parsons, C. Wright Mills and Peter Berger. While all would agree substantially on some aspects of the sociological calling, to do with subject matter, intellectual craft and so on, their reasons for studying sociology are somewhat divergent.

We begin with Talcott Parsons, who spent many years engaged in sophisticated theoretical study at Harvard University. His great aim was to show what holds society together. Sociology, for him, could contribute to its orderly balance by demonstrating the social basis of equilibrium. Unpacking the following (typically worded!) statement shows what I mean:

> An established state of a social system is a process of complementary interaction in which each conforms with the expectations of the other(s) in such a way that the alter's reaction to ego's actions are positive sanctions which seems to reinforce his given need dispositions and thus fulfill his given expectation (Parsons and Shils 1951: 204–5).

From this excerpt one clearly gets the impression of a smoothly running machine or a healthy body. If each person conforms to the expectations of the other, satisfaction can be had all round. What is needed for an integrated society, an established social system, is that values be shared. People may live together with shared values, despite other differences. Although these three do not appear to go well together, Parsons believes that people are variously pleasure-seekers, ordered or ruled, and idealistic. But if they will agree on values, then society can function as an efficient system. So the justification for doing sociology, it seems, is to study the conditions conducive to an orderly society. What Parsons does not emphasize is the way order is achieved and control maintained. Columbia sociologist C. Wright Mills attacked Parsons exactly at this point.

Mills concerned himself with precisely the issue he believed Parsons had fudged. According to him people feel trapped within the very system described in Parsons' heavy jargon. Sociology for Mills has a liberative justification. The 'sociological imagination', as he calls it, enables people to make connections between their individual biographies and history, between self and society. One or two unemployed persons may think of themselves as having personal troubles. The sociologist on the other hand would locate them in a wider context of 'public issues of social structure', in this case caught up in a general collapse of job opportunities. The root problem is not the personal make-up of the unemployed, but is a structural issue. Social forces have created this situation in which the unemployed person is a trapped victim. Thus 'it is now the social scientist's foremost political and intellectual task – for here the two coincide – to make clear the elements of contemporary uneasiness and indifference' (Mills 1959: 20). For Mills, the production of sociological knowledge is a means of stirring the social conscience (on this see Eldridge 1983).

A third example is that of Peter Berger, now at Boston University, whose concern is not so much control or liberation as 'the attempt to understand' and thus to increase others' self-awareness. Intellectual curiosity would seem to be an important justification for him. He would not agree with Mills' comment on the oneness of the political and the intellectual task. As a citizen he has values which relate to sociology's *vocation*, but as a sociologist he claims only one: scientific integrity. Berger's focus is often on the small scale, the everyday life experience of ordinary folk (although he is also well-known for his writing on social transformation in the Third World). As he says, 'things are not what they seem' – and that is worth exploring. An example he uses is of an American lecturer describing to white southerners the racial situation in the Southern states. Not until he compares it with the Indian caste system and its taboos, its economic interests concealed within the system, its effect on economic development and so on, not until then are their eyes opened. Perhaps *we* inhabit a world like this. Is *our* economic position maintained at the expense of blacks? Such questions might be asked, maybe angrily, by the students. Things are not what they seem. The sociologist, according to Berger, should be interested precisely in what is interesting: human social behaviour in all its facets. The more recent Berger does stress that sociology is both method *and* vocation. Scientific objectivity and value-freedom are methodological ideals, but this does not imply the 'stance of a detached, cynical observation of a disintegrating society' (Berger and Kellner 1981: 169). The goal of the sociologist should guide his or her sociological endeavours.

Contradictions and queries

In his popular classic *Invitation to Sociology* Berger saw the goal behind sociological understanding as the nurturing of individual freedom. Sociology may seem to portray us as puppets on strings, manipulated by society. But 'unlike the puppets, we have the possibility of stopping in our movements, looking up and perceiving the machinery by which we have been moved. In this act lies the first step towards freedom' (Berger 1963: 199). But how far is this compatible with a Christian *justification* for involvement in sociology? We need to go beyond Berger.

Parsons, Mills and Berger all raise important questions about the study of sociology. But we must also question them. Why should social integration be the goal of society, and does it not matter how such integration is achieved? Mills' quest for a just society, in which inequality is eradicated and the powerful few lose their grip on the puppet strings, is perhaps more appropriate. But how do we know what justice is? And should we treat all claims of oppression and demands for 'justice' equally? Mills rejects the idea that 'man's chief enemy and danger is his own unruly nature'. No, the enemy 'lies in the unruly forces of contemporary society . . .' (Mills 1959: 20). Berger shies away from such pronouncements, yet still sees 'freedom' as an ultimate goal towards which sociology may contribute. But is freedom itself a Christian goal or an existentialist one? Richard Mouw comments: 'The Christian's goal is not freedom as such, but obedience to the will of the liberating God. Sociological inquiry can also give us the insights necessary for faithful obedience' (Mouw 1981: 12).

The further back the questions are pushed, the more apparent contradictions emerge. Parsons seems to accept the *status quo*; the Bible appears to teach its own non-acceptance (Paul in Romans 12: 2: 'Do not conform any longer to the pattern of this world'). Mills suggests that the sources of injustice are external to the human action in a specific situation; the Bible locates the origins of social conflict in 'desires that battle within you' (James

29

4: 1). (Of course, we must not make the mistake of confusing structural contradiction and inter-personal conflict. But at the same time may we speak of structural contradictions in a manner which entirely ignores biblical teaching on 'internal battles'?) Berger's final justification for his sociological curiosity is the promotion of individual freedom; but Jesus linked freedom with the *truth* ('The truth will set you free . . .' John 8: 32). As we proceed I shall attempt to unravel these real and apparent contradictions and inadequacies from a Christian viewpoint.

Let us return for a moment to the three views of sociology's vocation. They are not dissimilar from the three kinds of interests which Jürgen Habermas argues are incorporated within three kinds of disciplines (Habermas 1971: 308). Parsons' approach is at times rather like what Habermas calls 'empirical-analytic' science, and his interests thus seem rather 'technical'. Parsons is a sort of social engineer, tinkering in the social machinery. Berger's work, secondly, appears to fall within the 'historical-hermeneutic' camp, whose interests are 'practical'. Berger is searching for a social hermeneutic – means of interpretation – to solve puzzles about social relationships. But Mills, thirdly, makes clear his 'emancipatory' interest and his 'critical science' method. Why is all this important? Because it indicates the impossibility of containing what passes as sociology today within one of these categories. And I wish to suggest that Christians may share, to some extent, all *three* interests.

The apparently moderate position of Berger cannot consistently be held by itself. For individual self-awareness and freedom requires appropriate social conditions which are unavailable in unjust and unequal societies. The practical interest leads to the emancipatory. In critical sociology, one stance is to state one's utopian aspirations, and then to see social situations and the desirable direction for change in that light. But this in turn generates a technical interest (if the critical theory be worth anything) in the means of creating the conditions for the practical aim.

This is precisely why I would argue that the primary Christian justification for sociology is to gain social understanding in order to facilitate the establishment of justice with peace. While I wish to distinguish between the roles of analyst and activist, I shall not claim that they can finally be separated. But a pre-liminary task must be to comment on why, from a Christian viewpoint, *any* engagement in sociology is justified. This inevitably begs the question: what is the relationship between salvation and sociology or, more generally, faith and scholarship?

Towards critical integration

As I see it[1] there are four options for Christians approaching sociology, though I suppose that the first does not really qualify as an approach at all: escapism. You avoid the sociological perspective by switching to some other perspective, especially if it is supposedly more 'Christian', like theology. This may defer the encounter. One price of this, however, is ignorance of a viewpoint increasingly significant in the modern world.

The second approach is compartmentalism. Based on a separation of 'sacred' from 'secular' thought it thus violates the basic confession of all Christians that 'Jesus Christ is Lord'. Early believers knew well enough that to make such a confession was to be a political and intellectual deviant in the totalitarian and idolatrous Roman Empire. Either Jesus is Lord or he is not. We have no right to carve up reality, insulating parts we fancifully call 'secular' from the influence of Jesus of Nazareth, our Lord.

This approach also betrays a sociological naïvety. It is enough to remark here that it involves role-splitting. The quest of objectivity may be valid, but if it means that the Bible believed on Sundays is irrelevant to weekday sociology, then this implies an incompatibility between the two roles. University of Wales sociologist David Berry's comment about any sociologist who 'compartmentalizes his roles in the pursuit of detachment' applies no less to the Christian who 'will in the end only succeed in detaching his sociology from the reality of the real world' (Berry 1974: 171).

A third possibility is that sociology along with other social sciences is accepted as a superior world view as a form of consciousness. Historically, this is possibly what has happened

---

[1]In my little book *Christians and Sociology* (Lyon 1975) I described four ways of approaching sociology. While I am unhappy with some things in that book, I still stand by its basic theses, and this is one of them. C. Stephen Evans has since produced a far more elegant and elaborate discussion of some of the issues in *Preserving the Person* (Evans 1977).

in the West, at least among the intelligentsia. Once upon a time people looked to theology as a resource for interpretation of social events and institutions. Nowadays we turn to empirical analytical approaches to social questions instead. The biblical documents are reduced to nothing but a set of historical curiosities. God is seen as nothing but a human projection of a father-figure. Reliable understanding may only be gleaned via the discipline of modern social science, decisively cut loose from any forms of supernaturalism. Church adherence is maintained in the interests of social status and respectability, or for the sake of the family. Only those teachings which survive the debunking scrutiny of so-called science are accepted. But this solution diminishes Christianity's relevance beyond recognition, and usually fails to be self-critical regarding its *own* assumptions and beliefs.

The approach advocated here I call 'critical integration'. By this I mean several things. The other three approaches are decisively rejected on the grounds that this is God's world. Nothing and no one, therefore, may claim immunity from his influence. Approach number one gratuitously discounts the value of sociology; approach three is equally dismissive of Christian faith. I wish to preserve the integrity of both. Approach two allows one to be both Christian and sociologist, but simultaneously denies both the relevance of sociological inquiry to Christian practice and that biblical belief has any bearing on the way sociology is done.

Exactly what is being integrated calls for comment. Sociology, as we shall see in the next chapter, may be thought of as existing on three levels, world-view, institution and intellectual practice. The dialogue, the integration, most evidently takes place on the world-view level. This is where deep but essential questions of the social aspect of humanness may be faced. The institutional contexts in which sociology is practised, which often worry students by their secularity or cynicism, is less in view. For some sociology promulgated in such contexts may not have a *necessary* relationship with those contexts – you don't have to be a Leninist to see the value of neo-colonial dependency theory! But by no means may this level be seen as neutral. The interests and values informing social science at this level still require evaluation. Something similar may be said of the level of intellectual practice. There is common ground on which all may stand to judge the adequacy of a concept of method. There will still be points of divergence. But the choice, say, to discard mathematical models in a study of social consciousness (of class and other divisions) would depend, not on intrinsic criteria, but on criteria relating to the world-view level.

The challenge of sociology to Christian faith may not be side-stepped. Equally, sociology may not be allowed to get away with claims to greater competence than it possesses, or with forms of theorizing which deny aspects of humanity as biblically understood. This is what I mean by 'critical integration'. Sociology and Christian believing are brought together and allowed mutually to enrich each other. But because we are starting from a Christian viewpoint, our fundamental orientation comes from the Bible in which we hear the very voice of our Maker. At the same time our ultimate reference point is not science, or society, or even the Bible. It is not an entity but a person, Jesus Christ himself (whom we come to know through the Bible). Christians have a deep conviction, born of faith and nurtured in the crucible of experience, that in him are 'hidden all the treasures of wisdom and knowledge' (Colossians 2: 3).

I stress this to show that our 'centre' or focal point in the Christian religion is Jesus Christ himself. Christians do not worship the Bible. Our supreme source book is the Bible, sure enough. But Christian commitment is a dynamic relationship with the living God, who communicates with his creatures in these major ways. He speaks generally in nature, with great clarity in Scripture and in a personal manner in Christ himself. Without the Bible we cannot properly understand the meaning of nature or the mission of Jesus Christ. Outside a relationship with Christ it is impossible properly to understand the Bible. And both the natural and the social world, about which we all know a lot, find their true meaning in relation to knowledge of God.

So our integration of Christianity and sociology is critical in that while dialogue is encouraged, social analysis and theory is not an equal partner with scriptural revelation. The former depends upon the latter. But not only is science criticized, so is society. As we shall see, a Christian approach has some resonance with what today is called critical theory. Our critical integration also implies social criticism. Christian faith may not be aligned with the powers-that-be, or used to legitimate the power of those who dominate in the decisions and directions of society today. By the same token, faith should never be aligned with a mere *status quo* sociology which is blind to the unjust or the immoral.

Critical integration is a model for dialogue, which deliberately implies two-way traffic. Christian practice benefits from a sociological imagination, and must sometimes be subjected to a social scientific critique. As we later touch on matters such as race, family and class it should become clear that Christian rethinking is called for in the light of social analysis. The record of the church in these and other areas is certainly not above criticism! With respect to the 'family', for instance, Christians need a sociological imagination to be sure they are not defending the indefensible. The church must be open to the possibility that it has wittingly or (more usually) unwittingly contributed to the development or persistence of biblically unwarranted social patterns.

Christian reasons for doing sociology

If critical integration is accepted as a general means of achieving a working relationship between sociology and Christianity, what is sociology's specific justification? In a nutshell: social understanding for human *shalom*. Spelt out a little more, this means two things: a quest for humanly appropriate tools for analysing society and a harnessing together of social analysis with the goal of justice with peace and the realization of true humanity. Let me stress, however, that this is a *justification* for doing sociology (in line with the directive to 'seek first the kingdom of God and his righteousness') and it requires immediate qualification. Perhaps the clearest way to state this is that we do not expect to see God's kingdom established on earth as an indirect result of our social scientific efforts. Why not? Because the biblical and everyday life evidence indicate the persistence of sin in the world; Christians have a sober assessment of human-social conditions which militate against the dawn of the age of harmony and justice. And yet we are called upon to struggle for the better world, intellectually as in every other way. As the apostle Paul says: 'we demolish arguments and every pretension that sets itself up against the knowledge of God, and we take captive every thought to make it obedient to Christ'

34

(2 Corinthians 10: 5). This includes scientific thought, of which sociology is one discipline.

Attempting to understand the social world is a worthwhile enterprise in its own right. Puritan forebears of modern science believed themselves to be 'thinking God's thought after him'. Something similar may be said about social science and discovering patterns of social relationships. An important difference, however, is that while the biologist may find out about the mind of the Creator, human society bears more obvious signs of having been distorted and disrupted by human disobedience against God. The social scientist is examining a world of divinely given raw materials which is nonetheless to some extent a human construction. Sociologists are unable to discern the Creator's intentions merely from observing social relationships.

Knowing about the social world may be understood as part of the human task of being caretakers of creation as described in the early chapters of Genesis. How can we be good stewards of the earth unless we know what is going on? Take the so-called 'professions' as an example. Professionals – be they doctors, lawyers or whatever – are believed to be highly qualified and moral persons, as befits their social position. But if doctors threaten to strike we are confused. This does not seem to fit the picture. We need to know where modern professions originated, how they maintain their exclusive hold on the right to practise, how they relate to other social institutions such as the education system and so on. Only then will we begin to comprehend the apparent anomaly. Once we see that their traditional means of maintaining their income and social position – having the credentials which effectively *exclude* others from their rank – have lost some efficacy in modern conditions, we start to see why they might resort to tactics normally connected with other social groups. Maybe the doctors have unconsciously made medical knowledge a scarce resource. Putting it in this context helps us see how social understanding is part of proper care and control of creation.

An understanding of the social world underlies many stories in the biblical account of God's people. Such statesmen as Joseph and David, prophets Amos and Micah, apostles Paul and Peter all evidence a grasp of social conditions and relationships in their writings. I have commented elsewhere (Lyon 1980) that the men of Issachar, government aides in the court of King

David, are typical of this. They 'understood the times and knew what Israel should do'. There exists in the present day a pressing need for the church to understand the times in order to act and speak appropriately. There is a sense also in which this extends beyond the church. For if the world is God's and humanity is ultimately answerable to him, then articulating his ways in society at large is part of the Christian task. But how may this be achieved without proper understanding of the process at work in specific societies at specific times?

This simply indicates the need to see the full justification which is to facilitate justice-with-peace and a more human world. This does not mean advocating the abandonment of social analysis in favour of social action. Sociology can be defended, not as a non-aligned discipline, but as a relatively reliable way of finding out. Some talk of 'pure theory' or 'scientific certainty' but I am talking of *quest* for objectivity. The scientific method does not lead to truth, but it does enhance the reliability of sociological findings. We shall enlarge on this in later chapters.

So what of justice-with-peace and humanization? Suffice it to say that God has revealed in the Bible his intention for the world. The Hebrew word *shalom*, meaning all-round well-being of people with God, with each other, with creation, is his desire. It is also the state of affairs he will eventually make a reality: 'Justice will dwell in the desert and righteousness live in the fertile field. The fruit of righteousness will be peace . . .' (Isaiah 32: 16–17). As we shall see, the content of this justice-with-peace may be made most explicit, and it is linked to the other theme: humanization. Berger once issued a humanistic invitation to sociology. But how do we know what it means to be human? Mills fashions sociological tools to make justice. But how ·is justice defined? Parsons seeks harmonious social integration. But who told him the requirements for true human *shalom*?

Moving forward

Let us pause to look back at where we have come from and then get a preview of where we head next. We began by examining popular images of what sociologists do. Some are very occupationally oriented, others relate to head-counting or revolutionary agitation. We suggested that a broader notion of doing sociology is gained from seeing sociologists as people concerned to understand our changing and complex contemporary world. This also yields important clues as to the disciplinary aims of sociology. But sooner or later this throws up more basic human questions. Sociologists in fact struggle with age-old human dilemmas and distresses.

We remarked that three major sociologists saw their task rather differently, either in terms of technical control for integration, emancipatory struggle for justice, or practical perception – demystification – for individual freedom. But this begs future questions which they do not answer. Is there a Christian justification which might help, we asked.

Before answering, we considered four different ways of conceiving the relationships between Christian faith and sociology: escapism, compartmentalism, capitulation and the one I plump for, critical integration. Sociology speaks to Christian commitment and vice versa, but the truth criterion is Christian, deriving from Christ and the Bible. Following this, I offered a Christian justification for doing sociology: social understanding yoked to justice-with-peace and humanization. As we move forward I endeavour to work this out in dialogue with contemporary social analysis and theory. This is not a thoroughgoing alternative vision of society. Rather, it is an attempt to let Christian belief shed light on the complex process of understanding the contemporary transformations of the world entrusted to us.

2
THE HUMAN CONTEXT

. . . presume not God to scan;
The proper study of mankind is man.

Alexander Pope

To explore the character of sociology . . .
requires us to identify its deepest assumptions
about man and society.

Alvin Gouldner

It is one thing to say *why* sociology is a worthwhile discipline, another to say *how* it might be approached. In this chapter I suggest that a 'human framework' is an appropriate way of approaching social science in a Christian manner. Of course this could mean a lot of different things. As British pioneer sociologist L. T. Hobhouse put it in his editorial article for the first issue of *The Sociological Review* in 1908, 'To the sociologist, "nothing that is human is foreign"' (quoted in Abrams 1968: 258).

One thing to avoid is sociology's shadowy side, represented by Auguste Comte's bizarre 'Religion of Humanity', in which humanity itself was the object of devotion. But this is more easily said than done. Comte's worship of humanity was only one expression of the ancient Greek idea which came decisively home in the nineteenth century, that 'man is the measure of all things'. This motif made its mark most profoundly on social thought.

While I wish to stress the importance of a *human* framework for sociology, I believe that Alexander Pope's 'proper study of mankind' is fundamentally mistaken. Nineteenth-century social thinkers took his advice and 'presumed not God to scan'. In so doing, however, they cut themselves loose from the very source of human meaning and purpose. The result is partly seen in the confusions and contradictions of current social science. This is not however to claim that a Christian alternative presents us with a stable standpoint of social certainties! No, the point is that a Christian perspective throws light on human personhood and human purposes, which in turn may be allowed to illuminate social analysis. Why pull the shade down over the light of Christian truth which, given a chance, could make a critical and constructive contribution to our understanding of the modern world?

Human images in sociology

Several perceptive sociological writers have stressed the importance of some human image in sociology. Alan Dawe, for example, writes that

> All sociological work, like all work of thought and imagination, is founded upon and derives its meaning from views of human nature, whether they are stated explicitly or remain implicit (and often unrecognized even by those whose work rests upon them) (Dawe 1978: 369).

Peter Roche de Coppens comes to similar conclusions in his study of *Ideal man in classical sociology* (de Coppens 1976). He argues, with reference to Auguste Comte, Emile Durkheim, Vilfredo Pareto and Max Weber that their concepts of 'ideal man' significantly affected their social theories and methodologies. Embedded in Durkheim's sociology, for example, is a view of how to be fully human. Against the nineteenth-century utilitarians, who said that continuous increase in individual pleasure provided human happiness, Durkheim argued for social restraint. Individual pleasures required socially approved limitation for people truly to be happy. Without such norms, for instance in times of economic crisis, individuals suffer 'anomie' (or normlessness). Durkheim believed that by discovering the essentials of social order one also thereby discovers the conditions appropriate to true humanity.

While sociologists may admit, however, to some relationship between their discipline and a view of humanness (or philosophical anthropology), the latter may simply be assumed (and therefore thought to be unproblematic). Geoffrey Hawthorn's understanding of sociology's history would support this view:

> Even the most deliberately modest works rest upon such assumptions [of what men are and may be], and although they may remain unchallenged for generations, there is nothing . . . to suggest they will always continue to be (Hawthorn 1976: 259).

His point is that sociology rests upon certain *essentially contestable* views of what is human.

The dominant nineteenth-century views of humanness arose from the Enlightenment. They rested on one common assumption, that humans are autonomous agents (that is, people who have no higher law than that which they choose). As Dawe says:

> Divinely ordered, universal situations become man-made, historical situations. Social relationships, institutions and systems became the subject and object of human action. In a word, the Enlightenment postulated the human, as opposed to a divine, construction of the ideal (Dawe 1978: 375).

This view, that humans could and should create their own world, liberated from the shackles of divine authority, lay beneath early sociology. As sociology developed, tensions within this view became increasingly apparent. One such tension, identified again by Dawe, is that between social system and social action. In the social system view, people are the products of society, imprinted with its values and manipulated by its forces. In the social action view, things are the other way round: people are the active creators of society, making it according to their meanings and intentions. We explore this particular tension between action and system, individual and society, in chapter six.

But sociology may manifest its human image in other ways as

well. For example, the hedonistic notion that people do things for what they can get is embedded in 'exchange theories' (often applied in micro-level studies of marriage and family). But a similar idea lurks in macro-level Marxian analyses of social situations which distinguish, roughly speaking, between the have and the have-nots. But is this the only theory of motivation available? No, others also exist which embody different forms of understanding and which may gel with different images of the human.

Theories differ on questions of humanity, and this includes human purpose and valuing. Marxian theory tends to be wedded to a view of the desirable *outcome* of social situations. The infamous American Project Camelot, which investigated the activities of Latin American revolutionary movements, was equally linked with a hoped-for scenario. Needless to say, because the project was sponsored by the Pentagon, its conception of the 'desirable' did not square with that of the revolutionary groups studied. In this and many other ways human images are found in the warp and woof of the sociological weave.

In later chapters we take up the question of sociology and humanness in different ways. As we shall see in chapter four, controversy over images of humanness has contributed to the rise of competing sociological perspectives or schools. A Christian perspective obliges us to evaluate these various positions in the light of a biblical understanding of humanness.

The vexing issue of valuing in social theory is the meat of chapter five. Although what we now know as the social sciences often began life as 'moral sciences', the twentieth century has driven a wedge between 'facts and values' or 'science and belief'. This now forms an obstinate barrier to a proper understanding of social science, although it shows signs of weakening in the later twentieth century. An important task for today is the attempt to re-connect some of the lost threads between humanness – in its ethical dimension – and social science. Another twist to this debate is seen in the chapters on Marxism and feminism, which have helped focus the issue in recent years.

The view taken here is that it is right and proper for sociology to be informed by images of humanness, but that it is also crucially important to examine the *kinds* of images presented. In a moment I shall clarify things by showing that the impact of the human image is felt at different levels. But the view that sociology should be related to some human image has recently been challenged.

Charles Lemert, from the University of Southern Illinois, following French social theorist Michel Foucault, has argued that no view of humanness is necessary to the sociological enterprise. Why not let sociology fall in line with other post-traditional thought? That is, relativity and indeterminacy in physics, the void in modern art, literature and drama left by the decline of representationalism and realism, and in music the silence which John Cage attributes to the death of a composer as the single source of musical texts. Lemert's proposed sociology, based on structuralism and linguistics, leads him to ask

> What evidence is there that when *man* makes himself the moral center that life is more human? What reason is there to believe that when sociology is done *homocentrically* that it is able to account reliably for the increasingly marginal position of human creatures in a technologically and biologically precarious world? (Lemert 1978: 231).

Lemert's stark-sounding questions are not insignificant. Queries like his are likely to be heard more in the future. But this book is committed to another position, that to understand the human social world aright, some human image ought to underlie sociological studies.

Levels of contact

First, let me repeat the distinctions made in chapter one, in order to avoid confusion. Questions about humanness do not immediately seem to relate to sociology as studied in a university context. It is not obvious how 'humanness' is linked with social mobility, the sociology of health and illness, or of informal economies. Sociology may be thought of at three interrelated but distinct levels. First, as a world-view, containing assumptions and presuppositions about society, individuals, change and so on. The dialogue with the intellectual content of a faith-commitment such as Christianity takes place most prominently at this level. Second, sociology is an ongoing social practice or institution involving social analysts, research institutes and university departments. At this level interests and values intrude to motivate and shape the findings produced. It is less easy to winkle out meanings and values at this level, because they are often less clearly articulated. They more usually exist as particles in suspension than as consistent philosophical platforms on which theories and explanations are built.

Third, sociology is an intellectual practice, in which measurement, data and immediate explanation are the major features. Although considerable controversy persists at this level, once particular methodologies have been agreed upon they may be shared by other social scientists operating over a broad area. Nevertheless, at this level too, questions of humanness are still important. After all, as we noted above, what *counts* as data makes a big difference to results obtained. The sociological debate over religion is an example. If religion is only thought of in terms of traditional Christianity, empirical studies will ignore not only the upsurge of new religious movements since the mid-twentieth century, but will also fail to take note of modern devotion to sexuality or family-centredness, which others take to be 'religious' phenomena. This illustrates how questions arising from this third level (of sociology as an intellectual practice) will always relate to prior questions located more properly at the first level mentioned.

Presuppositions embedded in sociology, at whatever level, seldom add up to a coherent philosophical position. So it is foolish to talk about 'secular sociology' as something monolithic. What we mean is sociology shot through with certain values and assumptions which are difficult to harmonize with (or sometimes quite hostile to) a Christian perspective. But one usually also finds much to commend a given piece of social science research. Thus the task frequently turns out to one of sifting and assessing material, of 'testing all things, and holding on to the good'.

Another caveat is in order here. Sociology ought not to be judged as some universal theory of the world (despite the cosmic claims of some notorious social theorists!). Sociology relates to the *social aspect* of humanness. It cannot properly be pursued without reference to the economic and political, or, for that matter, to the historical and geographical. But it is fundamentally concerned with the attempt to explain why some social situation persists or changes. Why factory workers become militant after what seemed to be an advantageous wage settlement. Why democracy is such an elusive ideal in newly industrial societies (or old ones for that matter!). Why women in cities are more depressed than women living in the countryside. These are the kinds of social explanations sought by sociology. This also implies that sociology cannot be content with explanations of an individualistic kind. A Christian perspective on sociology certainly does not attempt to snatch the sociological rug from under our feet by insisting that everything social can be adequately understood by referring to individual intentions and actions. As we shall see, Christian commitment relates to, and gives ground for defending, the reality of the social aspect of humanness.

So sociology may be thought of as existing on different levels. I am concerned to comment on all three, but particularly to show how sociology as an overarching perspective (level one) relates – positively or negatively – to a Christian understanding of humanness. That level, in conjunction with the interests and orientation of the institutional contexts in which sociology is manifest, tends to determine the ways in which the basic level – sociology as intellectual practice – happens.

An example: Chinese sociology

The changing situation in Chinese sociology illustrates this well. Chinese sociology, based largely on British social anthropology and Chicago school sociology, was taught in universities until 1949. But with the revolution such ideas were seen to be incompatible with Marxist-Leninism and sociology was crushed. Efforts to revive sociology met with no success. This was a conflict at the world-view level. In the mid 1970s, however, sociology began to stage a comeback, following the fall of the Gang of Four in 1976.

Marxist-Leninism is now seen as a 'framework' rather than a 'blueprint', so difference of opinion is possible at the world-view level. Strong interests are operating, however, at the institutional level, as Chinese sociology attempts to break free from dependence on western theories and concepts. The problems of modernization – in agriculture, industry, science-and-technology and defence – are paramount. But one of the big questions confronting Chinese sociology today is whether the 'tools' of sociology – the intellectual practice level – can be separated from their 'bourgeois essence'. Does world view determine which concepts and methods are appropriate? As I shall suggest, it often does, but we must refer to specific examples to see how. Which sociological flowers will eventually bloom in China remains to be seen seen. All, however, will relate in one way or another to some view of humanness.

The important thing, as far as we are concerned here, is to explore the *ways* in which sociology and human image are linked. Christopher Harris helpfully phrases his attempt to do justice to the uniqueness of our human capacities and limitations like this:

> Insofar as sociology is concerned with human life, and takes account of that life, ignoring neither its reflective and moral character nor its inherent materiality, sociology is a humanistic discipline (Harris 1980: 190).

But Harris goes on to stress that sociology does not aim to bring its practitioners into living encounters with individuals. This is not the point of sociology. Rather, by analysing social situations, sociology attempts to trace connections between them and their consequences. We shall not forget Harris's comments as we try to suggest how a Christian view helps us to maintain human uniqueness within sociological studies.

Humanness as a key

The above remarks may appear to be beside the point, however, if the biblical importance of humanness has not been appreciated. I have suggested that the question of humanness is a crucial one for sociology. But if it is not also an important element of a Christian outlook, then this proposed ground for dialogue is a mirage. In fact the question of what it is to be human may be seen as an interpretive key at the centre of biblical revelation. It not only opens up the Christian life in a meaningful manner (Barrs and Macaulay 1978), it is also a way of hearing God's voice as he speaks to the whole creation. Thus, as theologian Jim Packer says, we should not spend all our energies attacking humanism. In the sense that we care about humanness, personhood and purposes, Christians are humanists! (Packer 1980).

In considering this more closely, we may refer to what Richard Mouw has called 'the biblical drama' (Mouw 1976). Any social perspective which claims to be consistent with the teachings of Jesus of Nazareth will relate closely to the biblical drama. It consists of four main moments, theologically termed creation, fall, redemption and the future age. The Bible presents a dramatic account of God's relationship with humankind. The drama includes not only the human purposes and directives associated with the creation but also the limitations and distortions of the fall, the emancipation and renewal of redemption and the vision and hope of a new age. For sociological purposes we naturally concentrate on the intellectual and social implications of this biblical drama.

Creation

The first motif in the drama is creation. But to get the picture properly in focus, we must begin with the Creator. The proper study of mankind may not be divorced (as Alexander Pope's lines advocate) from an understanding of God. As Evans puts it:

> Although our human limitations require us, no doubt legitimately, to conceive of a personal God in terms of our familiar experience of finite persons, there is no doubt that an adequate understanding of man [as male and female] proceeds from an understanding of God, rather than vice versa (Evans 1977: 142–3).

Human nature and destiny are not in human hands, but divine: God's creative activity and purposes form the parameters of our spatial-temporal existence. Though the idea grates badly in today's culture, we are utterly dependent creatures, unable to exist without God.

People are creatures, sharing the fact that we are part of nature with the rest of creation. It is important to understand this in relation to a movement like socio-biology. The socio-biological mistake is not that human social behaviour is observed to have similarities with that of animals. Rather the error is to imagine that conceptually human society may be reduced to that level alone. Our creatureliness does, however, limit our activities. We are dust and to dust we shall return (Genesis 3: 19). We are finite, yet with a sense of the infinite; natural, yet able to reflect upon ourselves. This is a tension, compounded by the fall, which is at the base of many other tensions which work themselves out socially.

Human creatures are such because they are 'in the image of God' (Genesis 1: 26ff.). Human personhood and sociality depend upon this idea. If creatureliness indicates that we are unlike God, this notion shows ways in which humans resemble God. In distinction from things, humans act, are agents. That is, we make choices to do things deliberately in terms of purposes about which we are capable of reflection. We are also self-conscious; the reflecting we do includes thinking about our own actions. It would be incongruous to think of God providing people with the 'purpose' of 'filling the earth and subduing it' (Genesis 1: 28) if we could not think of ourselves doing it, and evaluating our attempts!

There is a sense in which sociologists like Alan Dawe are endorsing this active (and, God-like, creative) aspect of humanness when he stresses above all the 'self and socially creative capacities and possibilities of human agency' (Dawe 1978: 414). The dangers of such a stance, however, may be highlighted thus: if we focus entirely on action the future is seen as unconstrained ('the world is our oyster') and we imagine that we may ourselves create the best of all possible worlds. As Harris reminds us, if we forget the limitations of our physical nature (as well as ignoring our societal restraints which are mentioned before) we end with human apotheosis (or deification, Harris 1980: 141).

Which leads immediately to another point. God made humans in such a way that he expected an answer from them regarding their exploits (Genesis 3: 9). Humans are responsible (literally response-ible) as persons within the complexity of social arrangements. Human activity is not autonomous. Rather, we are created to act socially in particular ways. A good illustration of this is in part a negative one, and entails jumping for a moment into the next motif of the biblical drama, the fall, and looking back at creation and the image of God from there.

The story now involves Cain, notorious as the first murderer.

Cain had denied the neighbour and kin relationship existing between him and his brother by murdering him. He insisted, on being questioned, that he was not 'his brother's keeper'. The divine punishment was made to fit the crime. Cain would himself be socially cut off. He became a 'restless wanderer on the earth', the pain of which was more than he could bear. His response was to build a city, presumably in an attempt to mitigate the loneliness of a socially rootless person. God's intention for human life had been quite the opposite. Cain's very mother, Eve, had been provided as a wife for Adam with the authoritative pronouncement that 'it is not good for the man to be alone'.

This is at least an implicit affirmation of the reality of human sociality. Cain could have retorted that because he had not chosen to be in his family that he had no responsibility in that direction. But it was precisely for his response to the involuntary social relationship (which had no doubt shaped his character) that he was called to account. Stephen Evans put it neatly: the person 'is not only constituted by these relationships; he himself constitutes them. He plays a role in continuing them, modifying them for better or worse, enhancing or degrading their quality and character' (Evans 1977: 145). We return to this theme in chapter six.

We may also see that humans are active and social *within* a moral or normative framework. Space forbids adequate treatment of the framework yielded by the Scriptures. Suffice it to say that the framework is exceedingly rich and positive (contrary to popular imagination) and directed to human good (e.g. Deuteronomy 4:1). In the Bible there are guidelines as to how relationships may be fruitfully developed, some institutionally specific and others which are general. 'Neighbour love' is the most general guideline (and is, of course, re-emphasized by Jesus himself, Matthew 22: 39) while *shalom* is the societal and cosmic parallel. The latter includes the thought, not of a soft peace as the absence of hostility, but a strong peace based on 'justice and righteousness'. But it also means the societal 'working together' of persons, institutions and processes as God intended. The fact that Jesus himself referred back to the creation in dealing with social questions (e.g. Matthew 19: 8) underscores the significance of this aspect of the biblical drama.

Dislocation

The fall, as the second motif, does not negate so much as distort and constrict the possibilities of creation. The notion of 'fall' indicates the dislocation of humanity (represented by Adam and Eve) from God, due to their wilful disregard of what he had said and their attempt to put themselves in his place, deciding what was right and wrong. The dimensions of this act were nothing short of cosmic. Among other things, social relationships became discordant and misdirected. It is expressed in Genesis not only in fractured family relationships but in the relationship between man and woman. Once characterized by complementarity and equality of personal worth, the fall brought domination and subservience (Genesis 3: 16). Technological and linguistic aspects of the fall follow in the story of Babel (Genesis 11), and political aspects in the decision to have a king (the unintended consequence of which was the development of an élite class, see 1 Samuel 8).

So a new perception of reality, in which humans see themselves as independent from God and his ways, is complemented by a new social practice, in which power and interest relationships become dominant. The distorted perception of reality has implications today in that no humans may claim 'pure' knowledge (in sociology or anywhere) and ideology and idolatry are ever present possibilities (see *e.g.* Walter 1980). But the new social practice, involving self-seeking, domination and the absence of neighbour-love and *shalom*, is also the subject-matter for sociology. Sociology may teach us how, amazingly, certain social relationships are preserved despite everything, but it also highlights the complexities and contradictions of a world adrift, characterized by competing attempts to construct social reality in a cosmos which has lost its proper centre.

It is possible that sociological emphases have, in the modern world, led to a rediscovery of certain forgotten biblical themes. (And here we observe how sociology does a service to the Christian community and its perception of the world at large.) For social science has helped expose some of the complex social dimensions of alienation which biblically is called sin and which finds its historical origin in the fall. In the western world especially sin has come to have excessively individualistic connotations. This has led not only to the privatization of sin but also to the idea that Christ came *only* to redeem individuals. Now, however, some would recall us to the prophetic *social* message of the Old Testament and of Jesus. 'Social sin' or 'evil structures' has become vogue parlance. There is potential for confusion here, on which I comment in chapter six.

Few will have failed to notice that 'sin' is not a commonly invoked category in sociology. Given the secular aspects of sociology's birth this is not surprising. But the early American muck-raking sociologist Edward Ross did see some connections, documented in his *Sin and Society* (Ross 1907). Much more recently, Stanford Lyman has returned to the study of evil in his *The Seven Deadly Sins*, which is a sociology of waste, distortion, oppression and so on (Lyman 1978).

Restoration and the future

Thankfully, the biblical drama is not all tragedy. Why not? Because written into the curse itself is a promise, believed by the patriarchs, expressed in the exodus, repeated by the prophets and finally realized in Jesus Christ: a curse-reversal. Via regeneration through Christ's cross, a new humanity is formed, who strive to realize the social (and other) renewal also deriving from the cross (Colossians 1: 20). These other effects of the cross show how blinkered is the merely 'individual religion' view of Christianity. 'Amazing grace' to individuals is indeed a marvel. But the Scriptures do not allow us to stop there. God's purposes, centred in the cross, are for the whole creation! It is thus not unjustified to think of substantial healing (the phrase is Francis Schaeffer's; it is echoed by Bob Goudzwaard, 1979: 235) taking place today in the social realm, on the basis of Christ's work.

In terms of Christian response to Jesus Christ's claims, the beginning of a new perception of reality is accompanied by a radically different (communal) social practice. Increasingly believers are expected to shed old lenses on reality and to polish and wear new ones (Romans 12: 1–2). In particular, we come once more to see ourselves as in the image of God, and are recalled to the purposes of creation. We do so, however, with eyes open to the context of a fallen, broken and unjust world. Even in this situation Christians are called upon to 'seek the peace and prosperity of the city' (Jeremiah 29: 7, see also 1 Timothy 2: 1–2) in which we are found. The creation purposes are still operative, and social analysis and theory must be geared to understanding how they may be applied today. But Christians increasingly see themselves within the biblical drama; not just looking backwards to creation, but also forwards to a new age.

As in redemption, so in the new age, it is God's initiative which brings events into being. But Christians also participate in the renewal by living the life of the new age (2 Peter 3: 11–13). In fact, when the apostle Peter speaks of the 'new heaven and new earth', he refers explicitly to the old expectation of *shalom* which is the hope of the Old Testament. This hope gives dynamic to the old purposes. And in conjunction with today's possibilities presented by redemption, this means that sociology may take on an emancipatory style. The future is not foreclosed, it is open, under God, to the full potential of his original intentions (see Lyon, forthcoming).

Sociology can only have a sense of 'what is wrong' with society in relation to an alternative vision. The Christian hope yields just such a vision, but it is yoked tightly to the purposes of creation and the reality of an alienated world, *and* rooted in the conviction that the Creator has not yet finished with his creation. It is thus not self-consciousness alone which is the condition of human freedom, but an awareness of the God who is there, in whose image we are made, and, in Christ, remade.

All of the biblical drama is important. Neglect of one or more of these 'key acts' in the drama leads to serious imbalance. For example, if one thinks only in terms of creation, the moment in which the divinely-given possibilities for human existence are enunciated, the tendency will be for a stiffly rigid social perspective to develop. Moreover, such a limitation means neglect of the crucial dimension of the fall. The latter has huge ramifications in the social realm, in terms of dislocation and disruption of relationships. Its effects also spill over into the area of ideology, of distorted knowledge and perception, whose recognition is vitally important for social analysis.

A social perspective based solely on the disastrous slippage of the fall, however, would also be inappropriate. Some for example who seem to take this view end by seeing the role of government in human affairs merely as restraint. In this view, any authority exists to curb the innate human tendency to descend into a Hobbesian 'war of all against all'. What is missing here is an appreciation of the continued divine intervention in human history, the breaking-in of God's kingdom in the person of the Servant-King, Jesus. Surprising reversals of the fall do take place as substantial healing occurs in the social as in other realms, through the lasting work of Christ.

Of course, the offence of the cross cannot be side-stepped here. Jesus, the victim of history's grossest miscarriage of justice, allowed himself to become a blood-sacrifice. This was specifically on behalf of all who would trust him and who form the community of his followers. But this act also made possible present reconciliations and renewal and is a harbinger of the new age. And in this future hope we find reason to believe that, one day, the created order will undergo catastrophic and radical change. The new heavens and new earth, the fulfilment of God's promises (the Old Testament vision of *shalom*, unrevoked in the New Testament) which have only shadowy shape now, will eventually be the only reality. The point is, however, that our own aspirations for the social realm should be no less than *shalom* now. Jesus himself taught us to plead with the Father that 'your will be done on earth as it is in heaven'.

Persons and purposes

So much for the broad canvas of the biblical drama. It is also possible to spell out more specifically how its main 'acts' have a bearing on a social perspective. This perspective may in turn be used to inform and guide social analysis and theory. Three aspects, each of which receives fuller treatment below, deserve mention here.

The first aspect might be called *doing justice to persons*. From the creation account we learn that God made people in his image. Humans, then, are like God in certain respects. In particular, God *acts* and so do we, according to intention, desire or just habit. This tells us something fundamental about being human which we neglect at our peril. Of course there are also limits to individual human action, among which is social constraint. The view that humans can act freely, as if in a social, economic (or whatever) vacuum, is also alien to a Christian social perspective. This means that, from a Christian viewpoint, reductionism (saying, for example, that we are *nothing but* a bundle of roles or reflexes) is unacceptable. But by the same token social *hubris* (imagining ourselves to be infinitely capable of free action regardless of social context) is also inadmissible.

The second aspect could be referred to as *doing justice to gender*. With regard to sex and gender, the creation account is supplemented biblically with an understanding of the asymmetrical power relations between the sexes which developed at the fall, and also with some straightforward guidelines (backed by his practice) from Christ himself. Of course, the Bible is not a feminist manifesto in the sense that it could simply be appropriated by contemporary feminism. But neither is an anti-feminist document, as some would-be Christian defenders of the sexual *status quo* may discover to their chagrin! In the context of his era, in the Middle East, Jesus of Nazareth was a sexual radical, who challenged the patriarchal patterns of discrimination and exploitation outright. The whole basis of male and female roles and relationships is challenged by biblical Christianity. The 'woman question' is equally the 'man question'. The Bible emphasizes our humanness, and puts sexuality in that wider context. This is manifestly not unimportant for contemporary sociology, whose single most significant challenge currently comes from the feminist critique.

The third aspect worth mention here is *doing justice in society*. As we have seen, one of the basic motivations for pursuing social science at all is, from a Christian viewpoint, the quest for justice. True human welfare may be sought only if there is adequate understanding of social situations. This applies both at the level of interpersonal relationships (such as in families) or in social structural contexts (such as the attempt to abolish poverty on a societal level) or, at the widest extreme, in the international scene. Sociology must have an interest in all levels.

In the modern world, where, for instance, decisions made in New York or London *do* have such deep effects on manual labourers in Seoul or Sri Lanka, the international level ought to be prominent. Talk of a 'global village' often conjures up rural nostalgia. But global realities are more like those obtaining in real villages; inequalities, power struggles and half-hidden corruption. But the person praised by the Scriptures is the one devoted to justice and to righteousness. Such a concern is one evidence of an encounter with the living God, which has included a glimpse of how his good purposes will finally be worked out in human history.

Setting the scene

The point of what follows is to apply this fundamental view of humanness to contemporary social analysis and theory. The general framework of the biblical drama provides the plot, which must now be related to empirical and conceptual studies. All sociologies connect, especially at the world-view level, with human images. What is distinctive about this perspective is that it attempts to display the ways in which a Christian view of humanness – humans as the image of God – may contribute to sociological investigation. This task should also expand our understanding of 'the image of God'. But this is not an end in itself. The concern with personhood and purposes in social science has no truck with mere abstraction, but is bound up with a desire to delve into the dynamics of modern society in its concrete and conflicting forms. The hope is to make some small contribution to the realization of true humanity, in terms of biblical welfare and the justice of Jesus.

Part 2

Human image and social theory

This part of the book is itself in two sections. One examines sociology's development and its contemporary schools. The other looks at key philosophical issues in social science. Both sections relate 'human image' to social theory.

Chapter three digs down to some of the roots of social analysis and theory in the social upheavals of the nineteenth century. Social science was an intellectual attempt to cope with these social changes. The revolutionary age which ushered in the modern world was a time of questioning received religious ideas. Social science developed partly as an alternative to religious understandings of the social world. Pioneers like Saint-Simon, Marx, Weber and Durkheim forged their ideas on the anvil of science, frequently setting notions of humanness thus derived over against religious views. This chapter highlights both the exciting new insights of the 'sciences of society', and the weaknesses of attempts to build on inadequate understandings of humanness.

Chapter four takes up the story with the later twentieth century proliferation of perspectives in social science. Some clues are given as to how such perspectives can be evaluated. I am thinking not only of evaluation in terms of the data of the real social world, but also of the 'human image' embedded in each perspective. In practice, this helps us to steer a course between the twin dangers of sectarianism (believing there is really only one perspective which counts) and synthetism (trying to weave all perspectival threads into one grand world-embracing theory). Christian criteria assist the search for perspectives which do justice to a proper human image.

The idea of a *science* of society seems shaky to many of today's sociologists, especially if the science has to be modelled on physics or biology. What then is left of human distinctiveness? Chapter five considers some of the basic problems involved in the disputes over the *scientific* character of sociology. We find that, not only is sociology no threat to faith, but Christian commitment may be a guide in doing sociology. Some contemporary views of science may in fact be used to support this idea, which allows human distinctiveness to be taken seriously in social analysis.

Another fundamental issue in sociology, crudely put, is whether we make society or society makes us. Is there a *social* reality, or is society really just a figment of sociological fancy? This is the theme of chapter six. Again the human image is invoked as a framework for deciding whether social *action* or social *structure* or both should be the focus of sociological study. The issue is of considerable current interest to Christians and others struggling with the concept of social structure in relation to class, poverty and the Third World: are such social structures neutral, benign or evil?

3
CLASSICAL SOCIOLOGY:
RELIGION AND RECONSTRUCTION

*Stepping outside the Tao, they have stepped
into the void. Nor are their subjects necessarily
unhappy men. They are not men at all: they are
artefacts. Man's final conquest has proved to be
the abolition of Man.*

C. S. Lewis

*Don't put my faith in nobody not even
a scientist.*

Bob Dylan

Is the idea of a social science irrelevant or indispensable to the
proper study of human beings? Strong arguments have been
presented in support of both views. The nineteenth-century
founding fathers of sociology were almost unanimous in their
affirmation of the idea of a science of society. Beyond that,
however, the disputes begin. Contemporary sociology cannot be
understood without stepping back into the last century to
examine early social theories.

Two aspects of this must be borne in mind. One, the actual
social and political context of revolutions and reconstruction to
which sociology was one intellectual response. Two, the philosophical and religious problems raised by the idea of a science of
society. Among the latter, in keeping with the theme of this
book, the focus is on the human images implicit or explicit in the

various theories of society. The journey begun in this chapter runs along these tracks, which in fact also carry us into the present: the issues raised are unresolved today.

New world: new outlook

The pioneers blazing a social scientific trail in the nineteenth century are misunderstood if their ideas are simply located in intellectual history. In the fresh air of freedom following the French Revolution there was tremendous exhilaration, a readiness to conquer the world in the name of reason. Against this enthusiasm to burst all the bonds of the old order was an anxious conservatism which sensed that boats were being burned which might have carried the world to a truly civilized state. European thought in the nineteenth century is very much a debate over the French Revolution. This event, which finally overthrew the *ancien régime* of monarchic, clerical and aristocratic power, thus made way for the rise of a new class associated with business, industry and science. The question, however, was whether the revolution should be consolidated, completed or countered. By 1848, the turbulent 'year of revolutions' in Europe, the question was still open.

Not only was there profound political change, of course. The nineteenth century was also to be the age of steam and iron, depicted in Turner's evocative and romantic paintings. It was the age of Dickens and Zola, whose novels etch unforgettable memories of misery and helplessness among the newly-created urban working classes. Next to the triumphs of industrial capitalism which epitomized the successful application of scientific technology to production, we must also place the discontent and agitation of many who suffered in factories and mines, obliging the powers-that-be to have second thoughts about the supposedly unmixed blessings of this new world.

The workplace was separated from the home. Workers were separated from each other and from the direct struggle with nature which had previously preoccupied most of the human race. People were thrust into new relationships with each other as old local communities were broken up, and smoky cities grew where once there had been fields. Parishes and cities, once important administrative centres and places where information and welfare were disseminated, gave way during the century to the nation-state, in which increasing numbers indirectly participated through the spreading franchise.

This was the new world with which early social scientists intellectually grappled. What would hold the new society together since the old glue of city and community had been melted in revolutionary fires? How would people know their identity and their social place now that religion mixed with tradition had dissolved with the decline of churchly influence (either through political dismantling, as in France, or through failure to move with the people, as in England)? And how should we live and what can we hope for now that old beliefs have been discarded by rationalists and superseded by science? These questions and others, in various configurations, furrowed the brows of sociology's founding fathers, stimulating original efforts to understand the new human social context, and the proper position of humans in it.

The trouble was that the social and religious questions came together in two revolutionary packages. The transformations we have come to know as the French Revolution and the industrial revolution happened over a long period of time (even if their symbolic moments were brief) and the scale of change was massive. But it was precisely the old source of social wisdom – religion – which was losing public acceptability at that time. The early sociologists I shall mention in a moment – Saint-Simon, Marx, Weber and Durkheim – all felt they had to find other ways of answering the questions thrown up by modernity. As John Burrow says of early English social theorists such as Herbert Spencer:

Typically, the nineteenth century intellectual required from social science ... a basis for ethics and political theory and an account of the human situation in relation to the rest of creation. Social science grew ... out of the collapse or re-evaluation of the older theories, philosophical and religious, which in the past had satisfied these needs (Burrow 1966: 264).

The intelligentsia of the new age sought means of understanding society in the context of the apparent breakdown of old verities, especially Christian ones. The answers they came up with, for all their perspicuity, reflected this secular milieu with its peculiar dilemmas and distresses. As our C. S. Lewis epigram has it, they 'stepped into the void'.

This shift of outlook even meant that, according to some, social science itself came to be seen as an alternative mode of faith. Forerunners Saint-Simon and Auguste Comte were quite explicit about it, as we shall see. As social theorist Roland Robertson has pointed out, Max Weber and Emile Durkheim

> placed the study of religion in its broadest sense at the very heart of their analyses of sociocultural life. Both were concerned, analytically and 'metaphysically', about the relationship between their respective diagnoses of the significance of religion in industrial societies and the sociological perspective itself (Robertson 1978: 260).

Elsewhere he writes that 'The idea that sociologists of this period dealt in *religious* issues arrises because they sought to replace a conventional-Christian position by another position' (Robertson 1968: 196). Though this might be a controversial suggestion to some, it bears consideration.

A science of society

The early social scientists thought of themselves as such for obvious reasons: they wanted a science of society. Science had made such an obvious impact in explaining and conquering the natural world, why not have sciences of the human world also? Political economy already existed, and psychology soon followed sociology as a new discipline dealing with people and their problems and patterns of relationship. The very term 'science of society' carries with it certain problems, however. The idea of a *science* of society we shall look at in chapter five; it is worth commenting briefly on 'society' here.

It was probably because of the new conception of 'society', made possible partly through the changes mentioned above, that a breakthrough occurred into 'sociology'. 'Society' had previously had connotations of the political realm, or of particular 'civilizations', but now 'society' began to be viewed as some kind of separate entity in its own right. Even so, it could hardly pass as an innocent term.

The modern use of 'society' only began in the late eighteenth century to describe a system of common life. It referred to a collectivity of individuals linked only by agreement or common interest. 'Society' had once meant 'fellowship' or 'companion-ship', but such connotations were to be taken over in the new idea of 'community'. Even in the limited sense of an 'upper class' (with its connotation of active belonging) it was dis-appearing in the nineteenth century, as witness Byron's *Don Juan*:

> Society is now one polished horde,
> Formed of two mighty tribes, the Bores and Bored.

Why do I say that society is 'not an innocent term'? Because even the usage of the word 'society' can betray a social theory, and thus also a view of humanness. 'Society' in its early social scientific usage, referred not to social relationships welded together by traditional ties, but to contractual relationships between individual social atoms. For this very reason 'com-munity' had to be charged with new meaning in contradistinc-tion to the impersonality and abstractness of 'society'. The tension between 'society' and 'community' in nineteenth-century social theory represented a view of humanness in which a high premium was placed on togetherness, felt to be especially necessary amidst the fracturing forces of industrial capitalism.

As I proceed to sketch a vignette of a few founding fathers' selected ideas, I highlight two things. Against the backdrop of massive transformations taking place in nineteenth-century Europe, these men were making 'sciences of society', which one, reflected the rejection of religion, and two, proposed new images of humanness. The reader will have to look elsewhere for adequate accounts of these figures (there are plenty of excellent ones available; see *e.g.* Giddens 1971 or Coser 1977). Our pre-sent concern is with their relationship to religion and their views of humanness.

By 'human image', it should be clear by now that I do not mean some theory of 'individuals'. As many problems arise in talking of the abstraction 'individual' as they do with the abstraction 'society'. No, I am referring to an understanding of what it is to be human, in its 'social' and 'individual' aspects. I take it that human images are built into social science such that, as social philosopher Tom Campbell says, 'It is impossible to conceive of a theory of society without a conception of human nature' (Campbell 1981: 18). What is meant by this should emerge in the following pages.

Prophets of progress

As with any ideas, sociology required a congenial context in which to thrive. The soil in which it grew had been well prepared and contained important elements. The most significant are these: one, intellectual elements, which may be summed up as the belief in *progress*; and two, social elements, represented by the French Revolution and the development of industrial capitalism. Having said that, another dimension to these elements is the religious. I say 'dimension' because the religious is not separable from the other elements. This is why we may see sociology as an overarching perspective as well as institution discipline and intellectual practice. The intellectual and social conditions for sociology's emergence are also evidence of religious conviction. Though frequently forgotten, it explains why early sociologists either felt it necessary to attack conventionally religious belief (Spencer and Marx) or to suggest what would replace traditional religion in the society of the future (Comte and Durkheim).

The outlook of the so-called eighteenth-century Enlightenment was one of belief in progress. Into the darkness of religion and superstition of bygone eras shone the light of reason. As Alexander Pope put it:

> Nature and Nature's laws lay hid in night:
> God said, Let Newton be! and all was light!

The power of unaided human reason to conquer all practical and intellectual problems meant that God became 'an unnecessary hypothesis'. Things would get better without his intervention. Not only would reason ameliorate the human condition as far as material things were concerned; moral improvement, civilization, would occur.

The notion of progress represented a secularization of the Christian view of history (Bebbington 1979: 68–9). First, history is moving in a straight line, but not between the poles of creation and judgement. Second, confidence is placed in the future. But this is no new heaven and new earth following the return of Christ. Just a new earth in which humanity has finally perfected itself. Third, the idea of progress assumes that we know and assess what is and is not progressive. Harmony, happiness, rationality; whatever the goal of the specific ideologue of progress, that defined good and bad. Not, as in the Christian view, certain transcendent standards set by God himself.

The French philosopher the Marquis de Condorcet, one of the key exponents of progress and a 'science of man' entitled his creed a *Sketch for a Historical Picture of the Progress of the Human Mind*. In it he explained the ten stages through which humanity had passed during the upward march to utopia. And as the phenomena of the human and physical worlds are on the same plane, the next step was to discover the rest of the laws of social life, thus producing 'a science to foresee the progression of the human species'. If Engels was to pronounce Marx the Darwin of society-science, Condorcet believed that he himself was its Newton. Condorcet's optimism was the more ironic in that he composed his creed while awaiting execution during a French Revolutionary purge in 1793. Which reminds us that his ideas were no mere armchair day-dreams.

The Enlightenment merged with the French Revolution, providing it with many of its slogans and rationale. The new world could be made by the people. Popular sovereignty meant in its earliest days that notice need no longer be taken of the word of the king or of God.

Socially and intellectually two major processes emerged with Enlightenment and Revolution. One, associated with wider forces, but given legitimacy in revolutionary Europe, was social differentiation. This is the splitting of society into increasingly specialized segments, according to efficiency and expertise rather than any higher meaning. For sociology, this means that its very social context was one in which less importance was attached to traditional relationships of duty and responsibility – a social trauma which was to trouble Durkheim in particular. The second process would be termed the pluralization of world views. In simpler words, the Enlightenment and Revolution finally broke apart the more unitary world view of medieval times. Already severely streaked with cracks, this spelt its final dissolution. Whatever sympathy might or might not be entertained for the medieval world view, the point is that a new pluralism succeeded it. It became increasingly possible – and socially acceptable – to abandon old creeds and fashion new philosophies. This was reflected, as we shall see, in the nascent science(s) of society.

But the Revolution met different responses. Some wished to

put the clock back and, as Robert Nisbet has shown, provided a conservative impulse for some of the most significant nineteenth-century sociology. The question was how to preserve and revive what was good in the traditions of prerevolutionary society. But others, notably the new class of entrepreneurs and industrialists who had risen to power, wished to maintain the gains of the Revolution. 'Liberté! Egalité! Fraternité!' was their cry. But they meant *individual* liberty to mould one's own life, equality only in politics and law, and brotherhood (without much sisterhood) between particular interest groups. A third response was more radical. What use was political and legal equality if poverty still existed? The radicals wished to continue the Revolution until all wrongs were righted, all abuses abolished and all class differences dissolved. Marxism and socialism grew from this response.

But even if the other groups paid lip-service to progress, it was the second group, the industrialists, for whom the term was an article of faith. Indeed, while much ink has been spilt on the relationship between secularized Protestant ideas and the formation of capitalism, this belief was also crucial to it. Dutch social analyst and politician Bob Goudzwaard has convincingly argued that faith in progress constituted the decisive spark which ignited the engines of industrial capitalism (Goudzwaard 1979).

So-called mainstream sociology emerged above all in connection with this group. The very word sociology came to have the connotation of 'industrial society' theory (which shows that 'sociology' is not an innocent term either, Giddens 1977: 23–4). This group saw economic growth and technological development as good in themselves. They tended to relegate notions of justice and equity to a secondary place. Industrialism was unfolding according to its own so-called logic.[1] The most prominent representative of the new science of society, who predicted the rise of the society of science, was Henri, Comte de Saint-Simon (1760–1825).

---

[1] Ironically, had the more authentically 'Protestant Ethic' of John Calvin been the outlook of the day, something rather different might have occurred. He had shown the Bible's teaching in this area consistently to be focused around stewardship of resources and justice among all people, Graham 1975.

Saint-Simon: a sociology of industrial society

Saint-Simon stood on the shoulders of the Enlightenment philosophers to construct his science of society. Surprisingly pre-
scient, he foresaw the development of industrial society at a
time when it was only just being born. In fact some people read
him today as a prophet of post-industrial or information society,
where technical knowledge (and the class possessing it) rules
supreme. His work became a model of a particular way of
viewing social change. Societies were typified as having either
'pre-industrial' or 'industrial' characteristics. One implication
of this way of seeing things is that the fundamental 'cause' of
change lies in the process of technological innovation. Christian
thought is always wary of such mono-causal explanation as it
suggests that some item within the creation is giving a predominant skew to one's perspective. Having a before-and-after
kind of model also tends to foreclose the possibility of a further,
new kind of society coming into being.

Saint-Simon diagnosed social and moral strains of the transi-
tion to mature industrialism. So although he made pioneering
analyses of class, he did not take this to a Marxian conclusion.
Rather, he believed that class conflict would die, given time, in
industrial society. An optimistic view of humanness, indeed!
Distributive equality would mean classlessness. This has constituted a key element in 'industrial society' theorizing since
Saint-Simon, seen in the work of Durkheim and several of their
mid-twentieth-century sociological descendants (Kumar 1978).

A couple of other comments on Saint-Simon are called for.
First, his work anticipates that of his disciple (and plagiarist)
Auguste Comte. He also influenced Durkheim and Marx, who
were to produce such divergent accounts of industrial capitalism. Marx, though he took up some Saint-Simonian themes,
dismissed him as a 'utopian socialist'. And there is no doubt that
Saint-Simon was a utopian. He produced a progressive view of
the new world of industrialism in which harmony would
ultimately reign. He thus criticized surviving elements of the
ancien régime. He yoked his social science to his future vision
and thus justified intervention in the present society to speed up
change in the right direction. Through his and others' work
'harmony, integration, cohesion and co-operation become the
dominant paradigms with reference to which all social theory is

conceived, society operates, and to which all other principles are subordinated' (Goodwin 1978: 203).

Not only Marx, but other social scientists were later to complain that utopia had no place in a science of society. This has in fact sparked off a debate which is still hot in the present day. In so far as social scientists could show how Saint-Simon's ideas were unrealistic they were correct to dismiss his utopianism. Had he considered the consequences of capitalism more fully, for instance, he might have been less sanguine about 'classlessness'. But if by utopianism they meant that some vision of the good society, however vague, should be banned from social theory, they were on less firm ground. Social 'laws' are hopelessly unstable compared, say, with the law of gravity – human wills and purposes enter right into their constitution. Also, social science language, as we shall see, is never 'neutral'. So the question of utopia turns not on whether or not utopian strains should be present, but on how realistic is the image of the good society proposed, and, more important, what the contours of that 'good society' are. In any case, Marx's critique was somewhat misplaced. He himself was a closet utopian.

The second comment on Saint-Simon concerns an ironic contradiction. Though he foresaw the new world of harmony through industrialism, based on a rejection of the philosophy, politics and religion of the past, in the end he lost his nerve. He concluded that it would require a new religion: *Le Nouveau Christianisme* (the title of a book published in 1825). He argued that rampant egoism had, since the Enlightenment, created a need for a new altruism, founded on brotherly love. But somehow Saint-Simon had missed the point of the old, original Christianity, that ethics cannot simply be lifted out of the context of the totality of biblical religion. There, brotherly and sisterly love grows out of prior experience of a divinely devised rescue operation which releases from, as well as combats, egoism. This misunderstanding did not, of course, limit the impact of Saint-Simon's work. His followers were equally keen to ignore biblical Christianity.

What, then, is the human image in Saint-Simon's work? He followed closely the Enlightenment view that humans are physical and social beings subject to natural laws. Human vision and effort, unaided by God's power or providence, ensure the realization of human potential. Saint-Simon devoted himself to post-revolutionary social reconstruction for, as he said: 'Humanity is not made to live amidst ruins.' He suspected, however, that a new natural science of society would not be quite enough to guarantee the emergence of a free, rational, secular and just society; people would also require some reconstruction of religion.

Karl Marx: a crack at capitalism

Karl Marx (1818–1883) was more worried about capitalism than industrialism. He rightly observed that Saint-Simon's Achilles' heel lay in his failure to analyse the capitalist context of industrialism. Marx set about making good that deficiency by systematically examining the way in which capitalism inevitably breeds classes and class conflict. For him, the French Revolution had certainly not gone far enough. While the owners of capital continued to make profit at the expense of the workers who had nothing but labour-power to sell and nothing but chains to lose, Marx would never give in.

Marx produced some theoretical concepts in order to solve some fundamental practical problems. It was not simply the case that when the weary workers heard the news that they were exploited, and were given the address of the employers, or shown how to build barricades, they would revolt and attack. Marx used the theory of surplus value to show that capitalist society could not survive. The bourgeoisie could not exploit the proletariat for ever. Revolution had to come sooner or later.

There seems little point in denying that Marx constructed the beginnings of a science of society, and made a major and highly intelligent contribution to it. The fact that at certain points he may have been wrong, or even that (as we shall note in chapter seven) his view of humanity is fundamentally misconceived, does not alter that. Nor does the obvious horror of revolutions made in his name which now use his ideas as a rigid and doctrinaire means of justifying powerful élites and in ruthlessly crushing all dissent, including Christian dissent.

Does this sound contradictory? Elsewhere (Lyon 1979) I have endeavoured to show why Christians (and others) should take serious note of Marx and Marxism. One reason is that he was not content to live in a world of gross inequality where the poverty of some clearly related to the comfort of others. In industrializing Britain it clearly was not the case that moral failure alone caused poverty (as some, including Christians, seemed to believe). Chances of living a decent life with shelter and sufficient to eat depended to an extent upon an accident of birth. Marx believed this to be intolerable. So does the Bible. Marx rightly or wrongly believed that he had scientifically demonstrated the connection between wealth (capital ownership) and poverty in capitalist social arrangements.

The history of sociology is not, as some would have it, solely a debate with Marx's ghost. But the debate over Marxist social science is perennial. Engels clearly wished Marx's ghost to shoot a particular line. Even as Marx's mortal remains were being lowered into the ground, he announced to all interested that just as Darwin had discovered the laws of organic nature, so Marx had discovered the laws of history. Marx's ghost would have gone along with that quite happily. After all Marx himself had offered to dedicate *Kapital* to Darwin. (And Darwin politely declined, not because he doubted Marx's scientific credentials but because he did not wish the public to associate him with Marx's atheism!) The link with Darwin was very significant, as he represented the acme of Victorian science. Everyone progressive wanted to be scientific.

We shall see later that the 'laws' of capitalist society which Marx propounded are both descriptive and predictive. Marx and the Marxists claim that capitalism is deeply split by internal contradictions. Eventually the splits will widen as capitalism finally cracks up. However, Marxism itself is replete with contradiction (see chapter seven), often at critical points. In fact the contradiction of capitalism and of Marxism may be traced to the same source: the effort to live in God's world independently of him, the idea of human autonomy.

This relates closely, I suggest, to Marx's human image. While this is discussed later, it is worth inserting the core of Marx's view here, to give continuity. The debate over Marx's view of human nature, or whether he even held such views, is endless. Some key themes are undeniable, however. He held to the Enlightenment notion that humanity is the centre of the universe, 'the sun around which man revolves'. Humans are distinguished as a species, from animals, by our self-conscious activity, in transforming the environment. In seeing 'man' only in relation to 'man', however, he lighted on a point *within* the creation – labour – and inflated that out of all proportion. Rather than seeing that numerous contradictions arise from the basic tension between humans and nature (relating to human finiteness) and its exacerbation through the fall (relating to human sinfulness) he focused on only one. This Marx then wove into a (frequently insightful) theory of capitalist society which optimistically predicts revolution as a panacea for human ills. The relation between social world view and social analysis is, in Marx, rather clear. Put thus, an injustice would seem to be done to Marx's subtlety and sophistication. Such is not my intention; I merely wish to stress in a stark way where Marx's human image finally leads him.

I shall not proceed to make a catalogue of all the so-called founding fathers of social science. That would miss the point of this book. Comment ought to be made, however, on two other major figures: Max Weber (1864–1920) and Emile Durkheim (1858–1917). The range and depth of the work of each is immense. The ideas of both penetrated deeply into subsequent sociology. Theirs also are ghosts to be reckoned with. But they gave birth to quite different sociological ideas.

Emile Durkheim: are social facts things?

Durkheim's sociology pointed both backwards and forwards. His work followed the French tradition of positivism established initially by Auguste Comte. (By 'positivism' Comte meant various things. It is science cut free from all metaphysical trappings, having only to do with 'reality'. It spells certainty, arising from scientific logic, and it is constructive, having utility in the real world.) Durkheim's version of positivism anticipated twentieth-century developments, above all in functionalism. Durkheim's influence on British anthropologist Radcliffe-Brown is strong, and also on American sociologists Robert Merton and Talcott Parsons.

Durkheim's ambition was to establish sociology as an autonomous empirical discipline. Thus he built on Saint-Simon and Comte, although he disagreed with them on matters of detail. He did not accept Comte's law of three stages, that societies were first metaphysical, then logical, and lastly scientific, as an explicit philosophy of history, but it does seem that this was a practical guide to his outlook. For in his attempt to account for the new kind of industrial society, whose birth he observed in France, he not only noted, but also promoted, a new individualism and a new basis for moral authority. Here we see the 'constructive' aspect of positivism.

Durkheim saw his sociology as a means of guaranteeing the secular moral foundations of the Third Republic. According to his biographer, Steven Lukes:

> Durkheim believed that the relation of the science of sociology to education was that of theory to practice; and, in this respect, would become a rational substitute for traditional religion (Lukes 1973: 359).

Durkheim refused to compromise with religion, or to try to 'modernize' the church. He believed that the success of sociology depended upon its being radically separated from religion. From his evolutionary viewpoint, traditional forms of moral authority had to be superseded as they were irrelevant to the modern world.

But he desperately wanted a new moral code appropriate for humans in the modern era. As he said,

> Our faith has become troubled; tradition has lost its sway; individual judgement has been freed from collective judgement . . . the remedy for the evil is not to seek to resuscitate traditions and practices which, no longer corresponding to present conditions of society, can only live on artificial, false existence . . . Because certain of our duties are no longer founded in the reality of things, a breakdown has resulted which will be repaired only in so far as a new discipline is established and consolidated (Durkheim 1933: 409).

Durkheim insisted that his political programme of liberal and reformist socialism was scientifically grounded. On the basis of his version of social evolution he discerned the 'healthy' and 'sick' traits of society. The analogy between 'body' and 'society' is obvious in his work; he saw himself as a kind of social clinician, diagnosing social ailments. The task of deciding what is 'healthy' or 'sick' still confronts Durkheim's (functionalist) followers today, whatever their claims to 'impartiality'.

So where did the *scientificity* of Durkheim's work lie? His basic 'rule of sociological method' says it all: social facts must be considered as things. Society is part of nature, and may therefore be studied by detached and theory-free observation. One social fact is explained in terms of another. Two things deserve comment here: one, it is arguable that 'society' had become Durkheim's ultimate frame of reference in a post-Christian manner. 'Society' itself generates its own cohesion, its own rules of life. It is no longer possible, or necessary, to look beyond.

The second item, for more extended comment, is Durkheim's famous rule of sociological method, that social facts be treated as 'things'. When in everyday speech we speak of being 'crushed in a bureaucratic machine', we are near to Durkheim. Durkheim believed that social facts have a constraining power over us, 'imposing themselves' on us, independent of our individual wills (Durkheim 1950: chapter one). This idea is closely connected with his positivism; he was committed to the idea of a natural science of society. Early on he claimed that social constraint is like physical: as straps or walls constrain, so do social traditions or institutions. Later he acknowledged that his 'social facts' have a *moral* nature, which gives them their 'power'. Even this, however, did not lead him to abandon his methodological stance of 'social facts as things'.

The trouble is that, while social constraint is obviously an important theme for sociology, the 'thingness' of social facts is patently not like the 'thingness' of trees or candles. 'Gravity' is a term invented to describe a physical force. But in social science our language is not invented in the same way. Words like 'suicide' (the topic of one of Durkheim's celebrated studies) refer to aspects of a pre-interpreted world which we already know and in terms of which we act. We shall return to this theme in chapter six. But the point here is that Durkheim betrays a human image at his supposedly methodological level. People help to create social facts, and apply such categories as 'marriage', 'sabotage' or 'suicide' to their actions *before* the social scientist even enters the picture.

Durkheim seems to hold a fairly pessimistic view of persons, who, by themselves, are powerless to limit or direct their activities. Rather, they have to look to society to 'provide the linguistic, reasoning, and institutional requirements for ordering human life' (Campbell 1981: 19). In a sense, Durkheim

71

suggests we have two people inside us: humans are *homo duplex*:

> There is in us a being that represents everything in relation to itself and from its own point of view . . . There is another being in us, however, which knows things *sub specie aeternitatis* as it were, participating in some thought other than its own . . . our inner life has something like a double centre of gravity (Wolff 1960: 327–8)

So people have an individual, animal being, but also a social being (which, Durkheim speculates, distinguishes us from animals).

Both aspects may be comprehended, says Durkheim, in a natural science of society. 'Human nature' can be seen as a product of a particular type of society, because the social aspect tends to curb the individual. Whereas the English writer Thomas Hobbes had said that the egoistic individual sparks off a war of all against all, in Durkheim the processes of education and socialization can create new people for a new age. In the industrial age, what Durkheim called 'mechanical solidarity' would eventually bind people together after the disruption of its early days.

The stress which Durkheim gave to sociality as an aspect of humanness helped launch sociology as a credible discipline. He established an abiding agenda for sociological inquiry into industrial society. But he also had critics right from the start. Among these was his colleague, Gaston Richard, who helped him to produce the journal *L'Année Sociologique*. Richard, a dedicated sociologist who was also a Protestant believer, accused Durkheim of claiming too much for sociology and thus trespassing in other fields. For him, Durkheim was a social determinist, whose human image led to a denial that people act and choose according to their own will. Moreover, Richard complained that, in his treatment of religion, Durkheim openly denied its truth value. It is important to remember this early critique for it indicates that Durkheim's sociology was seen, like Comte's, as a counter-Christian weapon (Pickering, in Martin 1980). We do well to revive Richard's memory as well as Durkheim's.

A note on Talcott Parsons

It was Talcott Parsons (1902–1979) who, more than any other, carried the Durkheimian torch into the mid-twentieth century. Because for many years his work represented a synthesis of classical sociology, it is worth touching on his ideas in this chapter. He also worked with the functionalist notion that society is similar to a body, a biological organism, in which each part may be seen to *function* in relation to the whole. He developed the notion that all societies have particular 'needs' to be met: adaptation, goal attainment, integration and pattern maintenance. More sophisticated than Durkheim, he gained recognition for his attempt to draw together insights from the European tradition into a single, synthetic theory of society, cumbersome in prose, but not lacking in insight.

The continuity between Durkheim and Parsons is worth remarking. If Durkheim took 'society' as his reference point, Parsons does something similar with the 'social system'. Like Durkheim, he believes he can forge a fact-science of society, cut free from ultimately religious assumptions about human society. The result, as Ken Menzies neatly phrases it, is that

> Parsons has locked man firmly into society. Man is fully social . . .
> not only do others react to him in such a way as to control him –
> he also has internalized values and controls himself . . . The
> problem . . . is that it excludes human creativity (Menzies 1977:
> 67).

Again, like Durkheim, Parsons also had his Christian critics who bemoaned his neglect (rather than denial) of free human action, implying that his positivism had got the better of him. In one particular debate Parsons said that resisting the restrictions of positivism in the name of a 'Judeo-Christian image of man' was only to impose another set of restrictions on sociology. 'There must be a more generalized nonpositivistic image of man which can also be Islamic, Buddhist and Hindu in the sense of comprising them all,' he asserted (Parsons 1961: 28). In my view, Parsons failed to answer the main criticism. He also seems to have missed the intrinsic openness of a Christian perspective (a point to which we return in a slightly different context in chapter nine).

Again, let me warn against a merely negative critique of Parsons. His shortcomings notwithstanding, his efforts are laudable in so far as he sought to establish concepts or frames of reference to keep sociological analysis on a firm footing as a serious academic discipline. All too often, since the later 1960s – early 1970s vogue for Parsons-bashing, he has been criticized on ideological rather than social scientific grounds. The angry sociologists of the left dismissed him for failing to account for social change and for handing out a sociology which justified the preservation of the *status quo*. Such remarks, though they were not without basis, often left untouched his contribution to social explanation.

Max Weber: *dilemmas of action*

Weber had no truck with French style positivism. His was a German tradition which viewed sociology as a historical or cultural discipline, not part of natural science. What can sociologists understand? The actions of others, for they, like us, are human. For Weber, any activity with meaning is action; *social* action occurs when meanings are related to others. But while this could sound like a chaos of individual acts, Weber believed that there are categories of action which may be combined into social institutions and processes. His desire was to understand social action in its historical social setting. But he also wanted to transcend cultural disciplines like history by formulating more general 'laws'.

The Protestant Ethic and the Spirit of Capitalism is, among Weber's encyclopaedic output, perhaps his best-known work. There his method is well illustrated. Capitalism, he noted, flourished in areas where Calvinism influenced the popular outlook. At the level of meaning, contemporary German historians would have been happy with such a plausible account, which indicated these possible connections. But Weber wanted more. He tried to demonstrate in a more scientific manner that there was a significant relationship (he called it an 'elective affinity') between secularized Protestant ideals of hard work and self-denial on the one hand, and the dynamic ethos of early capitalism on the other. He also pursued comparative studies to show that the same could not also be said for other areas. Weber claimed that sociology should *scientifically* categorize and analyse *meaningful* actions as they contribute to the structuring of large-scale social patterns and processes. 'Meaningful action', in turn, has to be grasped through *verstehen*, or 'interpretive understanding'. But this disciplinary ideal betrayed a tension in Weber's life which was more than methodological.

Weber's life was brief, brilliant, but burdened. He produced numerous teutonic tomes and enjoyed widespread academic acclaim. Equally happy in law, economics and history, it is his contribution to sociology for which he is mainly remembered. On both sides of the Atlantic and in other parts of the world, he is regarded as a founding father, earning reverence from some, ridicule from others. But his life was disrupted by emotional turmoil, ill health and the Great War. Though he described himself as 'religiously unmusical', his work in fact betrays a deep understanding of the dilemmas of post-Christian humanism.

This is clearest in his famous lecture, 'Science as a Vocation': 'The fate of our times is characterized by rationalization, intellectualization, and above all, the disenchantment of the world' (Gerth and Mills 1958: 155). He saw that the old signposts had gone and that the new world had no means of knowing right and wrong, good and evil. Meaning itself seemed in short supply. He appeared to think that this problem of secularization was irreversible; one could not return to the old religion without committing intellectual suicide. The great dilemma of the post-Christian world is the following: Science is apparently the great liberator from the shackles of past tradition. But science seems to enslave by reducing people to 'things'. And the rationalization process becomes socially oppressive, Weber argues, in the form of the bureaucracy. Thus he countered Marx by commenting that it is not the dictatorship of the proletariat but the dictatorship of officials which is marching on. How can we bend the bars of this unyielding 'iron cage'?

One is not surprised that Weber found life such a struggle as he grappled with questions like this. The tragedy is that he seemed also to know why: 'The fate of an epoch which has eaten of the tree of knowledge is that it must know that we cannot learn the meaning of the world from the results of its analysis, be it ever so perfect; it must rather be in a position to create this meaning itself' (Weber 1950: 4). Thus, correctly in my view, he likened the Enlightenment to the biblical account of the fall. What happened was that those representative humans rejected their Creator's categories and action alternatives, proclaiming intellectual and moral independence. The cruel consequence was their subsequent inability to know or do anything in an undistorted or unopaque manner.

As with our other ghosts, the Christian response cannot be to try an exorcism. For a start, interpretive understanding (or *verstehen*) has an interesting and partly Christian history. Nietzsche observed that 'the Protestant pastor is the grandfather of German philosophy' (quoted in Bebbington 1979: 160). And William Outhwaite reminds us that this 'hermeneutic' approach began in theology, with the Protestant reformers' insistence that the Scriptures could be directly *understood* (Outhwaite 1975: 19).

A similarity exists between accounts of social action and biblical texts. Both are available, but both require principles for their correct interpretation. And just as biblical theologians insist on a hermeneutic which considers a text from different angles and in relation to its contemporary application, so Weber (and after him Karl Mannheim) maintained that looking at the same situation from a number of viewpoints is a necessary stage in interpretation. As we have seen, from the point of view of the *imago dei*, social science conceived in truly human terms must take account of the meaningful action of the subject of study. This entails interpretation.

But another similarity also exists: the potential pitfall of subjectivism. Contemporary theology's 'new hermeneutic' has fallen right into it. Weber could conceive no final way round this issue. In biblical interpretation this means that scholars suggest that we can know God, even though he does not really speak to us! In sociology it means that *evaluation* of human action is supposedly inappropriate. Weber bequeathed to us a terrifying vision of the contradictions of a human-centred world without indicating the exit from this claustrophobic cage. He never claimed his study was neutral, or free from ethical motivation. But what he did say was this: given the collapse of Christian certainty, we must fall back on our own individual choice. It is futile to wait for prophets and saviours now. Rather, he concluded his lecture: 'We shall set to work and meet the "demands of the day" in human relations as well as in our vocation.' This, however, is plain and simple, if each finds and obeys the demon who holds the fibres of his very life. But *without* prophets, we must ask Weber, who is to decide the 'demands of the day'?

It would be a difficult and possibly misleading exercise to try to identify Weber's image of humanness, though one does implicitly exist. Perhaps it is sufficient to point out that his view is quite different from Durkheim's on the question of human intention and meaning. Weber stressed the requirement of a sociology true to its subject-matter to work from some under-standing of action. He clearly saw persons as intentional and purposeful social beings. Although he can be criticized for opening the door to an over-subjective approach, his emphasis on action and *verstehen* is one which many Christians have found attractive. In chapter five I return to look at Weber on the place of valuing in human life and in social analysis.

Science, society and humanness

Unlike many contemporary social scientists, the earliest sociological pioneers were not shy about their linking together social analysis (as intellectual practice) and social philosophy (as sociological world view). But the biggest single change in social thinking during the nineteenth century involved the driving of a positivistic wedge between matters 'metaphysical' and matters 'scientific'. While a Saint-Simon and a Comte could propose an explicitly religious foundation for future society, Weber and Durkheim deliberately distanced their social analy-sis from any form of religion. In Weber's case this was not because he was a strict positivist, but because he simply could not accept the idea that science and religion were compatible. The irrelevance and outdatedness of religion were frequently *assumed*, never demonstrated.

All the classical sociologists felt keenly the sharp tug of the new industrial capitalist era, but also the nostalgic backward pull of time-honoured regimes and social patterns. While they each in their own way yearned for some satisfactory replace-ment for religion, there was general agreement that the demands of the present and future would have to be met without the benefit of religious wisdom.

What this meant for their views of humanness and their social theories has been touched on in this chapter. Rejecting religion certainly did not guarantee the emergence of a coherent view of humanness. The kind of human images revealed by nineteenth-century social theories are in fact contradictory and confused, reflecting the novel pluralism of world views characterizing the nineteenth century. The problem, as pinpointed by Hawthorn, is that in accounting for the place of humans in the scheme of things, from the Enlightenment onwards, theorists worked on the assumption that humans had to be seen as separate from any external realm. This conviction, says Hawthorn, 'detaches man and thus restates the question of his attachment, but does so from premises which make that attachment almost impossible' (Hawthorn 1976: 255).

This in turn leads to other difficulties. Can there be a science of society which considers social facts as one would the 'things' of nature? Of course I am no more suggesting that *all* the classical sociologists concluded that this question *had* to be answered before sociology as social *analysis* could begin, than I am suggesting that social theories are somehow 'built on' views of humanness. It is rather the other way round. The attempt to explain particular social situations – Weber on the development of capitalism for instance – *betrays* an answer to this question. Many argue that we can get on with social analysis without elaborating a particular view of humanness. No doubt this is true. The trouble is that leaving such questions on one side does not make them go away. As I shall argue in the following chapter, the problems bequeathed to us by our sociological grandfathers are still with us today.

4

CONTEMPORARY SOCIOLOGY: PERSPECTIVES AND PARADIGMS

The dissolution of the orthodox consensus has been succeeded by the Babel of theoretical voices that currently clamour for attention.

Anthony Giddens

The synthesis of classical sociology achieved above all in Parsons' grand theory came to be known in the later twentieth century as the 'orthodox consensus'. It was positivist and functionalist in orientation, generally having an image of humans as relatively passive cogs in a machine. There was a gaping rift between empirical studies and social theory. Since the 1960s, however, the orthodox consensus has been broken up, the fragments forming the numerous 'schools' and 'perspectives' which confront the bewildered sociology student today.

In this chapter I shall try to distinguish some of the voices in the present sociological Babel, once again relating them to images of humanness. I wish strongly to resist, however, the idea that these theoretical voices represent merely an intellectual squabble. Divergences of opinion in sociology are rooted simultaneously in problems thrown up by the real world and in ideological or metaphysical commitments. Just as, in the nineteenth century, it was the felt magnitude of social transformation occurring with the growth of industrial capitalism alongside the discrediting of religious world views which stimulated new social theory, so in the twentieth century continued upheaval has prompted people to ask new questions and seek new answers. The interplay between events in the real world, their social explanation and pre-theoretical commitments, is exceedingly subtle. It would be foolish and misleading for me to oversimplify things.

To try to illustrate this, I begin with an example, which I hope will show the interaction between social change, social analysis and social assumptions. After that I tease out some of the main differences between different sociological 'schools', again stressing that this is only a pigeon-holing device, not a reflection of reality. Inevitably, in a post-Kuhnian world, I must make some comment on 'paradigms', a notion of which we have all become confusedly conscious since the publication of *The Structure of Scientific Revolutions* in 1962. Let me remind the reader once again of the limited aim I have in mind by so doing. It is to show that controversies in sociology are not merely *internal* scientific disputes. They are echoes on the one hand of our conflicting, contradictory social situation, and on the other of deep disagreement as to humanness: origin, nature and destiny.

An example: the new sociology of health

Changes in the sociology of health and illness illustrate well the interaction between sociology and society. After the second world war, medicine became a key focus in the treatment of sickness. In Britain the National Health Service was established and in other advanced societies medicine became more specialized and bureaucratically organized.

Sociologically this meant that Parsonian theory seemed highly appropriate. In an era of optimism about human potential for post-war recovery, and that science could conquer after all, Parsons produced a theory of professionals in which doctors were prototypes. Medicine found its niche in grand theory, as an important aspect of the professionalization typical of capitalist development. The focus was firmly fixed on the doctor and of course on the patient who, it was assumed, would soon recover, given the right medicine.

But despite this optimism in many places rates of chronic disease seemed to rise. And patients complained of increasing impersonality and alienation in the process of treatment. Social scientists who examined this situation found that good health is unequally distributed along social classes and, to a certain extent, in different geographical regions.

Because the medical profession had geared itself to germ theory, searching for chemicals which would kill micro-organisms but not people, little attention was paid to the *social* context of health and illness. Faith in science was still high, and sociological attention was directed to physician-centred scientific healing. Sociology was a handmaiden of the medical profession, researching important but micro-level questions such as doctor-patient relationships.

Questioning the effectiveness of medicine, and its soaring costs, along with the ethical issues raised by new technology, led to a crisis of relevance followed by a shift in sociological emphasis. Whereas in the 1960s technological sophistication and complex health delivery systems were seen as human progress, unease set in in the 1970s. The quality of medical care, despite its new technology, was challenged. Doctors had gained immense autonomy and prestige, but this did not necessarily reflect evidence that people were any healthier overall. The whole profession was attacked in popular books such as Ivan Illich's *Medical Nemesis* (Illich 1975), encouraging a mood of (partly justified) cynicism about medicine in general. Competition from other healing agencies began to mount, so that today numerous new movements, such as 'holistic' medicine, have emerged.

The crises in medicine stimulated changes in the mode of sociological analysis. Concern shifted to what is now referred to as the sociology of health (Twaddle 1982). Medicine now tends to be seen as only one element associated with the health of individuals and populations. The focus has moved from the small scale to the social-structural constraints on health and influences on illness. The fact that health is unevenly distributed among social classes has made space for Marxian perspectives on health. They stress factors like the power of the professionals and the control of the health systems by small élites.

Others have emphasized what might be termed the humane aspects of health, highlighting questions about the quality of life. One practical example of this is the growth of hospices, dedicated to the personal care of the dying, including medical pain control. Another is seen in a recent Swedish report on health policy for Göteborg. This report suggests that alienation is the key health problem. Decentralization of public opinion, rather than medical care, should be the key to health policy, returning control to local communities and improving the physical environment (quoted in Twaddle 1982).

This example shows how changing social circumstances, in this case public disquiet over the effectiveness of medicine, stimulates changes in sociological approach. At the same time it shows how no new consensus emerges. For there is an ongoing debate over which perspective is most appropriate. The Marxist focus on power and inequality of health care is countered by the humanistic concerns of those emphasizing decentralization and quality of life. Meanwhile some traditional sociologists still cling to small-scale empirical study having little patience with either Marxist or humanistic perspectives. The sociology of health can scarcely be said to have a coherent identity!

A plethora of perspectives

The conflict of different perspectives in sociology can scarcely have been more evident than in the early 1970s. A debate occurred in the *British Journal of Sociology* in a series of articles beginning with 'The two sociologies', answered by 'Only one sociology', queried by 'How many sociologies?' and so on. Another way of settling the matter appeared when George Ritzer announced that sociology is a 'multiple paradigm science'. We shall comment on his view below.

All this constitutes a big problem for students of sociology. How does one decide which perspective is appropriate? The hopelessness is heightened by the realization that some sociologists are committed to 'their' brand as the *only* way of doing sociology. Functionalists, Marxists and ethnomethodologists are especially prone to this perspectival imperialism. Such sociological squabbles seem to detract from, rather than contribute to, the task of actually attempting to understand society.

In this section, I shall indicate the main tendencies or perspectives in sociology today, and attempt to suggest why there are such competing perspectives and how they might be evaluated. Two preliminary comments may be made. One, these 'perspectives', while they all derive, one way or another, from some aspect of the classical sociology of the founding fathers, may not exclusively be associated with any one of them in particular. The possible exception may be Marx, but many who follow in his footsteps have also incorporated ideas and techniques from other traditions into their work.

It used at one time to be possible to reduce the different perspectives in sociology to a handy trio. Increasingly this is proving less possible and less helpful. However, because they are still important, we shall begin with them, characterizing them in terms of the image of society embodied in each. In so doing, however, we shall also begin to uncover the image of humanness which is not far beneath the surface. I shall also glance at one or two other tendencies which have begun to make their mark on the sociological scene.[1]

Society as a body or system

The middle-class suburbanite, commuting daily into the big city to sit at a desk consulting computer print-outs, hoping for one more promotion before retirement, is said to be in a rat race. The group of anarcho-existentialists who have formed themselves into a self-sufficient rural craft and farming commune believe that they have got out of the rat race. But what exactly do they feel they have escaped from? The image of the rat race, in which laboratory rodents run along pre-determined paths to a predictable goal, is similar to the image of society as a body, or a system. People play out social roles, fitting in to what is expected of them, moving around (to change the picture) like cans on a conveyor belt, undergoing certain processes at regular intervals.

Theoretically this view of social relationships is known most generally as structural-functionalism. Its origins lie in the work of Durkheim and, to some extent, in Spencer. Both took an evolutionary view of social development; both viewed society

---

[1]For those wanting a more sophisticated introduction to different perspectives in terms of their image of society and image of humanness, Margaret Poloma's *Contemporary Sociological Theory* provides just that. She rightly recognizes that 'underlying the variety [of theoretical models] are different assumptions about the nature of people and the nature of society.' While I share her view that one should always seek out the worthwhile and abiding insights offered in all theories, I am unconvinced that she is warranted in being as sanguine as this: 'Each theory contributes to the mosaic of a better understanding of men and women and the social world in which they live' (Poloma 1979: 11).

as analagous to a body. The idea of social organism was taken up by British anthropologist Bronislaw Malinowski, and then American Talcott Parsons, who above all established the structural-functional perspective. Social institutions and processes, in this view, are believed to be 'functional' in relation to society as a whole.

An example is what such functionalists refer to as 'social stratification'. This process, whereby people are 'layered' into different social positions, is said to be functional for society in the following way. The existence of a stratification system enables the most qualified persons to occupy the functionally most significant niches in a given society. Thus doctors, lawyers and, increasingly, various technologists can command high remuneration 'in keeping' with their credentials and elevated social status. The social body, in other words, may operate in a smooth fashion given such a lubricant.

People within the social body appear to be constrained by the kinds of roles they act out – scripted for them by society. The connection with Durkheim's view of society as a thing in itself which seems to determine individual behaviour, is obvious. The relationship between the body analogy and the system analogy (its later twentieth-century descendant) is close. But it is not so much individuals who are constrained, as 'components' of the system, responding to change in other areas. David Moberg gives us a good example of ecumenism in church life:

> As the world 'shrinks' through improved transportation, religious organizations are brought closer to one another, and cooperation is thrust upon them. The ecumenical movement can be explained partly as an outgrowth of the same forces that brought the United Nations into being (Moberg 1962: 260).

This explanation is, of course, incomplete, but the influence of the systems perspective, not to mention its illuminative quality, is clear.

A view like this is, of course, very attractive to those who value prediction. If one can indeed predict what will happen in one area of society consequent upon changes in another, sociology holds hope of becoming a 'hard' science. In a limited sense this is precisely the genius of sociology, to explain one social phenomenon in terms of others. But the predictive capacity of sociology must always be limited by what functionalists have sometimes ignored, namely the mutability of social 'laws'.

The body analogy may also be initially attractive to Christians. One recalls that Paul the apostle often referred to the church using a body model. Should we not adopt this perspective, reflecting as it does the quest for an ideal society, where harmony and co-operation between mutually dependent parts is the order of the day? That my reply would be negative in no sense demeans the integrity of the body model as applied to the church (or even future society in the new heaven and earth). Big problems are involved, which, if pursued carefully, illustrate well the difficulties of lifting biblical ideas out of context and attempting to use them 'raw' in social (or any other) science (Daines 1975).

I shall mention only two problems connected with this perspective. The first has to do with the place and needs of individuals and groups. The biblical body model is *directly* related to the human needs and responsibilities of individuals and groups. Contrast this with the rat race which may again provide a useful analogy. In such an event, it is not the rats who benefit (unless one counts the exercise gained or the reward): the point is to stage the race. The needs of the rats are relatively unimportant compared with the smooth running of the race. Something similar is going on with regard to 'society' or 'the system' in this perspective. The needs of the system are paramount. The example of stratification is a good one. This process of placing the best qualified in the most influential positions is functional – for whom? Of course, some individuals and groups may gain (and do!) but the point is that the system is served by this process; society is thought to be 'working smoothly'. Social efficiency comes to be seen as an overriding value, an end in itself. But beyond this is the simple point that a society cannot itself be said to have 'needs'. Needs are imputed to it by individuals and groups and usually refer to sectional interests rather than the good of the whole society in question. This is why Christian social scientists must always have the biblical requirements for a just society in the back of their minds. They form a powerful antidote to the distortions of any ideologues who further their own interests in the name of society's 'needs'.

Which brings us to the second problem: the structural-functional model has strong affinities with conservatism.[1] That is, the focus tends to fix on ways in which social equilibrium is maintained and the *status quo ante* restored after some shock to the system. Sociologists working within this perspective are generally interested in discovering the conditions necessary for keeping the existing social order intact. Concern with the so-called 'return to normal' following the outbreak of industrial unrest during a period of economic recession or technologically induced lay-off would illustrate this. The justice of the situation is a question left on one side, but this is not due to the relative neutrality of the perspective. The perspective is historically and logically wedded to other kinds of priorities, 'order' being the chief. From a biblical viewpoint, order is not a virtue in its own right (any more than efficiency is). The 'orderliness' of *shalom* is produced by justice. In it, all groups and individuals are contentedly free to pursue their God-given tasks without being exploited or dehumanized.

The structural-functional perspective, which views society as a body or a system, has attractions and defects. I have necessarily only commented on a few of each. Understanding how diverse aspects of social life are interrelated is clearly an attraction. But the way in which this perspective seems to be locked into a rather deterministic, conservative outlook is a decidedly negative feature. Order, stability and equilibrium need not be the kinds of values built into sociological theory, especially when this is at the expense of understanding the real and felt needs and operations of specific social groups within a given society. In the next section, such needs and aspirations come more starkly into focus.

Society as class-divided

What would interest the Marxist in the example of industrial unrest given above? Marxists certainly share the concern to *interpret* such a social phenomenon, and indeed to understand the relationship between one social group and another, but

[1] As it happens, various brands of Marxism also employ functionalist-style argument, for example, suggesting that capitalism 'needs' an army of unemployed labour. Though Marxists sometimes fall into similar traps to Parsons, they could hardly be accused of bolstering the *status quo*!

within a rather different framework. Marxists often share the functionalist view that the system has certain 'needs', for example a willing, mobile and healthy labour force, but would insist that the system in fact works against the best interests of that labour force. The system operates at their expense. The questions Marxists ask are not so much along the lines of, 'Is the system running smoothly?' as, 'Who is running the system?'

Notions of power and conflict come clearly to the fore in Marxian sociological accounts. Power is held by those who have a controlling influence over the means of production, and thus conflict exists, either latent or overt, between classes with power and those without. Those at the top make the rules which limit access of others into their position. This is reflected in educational systems, for instance, which, despite explicitly egalitarian policies, succeed in ensuring that the sons and daughters of the power élite (as C. Wright Mills called them) themselves become members of that élite. Modern media too, especially the T.V. news, portray an image of society where those who are in power are given 'proper deference', and those in the lower echelons treated with less air-space and respect. An establishment, *status quo* view is thus purveyed, reinforcing the power of establishment domination of the media (Glasgow Media Group 1976).

Of course one does not have to be a Marxist to notice that capitalist (and state-socialist) societies are split by inequalities. Indeed many sensitive sociological studies of class structuring (such as C. Wright Mills' in the U.S.A. or Frank Parkin's in the U.K.) are more Weber-influenced than Marxist. The impulse to make class analyses, however, often comes in response to more distinctly Marxist studies, now increasingly significant in North America as well as in Western Europe.

Although Marxist social theorizing had been in process in several societies right from 1848 when Marx and Engels produced the *Communist Manifesto*, not until the later 1960s did various brands of neo-Marxism surface as serious contenders in the sociological arena. Despite the containing efforts of those threatened by the idea of a Marxist sociology, Marxism now catalyses much sociological analysis and debate. In fact the gap between empirical studies and theory, mentioned above as a symptom of sociological malaise, has sometimes been bridged in recent years by a confrontation with Marxism. While as a political doctrine Marxism may have lost some credibility through the failure of its predictions, this has done little to stifle enthusiasm for Marxism as a tool of social investigation.

Of course the very idea of a Marxist sociology appears contradictory to some, both for scientific reasons and political or ideological ones. As I remarked before, 'sociology' is not itself a neutral or innocent term. It has its strongest links with 'industrial society' type of theories, related to structural-functionalism, which see industrial society developing in an evolutionary manner, according to a supposed inbuilt 'logic'. Any class-related disturbance or conflict is, on this view, only a passing phenomenon associated with the disruptive shift from pre-industrial to industrial society. It may even be seen as functional to the operation of capitalist society. And this is why Marxism has to be distinguished from a new sociological hybrid which appeared from the late 1960s, called 'conflict sociology'. Represented for example by John Rex and Ralf Dahrendorf in Europe, and Lewis Coser in North America, it steers a respectful course between the Scylla of Marx and the Charybdis of Parsons. Marxism, on the other hand, stresses the inevitability of class conflict, not within industrial society as such, but within industrial societies organized on capitalist lines. Marxism is thus a theory of capitalist society.

This is not to say, of course, that state-socialist societies have successfully 'transcended' capitalism. On the contrary they have rather substituted capitalism with an alternative mode of organizing production. It is the relative freedom of market forces which allows for the development of classes in capitalist societies; classes as such are not formed in societies where economic life is politically controlled. The possibility of keeping power monopoly within certain families is less, and the gap between manual and non-manual workers is smaller. The greater problem in state-controlled economies is the limitation of freedom which has accompanied the effort to abolish classes. This represents a serious contradiction yet to be overcome in Marxist theory. Marx seems to assume that classlessness would be accompanied by the 'withering away of the state'. But in practice the opposite occurs. State power grows as the very means of abolishing classes. One form of social exploitation is thus frequently replaced by another.

From a Christian perspective, in so far as Marxist social theory stimulates attempts to clarify the nature of exploitation in the contemporary world (within state-socialist or neo-capitalist societies), it must be respected as a partner in sociological dialogue. For Marx meant something rather specific by 'exploitation', to be explored in chapter seven. The Marxist promise to relate theory and empirical data must not be resisted either. This too is highly congenial to a Christian approach. The contradictions within this perspective, however, may also prove insuperable. I commented above that the apparent alternative between class domination or political domination 'has yet to be overcome'. In fact it is doubtful whether it can be overcome *within* Marxism. A normative understanding of the role of the state which would limit class exploitation without itself becoming exploitative is not available in Marxism as such. It could well be an area for meaningful dialogue between Marxist and Christian social scientists. It is certainly of practical relevance to a large proportion of the world's population.

Society as socially defined

'If people define situations as real', goes W. I. Thomas's famous phrase, 'they are real in their consequences' (Thomas 1923: 41). This is the essence of the view of society as socially defined. What matters, in this view, is not so much what massive social forces are operating to mould the life of the individual, but how the individual perceives, and thus acts in, the social world. Society, instead of being seen as something which makes people what they are, turns out to be what they make it.

Power, in this perspective, does not so much flow from the barrel of a gun, as Mao maintained, but rather is maintained because the masses co-operate with the powerful. Gandhi, rather than Mao, expresses this view: 'All exploitation is based on co-operation, willing or forced, of the exploited . . . there would be no exploitation if people refused to obey the exploiter' (quoted in Rigby 1974: 1). As long as the members of a society have complementary definitions of their everyday social situations, a given social order will persist. When this taken-for-grantedness breaks down, however, for whatever reason, change will occur.

To return to a previous example, many commuting businessmen take for granted the naturalness of the rat race. Even though they may be aware of such characterizations of their existence, they accept it as natural; define it as real. But maybe the introduction of some automated office procedure causes the loss of such a person's job. Such an occurrence will seriously damage his taken-for-granted world and could even, given the right set of circumstances and acquaintances, lead to a significantly different way of life such as that of a self-sufficient communard. (A more soberly conceived likely outcome is that the person will continue to see the world as 'given' and 'natural', and to react with bitter resignation rather than optimistic reconstruction.)

The relevance of this perspective has been most fruitfully tested with regard to studies of deviance and crime. Remember the common assumption regarding juvenile delinquents is that bad kids come from bad homes? This represents a highly popular (plausible and in some cases no doubt true) 'definition of the situation', shared by social workers, magistrates and high-school personnel. Moreover, it is very 'real in its consequence' for the children who get sent away as a result of their misdemeanours. But it is also part of the socially constructed world inhabited by the social workers, for their very profession is defined in terms which assume the bad-home bad-kid thesis. If they come to doubt the thesis (and say, perhaps, that the run-down neighbourhood had a big influence on what happened), they could put their own jobs at risk.

Although the reader will recall that the three major founding fathers did not found 'three schools', it is true that each draws a basic insight from each of Marx, Weber and Durkheim. In this case, it is Weber's notion of 'social action' which lies at the back of this approach. (It must be stressed, however, that to identify the three theorists with the three schools is grossly to oversimplify.) In fact, this sociological tendency or perspective is, like the other two, only to be considered as a loose collection of somewhat similar insights. Weber would be on one end of the same continuum as some of his ideological opponents.

Weber tried to mediate between the German positivists of his day, who wished to reduce social science to science of the physical type, and the phenomenologists who stressed the uniqueness of the human spirit and thus believed that only sympathetic intuition and a concern with meaning can yield adequate understanding. Weber argued that interpretive understanding (*verstehen*) is vital in sociology, but that such understanding may also be connected with causal explanation. Because meaningful action is important to Weber he takes very seriously the intentions and motives of social 'actors'. But wider social ripples are caused by such 'actions' than we might at first imagine. In our previous example it is clear that the social worker's definitions and taken-for-granted assumptions about everyday life become incorporated in influential court reports which in turn largely determine the future of certain 'delinquents'. The long-term result may be that more young people are sent to residential institutions and thus prepared to enter criminal careers and eventually to swell the numbers in prison.

This perspective also includes diverse components such as symbolic interactionism (represented by persons such as Erving Goffman) and the elusive and sometimes eccentric ethnomethodology (the brain-child of Harold Garfinkel). In the case of Goffman we see not only how individuals act according to their definitions of situations, but how people try to persuade others that their definition is correct. The social worker, for example, may present herself or himself as a dedicated, sympathetic and non-judgmental family helper, quite unconcerned about financial gain. Consideration of intentions, encouraged in this perspective, is a corrective to the notion that we slot ourselves passively into pre-determined roles. As for ethnomethodology, this is concerned with the minutiae of everyday life; the tiny 'taken-for-granteds' which, though they seem flimsily insignificant, are woven into the web of recognizable social intercourse. Garfinkel's most notorious (because as research practice morally dubious) experiments involve the disruption of such routines in order to establish their reality. For instance, he has sent his students into their own families to act like lodgers in order to discover what is routinely taken for granted in parent-child relationships. It comes as little surprise that when taken-for-granted greetings or duties are neglected, anger and frustration are soon expressed!

The charge of 'distance-from-reality' can hardly be levelled at this school. Its adherents are intensely concerned with everyday life, human situations. This is the emphasis of John O'Neill who has said that sociology ought to be seen as a 'skin trade', sharing with hairdressing, dentistry, medicine, counselling and entertaining the craft of 'working with people'. In other words, sociology's direct concern should be with people and their needs. So '. . . the rhetoric of scientism in sociology as well as its humanism must be tested against the commonsense relevances of everyday life . . . society is richer than sociology . . .' (O'Neill 1972: 10). Moreover, in so far as this perspective reminds us of the uniquely human quality of 'social action' (concerned with the meaningfulness of behaviour), then it may foster sociology as a truly human science.

But drawbacks also exist. For one thing the Weberian concern with wider social processes is not always shared by those working in this perspective. The ethnomethodologists in particular seem to stray close to a social atomizing which is distinctly pre-sociological. Moreover, in the effort to demonstrate that people create their reality, sociologists often forget the Marxist lesson that reality is only created in circumstances not of their choosing. From a Christian perspective people certainly construct their social world, but they do so not only in a historical, but also a normative context. People do respond to human definitions of situations, but those very human definitions are only made possible by divinely bestowed possibilities and directions not unknown by them. It would not be inappropriate therefore for the sociologist to hint at the 'bad faith' of our social worker who may rather risk the future of her young client than her own job.

Sociobiology and other stray schools

As I commented earlier, there are many plausible ways of cutting the sociological pie. Some might object that to focus arbitrarily on three tendencies is to do a grave injustice to some persuasions – such as ethnomethodology – which may seem to feature only as 'also-rans'. This is not intended to indicate any intrinsic irritation with, or insult to, ethnomethodology. As I suggest below, however, the only strong reason why one might think it deserved more space is if it is seen as somehow superior to other sociological schools.

'Conflict' sociology, though very popular in some quarters, has not been dignified with special and separate attention either. Again some may wish to take issue with this. John Rex,

Contemporary sociology: perspectives and paradigms

who acknowledges that 'some would say that (social conflict) should be the central theme' in sociology (Rex 1981: ix), has high hopes for it himself. He claims that his 'paradigm . . . is a more inclusive one than that of functionalism, interpreting the social order which it perceives as the outcome of balances of power and of truces' (Rex 1981: 125).

Other tendencies which undeniably mark shifts of emphasis or changes of direction have appeared in recent decades. The most significant, however, are both associated (in social thought) with strands of Marxism: neo-Marxist critical theory on one hand, and structuralism on the other. As I give these an airing later (some in chapter six, more in chapter seven), I refrain from discussing them here. It would be a mistake, however, to minimize their importance.

This leaves sociobiology, the effort to trace all social activity to its supposed biological bases, which in several respects is the odd one out. Or is it? One would be forgiven for thinking that the social aspects of Darwinism would have had plenty of time to become extinct by the late twentieth century. Who reads Herbert Spencer today? Who indeed? The new mood of free enterprise in economic practice would have gratified Spencer. He maintained that the struggle for survival in the economic realm was an inevitable part of progress. Evolutionary law decreed that the weakest should go to the wall; for a welfare state to intervene is to block progress. As Philip Abrams once pithily put it, Spencer 'turned Adam Smith's invisible hand into an invisible fist'.

If Marxism can still hold its own in the late twentieth century, why not social Darwinism? Though it may not be as popular in Europe, American Daniel Bell credits sociobiology with being one of the four developments with the greatest potential impact on future social thought. He says (in *The Social Sciences since the Second World War*) that these efforts (the others are neo-Marxism, structuralism and the new macro-economics) are 'major new synoptic attempts to provide some master keys to the understanding of social behaviour' (Bell 1982: 57).

Sociobiology is the endeavour to explain human societies in terms of the evolved drives of the human 'animal'. E. O. Wilson, its best-known proponent, frankly wants to 'biologize' social science: 'Sociology and the other social sciences, as well as the humanities, are the last branches of biology waiting to be included in the "modern synthesis"' (Wilson 1975: 4).

93

'Biological' drives, such as aggression and sexuality, are seen to be behind all social behaviour. Animal groups are likened to human societies, and humans are considered above all as complex animals. This is not merely the 'instinct-domination' idea of a Konrad Lorenz (which suggests we all have aggression which needs an outlet). Nor is it a B. F. Skinner type of stimulus-response theory (which suggests that humans are rather like rats or pigeons in the way we learn rules). Wilson bases his ideas on our genetic structure, by which social behaviour is 'reproduced' in succeeding generations. Human social relationships are thus seen as determined by each individual making the most of the reproductive success of his or her genes. This is done both through personal reproduction and through aiding the survival of others with similar genes.

As with Marxism and Parsonianism, critics are frequently as worried about the uses to which sociobiology may be put as they are about its intellectual strengths. Although the two factors are related in some ways, the two types of criticism can be distinguished. Not without reason social Darwinism is seen as a threat. The controversy surrounding Arthur Jensen's views on I.Q. and race should be enough to demonstrate this. Crudely put, the fear is that Jensenism (or aspects of Wilsonism) could be used to suggest that certain people are *racially* superior to others.

Intellectually, sociobiology is questionable on various counts. Are we justified in supposing that human kin selection is sufficiently like that found in animals? How do we explain the endless variety of codes governing kinship? Is not 'culture' in humans rather different – because rooted in self-consciousness – than biological behaviour patterns in animals? Who says that biology gives a 'more ultimate' explanation than sociology or anthropology – is this not sheer 'nothing buttery'? (Donald MacKay refers to reductionism, the argument in this case that social activity is 'nothing but' biological drives, as 'nothing buttery', MacKay 1974).

Once again the question of the human image comes to the fore. It would be dangerous to deny that human society is similar *in certain respects* to ant or ape colonies. The question is, are we more than genetically-determined animals? Christian thought, however much of evolutionary theory might be accepted, would be unanimous in saying we are more than naked apes.

Self-interest and altruism on a personal level, let alone social practice and cultural belief, are not seen, biblically, as genetically-rooted. Belief that we humans are the *imago dei* entails commitment to action, reflexivity, sociality, morality and so on. Neo-evolutionary ideas stand in contrast to this at the level of presupposition – of basic belief. This does not mean that sociology should take no account of biology. On the contrary, debate may help to clarify the issues at stake. But when they do become clear, it is imperative that Christians stand by what is non-negotiable (see Isbister 1978 for a preliminary critique).

Paradigmitis

A new disease has spread rapidly through social science and indeed into wider journalistic parlance. Occasionally reaching epidemic proportions, 'paradigmitis' seems to occur whenever someone is searching for a trendy synonym for 'school', 'approach', 'framework', 'outlook', 'belief-system', 'theory' or 'perspective'. Talk of 'paradigms' scientifically sanctifies what in more primitive times used to be known as 'pigeon-holing' or 'classifying'.

While it could be said that Thomas Kuhn's controversial book, *The Structure of Scientific Revolutions* (Kuhn 1962) led to the outbreak of paradigmitis, he can hardly be blamed for the abuses to which 'his' concept has been subjected. Kuhn's work is intended to show how the *process* of production of science occurs. He says that most of the time 'normal science' reigns, in which an accepted and established theoretical framework is used and taught fairly unquestioningly. 'Scientific revolutions' occur, however, when science can no longer cope with its own products – when theories begin to contradict themselves, or when they seem incapable of explaining a problem. Scientists then engage in an imaginative switch to another framework, not one which is logically 'proved', but which seems able to 'cope' better. Thus science moves on, according to Kuhn. Galileo, Newton and Einstein are key figures for important 'revolutions'.

All this happens within a scientific community, of course, which Kuhn also pointed out. Any paradigm shift is resisted by other scientists, and thus a conflict ensues between adherents of the incompatible paradigms. Whether or not Kuhn is right, the difficulty of talking about 'paradigms' in *social* science is beginning to emerge. For one thing what I have referred to as perspectives (but Ritzer calls paradigms – all *within* the 'multi-paradigmatic' discipline of sociology) exist *at the same time* in social science. Either sociology has not even taken off as a 'normal science' discipline yet or else Kuhn is wrong about the 'monopoly' of paradigms. In the latter case there is clearly no point in clinging to Kuhnian terminology.

To use 'paradigm' to mean 'pigeon-hole' is to miss the whole point of Kuhn's analysis. Paradigm, in his sense(s) (Masterman 1970) has to do with the *process* of scientific change (Harvey 1982). The best-known – and in many other respects excellent – attempt to apply Kuhn to sociology (Robert Friedrichs' *The sociology of sociology*, Friedrichs 1970) falls foul of this criticism. This is why I have avoided the issue here by unashamedly 'pigeon-holing' different kinds of sociology as 'perspectives'.

Nevertheless the Kuhnian debate over paradigms does raise some important questions from a critical Christian perspective. If there *is* an overarching sociological paradigm then, as Hawthorn hints, it has not changed much:

> Not only have the guiding assumptions about man's relations to nature and the status of his sociability changed little since the beginning of the nineteenth century, but contrasting sets of assumptions have often coexisted in the same places and even occasionally in the same men (Hawthorn 1976: 253).

Perhaps the re-situating of sociology in structuralist or sociobiological terms *might* count (if it occurred) as a Kuhnian revolution? Whatever the case, the crucial thing, as I see it, is to attempt to assess specific theories in a Christian manner. It does not appear at present that the whole sociological edifice is in need of dismantling and reconstruction. Aspects of it, however, sometimes rather significant ones, are due to be weighed in the balances. From a Christian viewpoint at least they will be found wanting.

This brings me to the second general point arising from Kuhn, the question of what else, as well as logic and evidence, determines theory-choice? What exactly *is* scientific 'rationality'? Does it involve 'shared values', as Kuhn suggests? This is a burning issue in philosophy and social science today. As Richard Bernstein says, even Kuhn 'would agree that what is required is

a more comprehensive and subtle understanding of rationality'
(Bernstein 1976: 93). Neither space nor competence in philosophy enables me to offer a lot here, but discussion of the issues is
the task of the following chapter. Before we get there, however,
let us return to the issue of perspectives – what do we do with
the baffling variety on the sociological menu?

Sectarians or synthesizers?

What constitutes an authentic response to the persistence of
competing perspectives in today's sociology? How may a Christian approach guide us through this rather perplexing array of
plausible but partly contradictory positions? A route taken by
some is entrenchment in a *sectarian* stance. Functionalism,
Marxism or interpretive sociology, some insist, is the only way
to do sociology. Other modes are logically or ideologically
improper. Another route is that of the *synthesist*. This attempts
to draw together the competing perspectives in a grand scheme
which overcomes the disarray and at last is able to present the
supposedly waiting world with a coherent discipline. A third
alternative is the *pragmatic approach*. This the way of searching
out theories appropriate to the subject-matter and chosen
according to imperatives outside the discipline. I shall commend a version of this third way which goes beyond the political
and social orientations usually chosen as 'imperatives outside
the discipline'. This approach seems to be compatible with the
critical integration model of relating belief and science.

Before going further, it is well to remember that social science
aims not to reflect on the possible logical connections between
abstract categories, but to explain aspects of the real social
world. So an important test of a sociological perspective is
whether theories derived from it are appropriate ways of dealing
with the data. Social science embraces such a wide range of
phenomena, from schools to cities, and from social work
strategies to international economic systems, that it would be
surprising if any one approach or theory could comprehend
them all.

Nevertheless sectarians, as I am calling them, believe that they
have discovered the essential hermeneutic key to unlock all the
mysteries of social life. They at least find some security amid the
shifting perspectival sands. Moreover, they clearly recognize

that philosophical debate is inseparable from social analysis. (Others, ostrich-like, react to the plurality of perspectives by maintaining that they can 'get on' with social research without being troubled by theoretical wrangles. Thus they pretend that philosophical winds blowing above the surface have no shaping effect on the sand of data in which their heads are buried.) But the trouble with sectarianism is that certain problems simply have to be shelved. The most skilful sociological sleight of hand cannot conceal the ethnomethodologists' inability to comment on the relevance of the pre-revolutionary religious monopoly, on the nature of contemporary French educational practices or the Marxists' lack of interest in the different ways institutionalized psychiatric patients present themselves to doctors and to each other. The price of sectarianism is the shrunken scope of sociological imagination. There may also be a political cost in that sociology becomes tied to conservatism, anarchism or revolutionism.

Like sectarianism, synthesizing also represents a response within a response. If the former withdraws from diversity, the latter welcomes it. Rightly the diversity is seen as a reflection of the diversity and dispute characterizing the social world; to minimize that is falsely to straitjacket social explanation. But the true synthesizer goes beyond a mere acceptance of diversity to an attempt to show how the different perspectives fit into a grand overall scheme in which inter-school contests lose their significance. This is both arrogant and blind. On the one hand it implies that, once established, the synthesis is one which *ought* to be adhered to by all sociologists. On the other, it ignores real differences between perspectives and is also likely to entail a further distancing from everyday life.

Two points deserve mention here. One, the different perspectives illuminate different (and often complementary) aspects of social life, so that they cannot be reduced to each other. For example, in the sociology of education, interactionist accounts of classroom relationships may complement Marxist studies of the role of schooling in a capitalist society. Light may be thrown on the schooling process which would not be available without the existence of both perspectives. But the second point is that real divergences exist between the perspectives, which are far from trivial, and which therefore rule out any simplistic synthesis. The second point invites closer inspection.

Those sociologists who sensibly acknowledge that some mod-est pragmatic approach characterizes all the best sociological endeavours still do not go on to spell out *why* one combination of perspectives is more appropriate than another. The nearest we get is this: an introductory text cautions that 'sociology should remain open-minded enough to allow new perspectives . . . but firm enough to retain a sense of what it is to be rational and reasonable about human beings' social worlds' (Bocock *et al. 1980:* 9). It is as if a plate of cakes is passed round and one chooses whatever that moment's taste finds appetizing and appropriate. Or the plumber's assistant passes an array of cop-per joints to the prostrate plumber who chooses the one which will most adequately connect the two protruding pipe ends. But in sociology this simply will not do. 'Taste' and 'fit' are inappro-priate images for a task which is both socially located and in which the sociologist is socially (and thereby ethically) respons-ible. Of course there are the important criteria of data which theories must 'fit'. But in social science perspectives and theories help to determine what counts as data, so the question is always more than merely technical. Perspectives and theories make sense (or 'fit') according to *other* criteria than the 'rational and reasonable'.

The criteria by which sociological perspectives seem appro-priate and social theories 'make sense' are embedded in the perspectives and theories. A strong relationship exists between 'purposes' and 'perspectives'. As Steven Lukes observes, such issues 'form the roots of the tree of social scientific knowledge' (Lukes 1977: ix). It is therefore important to dig down to dis-cover exactly what those roots are.

The functionalist perspective, for example, has apparent affinities with the scientistic motif of prediction and control. Its roots lie in the notion that people can know about and fashion society according to discoverable laws, without reference to any metaphysical reality (such as God). Every social event is, in principle, explicable according to natural laws; science has no limits. The interactionist perspective may be seen as a reaction against this. From experience alone we tend to resist the notion that humans are determined in this way, and thus freedom is asserted as an alternative motif to science and forms the basis of a contending perspective in the sociological arena. Some Marx-ists or Weberians might claim that their perspective mediates between scientistic control and reality-constructing freedom, and this claim has some validity. But such views are still rooted in specific views of what it is to be human. Marxism cannot ultimately break out of the dialectic of post-Christian humanism with its swing between control and liberation because it refuses to acknowledge that there is any more to life than that dialectic. Only if repeatedly pushed to uncover the *origins* of inequality, or when driven to acknowledge that Marxism ultimately derives its power from the *hope* of a new kind of social world, might the Marxist admit that some non-empirical beliefs enter into his agenda.

Knowingly or unknowingly, then, social theorists working within a particular perspective promote viewpoints which may be shown to be religiously rooted. For instance while the symbolic interactionist may give a very detached account of his or her efforts at social understanding, the conspicuous connection between such an outlook and the existentialist and counter-cultural trends of the later 1960s and early 1970s may not lightly be overlooked. For one thing, while it may not be the intention of sociologists to contribute to such a movement, it is necessary that they be aware of the possible *effects* of studies which emphasize, say, the fragility and precariousness of the taken-for-granted world. And, for another thing, it is all too easy to allow metaphysical commitments to seep into methodological statements; as Mary Stewart Van Leeuwen says, people get 'seduced by their own metaphors' (Van Leeuwen 1982: 90). Talk enough about people being 'socialized', and sociologists may begin to believe that people really are the passive mechanical items which socialization theory has often implied.

Thus great danger lurks in the unthinking usage or acceptance of some plausible perspective in sociology. Christians, committed to a specific understanding of humanness, dare not compromise with views whose roots are quite different from theirs. But while we should be aware of this danger, it should not cause paralysis, precluding further sociological endeavour until some 'Christian' alternative is developed. And neither should it lead to a lifetime spent in digging at roots, subjecting them to increasingly minute inspection before final rejection.

If we grant that perspectives, just like concepts, are contested because they are related to moral and religious stances, then it follows that part of the sociological task is to ensure that the moral and religious stance implied by the concept or perspective is consistent with the outlook of the sociologist. The fundamental commitment of the sociologist should provide some of the criteria of acceptance or rejection of concepts and perspectives. And, as it is not the case that to accept *part* of a perspective commits one to the *whole* (let alone to its religious roots), a modest pragmatism is in order. But this approach is followed according to certain (explicit) criteria. The notion that 'all truth is God's truth' (the subject of an excellent book by Arthur Holmes, 1979) is not an excuse to baptize every attractive idea with a Christian seal of approval. It rather expresses the conviction that, as God is the author of truth (and Jesus himself personifies truth), true ideas and actions, wherever they are found, belong to him. Thus true insights may be yielded by a perspective which itself is oriented away from biblical revelation. They ought to be *claimed* as such by Christians and woven into their explanatory account.

Three guidelines

First, remember that all perspectives have some world view presuppositions. They are not neutral. Max Weber recognized that different perspectives could be traced back to competing 'gods and demons'. Subsequent social theorists have tried, unsuccessfully, to find a fixed vantage-point for assessing the worth of all perspectives and theories (Lukes 1982). For instance, Marxists think that the 'proletarian perspective' is ultimate, whereas Habermas believes we can judge from the Archimedian point of an 'ideal speech situation', where there is harmonious communication between persons. My proposal, once again, is different. Rather than resorting to merely political or utopian criteria, a Christian view of humanness is available, offering a framework by which different perspectives may be evaluated – and sometimes critically utilized.

Two, do not prejudge the perspective. I doubt the wisdom of rejecting any sociological perspective out of hand. Despite their often being traceable to secular roots, they may contain undeniable insights on the social world compatible with (and maybe illuminating for) Christian commitment. I sympathize with those so disillusioned with some specific perspective that they advocate a 'clean break' with all 'humanistic' thought. But I also beg them to remember Balaam's ass. Genuine perceptions can come from very unsuspected quarters! The task, again, is to 'test all things and hold fast to the good'. The 'testing criteria' which have been considered here derive from a Christian view of humanness. Sectarianism and synthesizing are thus inappropriate. The third way, of empirically-sensitive and Christianly-guided pragmatism, is nearer the mark.

Three, do not succumb to perspective-paralysis! Embark on some programme of social research. David Wolfe offers some sound advice for those perplexed by pluralism:

> Start where you are. Continue with (or choose, depending on where you are) the interpretive scheme which is personally most important or interesting to you and pursue it as long as it does not succumb to active criticism . . . Why not go with the scheme that seems to you to offer the richest view, the greatest hope, the most powerful values? (Wolfe 1982: 68).

Remember that the aim is not mere social speculation, but to find coherent explanations of social phenomena, using concepts and theories. This 'principled pragmatism' must do justice both to a Christian social perspective *and* to empirical data. What I have written is supposed to be a first stab at the problem, but its development must occur in the context of understanding events, institutions and processes in the real social world rather than in 'the abstract'. Nevertheless, other aspects of the same problem have yet to be tackled: in the following two chapters we grapple first with beliefs and valuing in social theory, and second with social action and social structure.

5

SOCIAL SCIENCE:
SEEING AND BELIEVING

Thou shalt not sit
with statisticians nor commit
a social science.

W. H. Auden

. . . in a theistic universe no facts are meaningless
but everything is value-laden.

Arthur Holmes

Most people are familiar with Rodin's famous sculpture of 'the thinker'. There he sits, his chin propped on the back of one clenched hand, his elbow resting on one knee. Lost in thought, he ratiocinates in splendid isolation, producing knowledge in a social vacuum. Rodin's sculpture represents a myth. But it is a myth shared by more than one of sociology's founders, including Auguste Comte. He deliberately read only poetry during the composition of his *Positive Philosophy*, in the belief that this would preserve his 'cerebral hygiene'! Knowledge is ever produced in the context of cultural belief and social milieu. Such knowledge may or may not be true, but either way, it bears the mark of its time and place.

In this chapter the notion of critical integration is developed in relation to one's stance in science. I shall suggest that social science is built on more than accurate observation. It involves seeing and believing. Once again, while two-way traffic ('critical integration') is encouraged between sociology and Christian commitment, I take it that a case has already been made elsewhere for sociological penetration of Christian social understanding. Modern Christians who work away from their native land, for instance, tend to be much more sensitive about the danger of imposing alien western life-styles in the name of Christianity. Similarly, those who choose to remain with their congregations in inner-urban areas tend to do so with their eyes open to the huge historical hiatus between traditional middle-class churches and the typical inhabitants of pre-cast concrete deserts or the tight-knit tenement territories. The formulations of theology itself, while dealing with some abiding verities, are increasingly recognized as products of time and place. In other words, the sociological imagination has begun to deepen Christian awareness of our modern social situation. The case can scarcely be made in reverse. Christian imagination has as yet had little self-conscious impact in social science.

In fact, in order to make a case at all, we must first dispose of three major obstacles. The first obstacle is the notion that sociology is inherently incompatible with Christian commitment, that sociology denies the claims of Christian truth. The second, and related to it, is the tactic some adopt in order to overcome the apparent hostility – the wearing of different hats, sociological and Christian. This is the tactic of 'methodological atheism'. The third obstacle is the empiricist idea that social theory is in any case neutral with regard to beliefs and values. Such qualities are external to the science and thus, it is claimed, should have no place in the scientific process. To avoid confusion the three levels at which one may speak of sociology are borne in mind; the levels of world view or over-arching perspective, of discipline or institution and of intellectual practices.

Sociology as a threat to belief

As we saw earlier Durkheim, among others, was convinced that sociology should become a secular alternative to religion as a guide to social conduct. In Britain the chief exponent of a similar view (though the two men had severe disagreements) was Herbert Spencer (1820-1903). He attempted to found a systematic sociological discipline on the basis of Darwinian evolution. T. H. Huxley, who did more than any other to popularize Darwin's

views as an alternative to certain Christian beliefs, encouraged
Spencer in his work. Spencer, who had come from a Free
Church family in the industrializing English Midlands, saw
himself as an antagonist of Christian faith in the late-nineteenth-
century battle of religion and science. In fact he did much to
help establish the popular myth that the battle was 'won' by
'science'. His views were also popularized in the U.S.A.,
especially by Graham Sumner, teaching at Yale. Sumner tied
Spencer's work into an elaborate evolutionary justification for
competitive capitalism.

One way and another, sociology came to be seen as a threat to
Christian faith, even though the content of that threat was often
ill-defined. It was rather an assumption about the self-evident
weakness and inappropriateness of faith to the new industrial-
capitalist world. Such an assumption was common to the *philo-
sophes* (or, better, 'sociologues') of the French Enlightenment.
Their ideas in relation to the social sciences were best represented by German philosopher Immanuel Kant, whose influence is documented below. And of course progress seemed to
be on the side of science, which helped confirm the view that
God was superfluous. The tradition continues. In the 1940s,
leading American sociologist Kingsley Davis denounced
religion as 'withering like a leaf before the flame' of science
(Davis 1948: 536). In the 1970s a popular sociology text announced that all sociologists

> accept a naturalistic view of man . . . he is not endowed with
> some special spirit or some special portfolio from heaven which
> removes him from nature's processes . . . any mysterious event,
> any miracle, can ultimately be found to have its origins in natural
> conditions available to man's observation . . . where mysteries
> exist, it attributes them to ignorance of how things 'work' in the
> real world (Cuzzort 1969: 8).

By the 1980s, a little more guardedly, a British text commented
that sociology 'will always appear as a threat to those who do not
want, or cannot cope with, the open-ended but often irreverent
discussion of social problems and human societies. This now
includes those who claim to know truths about human societies
on the basis of . . . revelation from a supernatural source such as
the Bible' (Bocock *et al.* 1980: 9). Sociological scepticism, they

105

contend, is necessary for an unprejudiced understanding of social life. Apparently faith must be left behind in the sociologist's enterprise. The assumption is that faith is 'closed-minded' while sociology is 'open'. At this point let us briefly examine the nature of the 'threat' of social science to Christian belief.

Sociology is a weak weapon for use against Christianity. Most of the supposed sociological arguments against the existence of God or the truth of Christianity are far from complete. The better sociologists frankly admit that there are strict limits to what may be said about the truth or falsity of religion. At the same time some imply that invincible sociological artillery may be wheeled into offensive positions against Christianity. Thus it could be the antagonistic atmosphere of the university department, rather than the social analysis itself, which appears as a threat. Eileen Barker has commented helpfully on these limits in a discussion of the sociological 'explanation' of religion. Her remarks inform the following discussion (Barker 1980). The 'explanations' may be of various kinds; we mention but two. First, correlations. It may be suggested that, for example, adherence to Christian churches in Australia, Britain or the U.S.A. is overwhelmingly a middle-class trait. Does this mean that Christianity is merely a reflex of the bourgeoisie, a social epiphenomenon? If I claim to be a Christian, is this *explicable* in terms of my middle-class origins? Far from it. The statistics cannot *predict* anything about my individual behaviour. And even probability claims depend on an 'other things being equal' clause. Moreover, the 'other things' usually are not equal. There is no limit to other variables which could intervene to yield different results.

So-called functionalist 'explanations', deriving from Durkheim, are equally undamaging to religion. Christianity, it may be said, *functions* to produce social cohesion. If 'functions' here implies 'consequence' then this may comprise a limited explanation for the persistence of religion, but not of its origin. And if 'purpose' is meant, then this is an explanation in terms of someone (human or superhuman) who had the purpose of bringing about cohesion in mind. Moreover in this case the purpose would be the 'cause' of the religion; the cohesion the consequence.

Even if one uses more than one explanatory mode, 'total'

explanation remains an impossibility. So anyone who alleges
that religion is 'nothing but' this or that is engaging in the
logically illicit practice of reductionism. In fact, as Eileen Barker
rightly concludes, sociology (as intellectual practice) presents
not a threat to Christian beliefs, but rather a challenge to the way
in which Christianity is lived out. Sociology could act as a
Balaam's ass. A discipline which is assumed to be incapable of
saying anything worth hearing – and in fact deserving only
insults – might utter some discomforting brays in the direction
of the church. Perhaps it takes a sociological imagination to see
how much like secular bureaucracies some big denominations
have become. If all clerical pronouncements relate to efficiency,
cost-effectiveness and results, then this might be evidence that
the church, like Balaam, is heading the wrong way!

Perhaps the more insidious threat of sociology to faith is that
of 'relativism'. The challenge from those who wish to deny the
reality of Christian faith by explaining it away in functionalist or
reductionist terms is more blatant. But relativism is a creeping,
cancerous academic affliction from which social scientists are
particularly prone to suffer. It can corrode the core of faith by
suggesting, for example, that Christianity, being only one faith
among others, must limit its exclusive claims. But in fact a little
relativism, used the right way, is a handy cure for social scientific dogmatism or overreaching claims. In this case it simply
exists as a reminder of human finitude, and our incapability of
arriving at unassailable answers in science. On the other hand,
too much relativism, as we shall see, is counter-productive. A
thoroughgoing scepticism is impossible to live with. So where
does the problem lie?

The art of suspicion

It is the sociology of knowledge, especially in its popular forms,
which provides us with the basis of this threat, appearing as it
sometimes does in the guise of mistrust, cynicism, debunking
and suspicion. Religion comes to be seen merely as a socially
constructed reality, serving as an agent of social control and
solidarity, and providing legitimacy for things-as-they-are. Put
this way, we can sense the spirit of reductionism. But the
reductionists do sometimes make a very plausible case. We
cannot but agree with at least part of their analysis.

As I have indicated, there are knotty logical problems connected with the sociology of knowledge. In a reductionist account, the Christian ideas may be seen as nothing but fortuitous products of certain historical circumstances, now moulded by the surrounding culture. But the Protestant Ethic thesis alone should remind us that the direction of influence of social location and ideas may be both ways! Other studies also indicate that a Christian perspective can have a social impact. Carefully documented studies such as David Bebbington's on the role of the 'nonconformist conscience' in British politics at the turn of the century, are cases in point (Bebbington 1982). Another example is Kevin Clements' conclusions about the role of theology after the Depression in New Zealand. Once supporters of the *status quo*, by the mid-1930s religious opinion leaders lent legitimacy to the Labour Party – who were change-agents at the time – and contributed to their political victory in the 1935 election. Thus the so-called 'religious variable' had a considerable independent influence on social change by suggesting what the Labour Party might do to bring about a Christian solution to the then current malaise (Clements 1971).

The fact that the church may exhibit certain characteristics does not mean that those characteristics exhaustively define what the church is. Related to this is the supposed assessment of the truth of some doctrine in terms of its origin or why some people hold it. To show that oppressed and exploited peoples, such as the millenarians (Cohn 1965), were enthusiastic about the imminent return of Christ with its reversal of social conditions and release from misery, is not to explain away belief in the second coming.

Probably the most abiding tendency in the sociology of knowledge is the self-referential fallacy. I hinted at this above, in saying that a thoroughgoing scepticism is impossible to live with. Somehow, the sociology of knowledge must avoid eating its own tail by denying so much that it cannot itself survive. C. S. Lewis invented the character Ezekiel Bulver as the discoverer of the sociology of knowledge type of approach.

Bulver ... heard his mother say to his father – who had been maintaining that two sides of a triangle were together greater than the third – 'Oh, you say that because you are a man.' 'At that moment', E. Bulver assures us, 'there flashed across my opening

mind the great truth that refutation is a necessary part of argument. Assume that your opponent is wrong, then explain his
error, and the world will be at your feet.' (Lewis 1970: 225).

Marx and Freud are the great Bulverists, according to Lewis.
Artists of suspicion they may be, but they have not fully
explained themselves:

> Now this is obviously great fun; but it has not always been noticed
> that there is a bill to pay for it. There are two questions that people
> who say this kind of thing ought to be asked. The first is, Are all
> thoughts thus tainted at the source, or only some? The second is,
> Does the taint invalidate the tainted thought – in the sense of
> making it untrue – or not?
>
> If they say that all thoughts are thus tainted, then, of course, we
> must remind them that Freudianism and Marxism are as such
> systems of thought as Christian theology or philosophical
> idealism. The Freudian and the Marxian are in the same boat with
> all the rest of us, and cannot criticize us from outside. They have
> sawn off the branch they were sitting on. If, on the other hand,
> they say that the taint need not invalidate their thinking, then
> neither need it invalidate ours. In which case they have saved
> their own branch, but also saved ours along with it (Lewis 1970:
> 224).

The point is that, in the end, the sociology of knowledge cannot
be a 'place to stand' which is immune from the influences and
distortions which it attributes to others. It can be no more than a
(albeit valuable) perspective. In fact we can find no such solid
place to stand *within* the discipline of sociology. We stand on
extra-sociological commitments in the last analysis. I wish to
argue here that, far from sociology invalidating Christian faith,
Christian faith can provide that 'place to stand', from which
sociology may be practised. Needless to say, not all will agree
with this view. A prominent exponent of a rather different
position is Peter Berger.

Methodological atheism

Peter Berger, author of a number of popular sociology books, is
sensitive to the questions raised by Christian faith in relation to
sociology. He admits that sociological analysis of religion can

prove unsettling to believers. Though he did not intend it, he confessed that one of his major books, *The Sacred Canopy*, read like a 'treatise on atheism' or a 'counsel of despair for religion in the modern world' (Berger 1970: ix). It is not difficult, however, to see how his so-called 'methodological atheism' could be construed as naked atheism *tout court*. He asserts that

> sociological theory must, by its own logic, view religion as a human projection, and by the same logic can have nothing to say about the possibility that this projection may refer to something other than the being of its projector (Berger 1967: 180).

On this view sociology itself can never be more than a thoroughly pagan way of understanding the world. Michael Cavanaugh has recently reasserted this view, calling it 'sociological Euhemerism' (Cavanaugh 1982). Euhemerus of Messene was a Greek who reinterpreted the mythic deeds of the gods and heroes in terms of mortal history. For his pains he was branded as 'a hoary braggart, penning wicked books ...' Cavanaugh, like Berger, argues that sociology should follow in the footsteps of Kant and Weber, who in turn are intellectual descendents of Euhemerus.

Berger has not lacked opponents, however. The main thrust of their arguments is based on the logical impossibility of 'bracketing' beliefs about religion when trying to describe it (Smart 1973). Against Berger and his ilk Robert Bellah made this claim:

> [To] put it bluntly, *religion is true* ... since religious symbolization and religious experience are inherent in the structure of human existence, all reductionism must be abandoned (Bellah 1970: 253).

Unfortunately, although this represented something of a breakthrough, Bellah's contribution raises as many problems as it solves. For while religion may be true, in a subjective sense to its adherents, what about the truth-claims of individual religions? Rastafarianism, Shintoism, biblical Christianity and the Unification Church cannot all be 'true' in the same sense. Nevertheless, Bellah's challenge to the reductionists involved pointing 'out instead their own implicit religious positions'. Much better, he suggests, to make one's own position clear, and not to obscure things under a cloak of methodological atheism.

A difficulty also exists with regard to the object of study, as Robert Towler makes sharply clear: 'Avowed methodological atheism is a fail-safe device which protects the sceptical researcher from taking the beliefs of others too seriously . . .' But at the same time, returning to the question of the beliefs of the sociologist, methodological atheism 'protects also the religiously or ideologically committed researcher from allowing his own beliefs to pollute his research' (Towler 1974: 2).

Despite its widespread popularity, one does not have to follow Berger's methodological atheism in sociology of religion or, for that matter, in any area of sociology. Gerard Dekker, a Dutch sociologist who participated in an Oxford dialogue between sociologists and theologians, made a proposal which deserves a sympathetic hearing. Without abandoning sociology as an empirical discipline, Dekker argues that 'methodological theism' would be just as valid as methodological atheism, but one would *not* have to proceed on the working assumption that there is no God. Thus he says:

> The methodologically theistic approach studies reality from the supposition that there is a God and that people think and act from a relation with that God. For the sociologist who chooses this approach the task remains to describe, to 'explain' what happens *in this reality*: so it remains an empirical approach (Dekker 1978: 6).

Admittedly, Dekker's is little more than a proposal, and we have yet to see an empirical study which exemplifies the approach. Also he was writing mainly for the sociology of religion, while I wish to broaden his case to apply more generally in any sociological area. But before we focus on that we must deal with the third obstacle to the admission of Christian ideas into sociology: the legacy of Kant.

The legacy of Kant

It is no exaggeration to say that, philosophically, classical sociologists stood on Kant's shoulders. And Kant himself straddled the eighteenth and nineteenth centuries in thought as well as biography (1724–1804). A child of the Enlightenment, he

111

taught at Königsberg University in Germany. His ideas returned to popularity after the nineteenth-century enthusiasm for Romanticism, exerting a strong influence on Weber and Durkheim in sociology. As Colin Brown says, Kant 'personifies modern man's confidence in the power of reason to grapple with material things and its incompetence to deal with anything beyond' (Brown 1969: 91).

Following Descartes, Kant took human reason as his central point of reference. And while he shared the Enlightenment optimism about the power of reason, he believed it had strict limits. Specifically, the human mind cannot, according to him, attain rational knowledge of anything beyond its immediate experience of the material world. In his *Religion within the Limits of Reason Alone* (1793) he declared in effect that enlightened people could only accept a religion with no frills such as faith in a supernatural God who intervenes in human history. Like Euhemerus, he fell foul of the Powers that be – in this case the King of Prussia – but this did little to reduce the baneful influence of his ideas.

Classical sociologists responded to Kant in different ways, which cannot be explored here (on Kant and Durkheim, e.g., see Tiryakin 1978). But Max Weber's famous distinction between facts and values is one example of the impact of Kant's distinction between 'is' and 'ought' statements. We can say something about the former, what is, but this has no connection with what ought to be. Yet the question vexed Weber deeply. He was profoundly convinced that sociology should be value-relevant (addressing the pressing issues of Bismarck's Germany) but also that it had itself to be value-free. His neo-Kantianism comes across forcefully in his consideration of the question, What is the meaning of science as a vocation?

Tolstoi has given the simplest answer, with the words: 'Science is meaningless because it gives no answer to our question, the only question important for us: "What shall we do and how shall we live?" ' That science does not give an answer to this is indisputable. The only question that remains is the sense in which science gives 'no' answer, and whether or not science might yet be of some use to the one who put the question correctly (Gerth and Mills 1958: 143).

Thus for Weber science can only tell us about effective ways of achieving a purpose, or what the consequences of that achievement might be. Science cannot help us to decide which purpose is right.

Weber's view, often domesticated as a trivial defence of neutral science (which is not even value-relevant) achieved dominance in twentieth-century sociological studies. Since the 1970s, however, especially following the reception of 'Frankfurt School' 'critical theory', such neo-Kantianism has come under fire. (Critical theory claims that all knowledge is rooted in, and affected by, human interests. Social science can never be neutral, but is ever critical of the object of study.) As Habermas, a stepchild of the Frankfurt School, puts it:

> the philosophy of science that has emerged since the mid-nineteenth century . . . is methodology pursued with a scientistic self-understanding of the sciences. "Scientism" means science's belief in itself: that is, the conviction that we can no longer understand science as *one* form of knowledge, but rather must identify knowledge with science (Habermas 1971: 4).

Habermas and others are raising a new challenge to Kant. The scientific monopoly on knowledge is an artificial exclusion of other kinds of knowledge, and perpetrates the myth of 'uncontaminated' knowledge. One does not have to believe all that critical theorists like Habermas assert in order to see that they possess a powerful critique of Kantianism.

More generally, we turn now to the post-empiricist debate (generated in part by critical theory) to explore further the ways in which commitments may affect sociological research.

Sociology guided by commitments

At first blush such a heading sounds incongruous, especially to ears tuned to Kantian airwaves. But in the later twentieth century a major reappraisal of the philosophy of science, especially social science, makes such questions very relevant. Alvin Gouldner, very much an international figure in the sociological world of the 1970s, argued fiercely for a value-committed sociology. Impatient with the supposedly value-free position of Talcott Parsons (which he suggested was in fact

113

deeply impregnated with a notion of social control via state welfare), he refused the Weberian split between scientist and citizen, or 'is' and 'ought'. He sought instead 'a new self-image and an historical mission that would enable sociology to act humanely in the larger world' (Gouldner 1970: 512).

Of course, such talk could be construed as Comtean bluster, only replacing Comte's priestly pontifications with the rhetoric of prophecy. While it is perhaps too much to expect sociology to provide such a 'mission', a modest version of Gouldner's message could well be taken to heart. But what was largely missing in Gouldner's gut-level critique of value-free sociology was a philosophical foundation for his position. While he marshalled sociological arguments with masterful panache, he acknowledged the need for some philosophical filler to make good the gaps between them. Contributors to the current post-empiricist debate are providing just that (e.g. Giddens 1977, Hesse 1978, Thomas 1979 and Tudor 1982).

It must be stressed that the better post-empiricists reject neither the importance of empirical data, nor rationality, nor even objectivity. However, all these ideas require some reinterpretation. First, empirical data – the facts of science – are not simply 'out there' awaiting observation. Let us refer to an example to illustrate this. Tepoztlan, a village in the mountains of Mexico, has received quite contradictory sociological treatment. Community studies made there remarked on different 'facts' about the same village. Robert Redfield's study found a bucolic pastoral paradise; Oscar Lewis's, a confused and conflict-ridden network of family-feud and violence (Redfield 1947, Lewis 1949). This was due to a number of factors, not least of which was the different world view and human image of the two researchers.

Second, rationality involves more than its formal properties. We say that something is rational if it is not self-contradictory, is supported by relevant evidence, and is subject to rejection if good reasons are found for so doing. Take for example the notion that people in poverty must feel relatively deprived before they will revolt over their condition. This statement appears to be internally consistent, and historical evidence may be produced to show that it is a useful generalization. People may know they are in poverty, but unless they also feel a sense of injustice about their situation, will tend to accept the situation as inevitable.

114

Contemporary social analysis seems to give no ground for rejecting the idea (Runciman 1966).

But there is more than this to rationality. Sociological notions must also 'make sense' of social situations. And this 'making sense' will vary from one group of assessors to another, depending on social location and, we might add, our fundamental commitments. We all have different reasons for deciding what to accept and what to reject. As Donald Hudson suggests, one of the things we mean by 'rationality' is that it is *appropriate* to believe something to be the case (Hudson 1980).

Third, the quest of objectivity. This is a key characteristic of modern science. But in social science, argues Mary Hesse, the definition of objectivity may need refinement. That scientific theories are under-determined by facts is old hat. It simply means that no amount of data collection 'adds up' to a theory. Theories are only (or should be) *constrained* by facts. But Hesse and others insist that *all* facts are theory-laden (Hesse 1978). The 'facts' about Tepoztlan are only 'facts' because they relate to some theory (albeit pre-scientific) about village life.

Theories, in turn, contain value-judgments. Hesse points out that in natural science they tend to be filtered out over time, largely due to its commitment to prediction and control of the environment. But in social science, as we have already seen, prediction on the natural science model is scarcely possible. The most important reason for this is what Giddens calls the 'reflexive incorporation of social science knowledge into the rationalization of action' (Giddens 1977: 28). By this he means that people may act on the basis of self-knowledge derived from social science, thus potentially altering that very knowledge.

But even if prediction and control were possible in social science, it may not be desirable. Natural science is committed to prediction and control, and this, says Hesse, could itself be seen as a form of valuing. If it is, then why not choose to reject that value in preference for another, such as 'justice' or some other value-goal such as Weber might identify for the value-relevance of sociology?

Elsewhere I have suggested a Christian response to this, in which I argue that 'the whole spectrum of biblical insights on humanness be allowed to penetrate social science as evaluative criteria' (Lyon 1983b). I have also tried to meet some potential criticisms which might come from Christians more enamoured

115

with empiricism than I am. In particular, it is noted that an important component of a Christian view of objectivity is the idea of striving to approximate to seeing things the way that God does (although we must also bear in mind the effects of the fall on our thinking). Allowing biblical evaluative criteria to enter the picture would in this view enhance, rather than detract from, objectivity. The debate goes on. These comments are offered as tentative contributions, very much subject to clarification and refinement.

Kant's reversal: reason in religion

If sociology as a set of intellectual practices is not inherently hostile to Christian commitment, and if it is the case that beliefs and values of some sort always enter into social science theory, then what might constitute a Christian response to this?

For a start, doubt may be cast on Kant's position. While it may look logically nice to separate 'is' and 'ought', this distinction seems to rest on a rather flimsy foundation. There is the fact that subjects of a certain theory could potentially invalidate that theory by acting on their knowledge of it. Beyond this, however, is the matter of the language in which theory is couched. A. R. Louch, among others, has argued that there is no neutral meta-language using which social science can ride above the moral connotations which its explanatory vocabulary necessarily adopts (Louch 1966). While it may be possible to present some (supposedly) raw information about a social situation ('the wealthiest 10% of the British population own 80% of British wealth') any theory which explains why this is the case has to be made using the morally loaded language of everyday life. 'Ought' tends in practice to be very mixed up with 'is'.

Consider the following example, pointed out by David Thomas (Thomas 1979: 127–8), concerning Young and Wilmot's famous study of *Family and Kinship in East London*. The authors try to answer the question why former slum-dwellers do not like living in new housing projects. Young and Wilmot's answer lies in the strongly mother-centred kinship structure of the slums, which is broken up along with those slums. Loneliness then breeds discontent. David Thomas argues that this illustrates how value-judgment logically enters the internal structure of the theory. Young and Wilmot reveal that they

116

themselves value considerations of 'community spirit' more than those of the physical standard of housing, which helps to explain why they chose their particular theory of the unhappy relocated slum-dwellers. Equally plausibly they could have referred to the preference for staying in a familiar locality, where one's sense of control over circumstances and environment was greater.

Thomas is also at pains to indicate the penetration of values into Young and Wilmot's factual statements. They say that Bethnal Green (East London) is a 'highly integrated' community, on the grounds that 55% of married women with mothers alive had seen their mothers during the previous twenty-four hours. Yet they elsewhere admit that few of these daughters had any contact with non-relatives. So what they mean by an 'integrated community' (an innocent-sounding term) is closely bound up with contact between *kinsfolk*. If, alternatively, they had valued contact between non-kinsfolk as a sign of community integration, a different 'factual description' would have emerged.

It would seem that the choice or proposal of a social theory must be along lines offered by Mary Hesse:

> I suggest that the proposal of a social theory is more like the arguing of a political case than like a natural-science explanation. It should seek for and respect the facts when these are to be had, but it cannot await a possibly unattainable total explanation. It must appeal explicitly to value judgments and may properly use persuasive rhetoric. No doubt it should differ from most political argument in seeking and accounting for facts more conscientiously, and in constraining its rhetoric this side of gross special pleading and rabble-rousing propaganda. Here the inheritance of virtues from the natural sciences comes to the social scientist's aid, and I hope nothing I have said will be taken to undermine these virtues (Hesse 1978: 16).

A Christian argument which parallels Hesse's in several respects has been made by Nicholas Wolterstorff. He neatly reverses Kant's book title by writing of *Reason within the bounds of religion* (Wolterstorff 1976). Assuming that the critique of empiricism is well founded (he demonstrates the inadequacy of what philosophers call 'foundationalism'), he proposes that Christians should allow their beliefs and commitments to guide their evaluation and proposition of theories. He helpfully unpacks the process whereby a theory is 'weighed' or evaluated. He has in mind some distinctions about different kinds of beliefs which we all hold when undertaking theory evaluation.

First, we hold *data* beliefs. Say we wished to test the idea that changes in the law on abortion prevented doctors with certain kinds of convictions from obtaining posts in obstetrics and gynaecology. We must believe that certain kinds of data (interviews, appointments records) relate directly to this hypothesis. Second, we have *data-background* beliefs. That is, we would assume that our statistics are correct, our respondents not lying and so on. But, third, we all have what he calls *control* beliefs which determine whether we have an acceptable *kind* of theory or hypothesis. Like Hudson he asks whether this explanation is an *appropriate* one. Does it 'make sense'? Most sociologists would reject the explanation which the hospital administration might issue, that doctors who failed to get appointments did so because they lacked the appropriate qualifications, and not because they held moral objections to doing abortions under certain circumstances.

The point of Wolterstorff's argument is that Christians *ought* to allow their Christian commitment to decide what are their 'control' beliefs. Thus both the assessing of existing theories or concepts and the generation of new ones should be guided by criteria derived from biblical Christian commitment. He is not saying that they come *direct* from the Bible. Neither is he claiming that Christian faith is a precondition of science. He is saying that, as science depends in part upon the role of control beliefs (such as the value of prediction-and-control), Christians should let their beliefs determine their mode of weighing and devising theories.

An example: explaining poverty

Rodin's 'thinker' represents the myth of uncontaminated thinking, of Comte's 'cerebral hygiene'. In the course of this chapter we have noted the mounting post-empiricist argument against this myth. The more careful theorists certainly do not wish to abandon attention to empirical data, the quest of objectivity, or any other dimension of scientific rigour. But with the greater realization of the internal role of beliefs and values in theory has come a renewed debate over social purposes and thus what constitutes an authentically 'good life'. The moment has arrived then for the entry of Christian evaluations into the social scientific arena. They, no less than others, are capable of rational defence and articulation.

Robert Holman's sociology of poverty (Holman 1978) is an example of how this might occur. The existence of a poor sector within a given society has always been cause for concern – and controversy. What accounts for the miserable conditions in which millions exist in cities like Calcutta or Buenos Aires? Furthermore, though the conditions of the poor in advanced societies are less wretched, their existence is more surprising: how can it be that poverty exists amid plenty? Holman examines various social scientific explanations of social deprivation, evaluating their adequacy in accounting for poverty. But he does so, and here is the interesting point, making explicit reference to the way in which his Christian stance commits him to the project of eradicating poverty. He clearly (and rightly!) does not see Jesus' statement: 'You will always have the poor with you' as an excuse for unconcern! His motto would rather seem to be that of Proverbs 29: 7: 'The righteous care about justice for the poor.' It becomes clear how his Christian perspective affects his conceptualization and explanation of poverty.

Holman discusses various well-known solutions to the puzzle of poverty, including individual failure, a self-perpetuating 'culture of poverty', and deficient welfare agencies. He concludes that while each has some plausibility, none is adequate to explain the extent or the persistence of poverty today. Rather, he argues, poverty must be seen in a social structural way, in relation to wealth. 'Too many studies of social deprivation have simply studied the poor and have deduced that the characteristics which distinguish the poor are therefore the cause of poverty' (Holman 1978: 241). Of course he would not deny that, on an individual level, laziness or fecklessness might be a cause of personal poverty. But to understand the widespread incidence of poverty only a structural explanation will do.

Holman opts for a structural explanation for two reasons. One, his Christian commitment leads him to view things in terms of the biblical drama. The theme of creation shows that the earth's resources have been placed by the Creator at the disposal, and under the care, of all humans, without partiality. God values all men and women – and, we might add, is concerned that all have 'enough' (see Taylor 1975). Thus, says Holman, 'social deprivation – because it means distress and disadvantage for valued people – should not be tolerated' (Holman 1978: 252). He holds that biblical teaching militates against tolerance of gross social-economic inequalities, which in turn are biblically related to societal circumstances and not merely to individual or other failure. Thus a sociological theory which explains poverty in a social-structural fashion is exactly what one might expect from a Christian social perspective. This *kind* of theory would seem appropriate.

The second reason why Holman chooses such an explanation is precisely that of empirical constraint. Other explanations are tried and found wanting – they fail to fit the facts. This sort of theory makes more sense in empirical terms. As already observed, poverty is a controversial topic, and much disagreement exists as to the nature of the facts. There is always space for discussion and development of theories. The point is that Christian 'control beliefs' may be allowed to enter the logic of theory-choice and concept-formation in an effort to define and make sense of the empirical facts. Thus theories may be produced which comport well with Christian commitment. Some theories may in the end look rather similar to others which are available, but this is beside the point. The important thing is that Christian minds are brought to bear on the process of social scientific research and discovery.

6

POWER TO THE PAWNS?
SOCIAL ACTION
AND SOCIAL STRUCTURE

By the fact of his living [every individual]
contributes, however minutely, to the shaping of
this society and to the course of its history, even
as he is made by society and by its historical
push and shove.

C. Wright Mills

Are we really only pawns in the impersonal game of some
sinister social structures? Or is it misleading to think of 'structures' at all; perhaps our decisions and choices do count for
something? People claim both positions as their reality. Some
feel hopelessly trapped by forces beyond their control,
especially if they are unemployed, part of an ethnic minority,
poor – or all three at once. This is the Kafkaesque world where
mysterious powers seem to grip one's life, manipulating every
move according to an unknown plan.

Other people feel that their choices do mean something. They
think positively, act decisively and believe that they are in
control of their circumstances and the direction of their lives.
They would tend to doubt the constraining capabilities of so-
called social structures, insisting that their individual action is
what really makes things happen.

Sociologists may be found who take either the puppet
(manipulated) or the plutocrat (manipulator) view. But most are
located somewhere between the extreme ends of the spectrum.

121

The very act of trying to make a science of society can force individual action into a structural strait-jacket. As Giddens puts it, 'the knowing subject, freely undertaking inquiry into the conditions of his own social existence, rediscovers himself as the outcome of determinate social causes that operate with impersonal force' (Giddens 1977: 26). Others would retort that this view is exaggerated and that individuals in fact exert considerable impact in social situations.

This question is at the centre of our present concerns. Do the pawns have power or not? We shall examine sociological debate over this question of individual and society, or action and structure, trying to evaluate it in terms of the Christian image of humanness. Time was when some social scientists thought of such 'philosophical' issues much as the average citizen thinks of sewers. While they were aware of their dependence upon them, assumed they worked, and were grateful for them, they seriously questioned the sense of anyone who wanted to go poking about in them. Sociologists are now realizing more and more that they ought to poke around in this area, dark and murky as it appears. Moreover it is not only a philosophical issue. Practical platforms for action depend in part upon how certain problems are conceptualized. As soon as 'poverty' or 'unemployment' are seen as 'public issues' rather than as 'personal troubles' (the terms are C. Wright Mills's) the way they are tackled will tend to alter. This reminds us that even terms like 'structure' seem to possess evaluative overtones. People begin to perceive 'structure' as something alien, oppressive or evil. So we must also ask the question, can social structures be said to possess evil or benign qualities? Is it helpful to speak of social or structural sin, as some do?

Short-sighted sociology?

It is said that sociologists, for all they pride themselves on their perceptive powers, often fail to notice real people. While they might precisely pigeon-hole you as a member of a socio-economic group characterized by reactionary political views and frustrated aspirations to social mobility, they might fail to notice the human being standing before them. C. S. Lewis provides us with a penetrating example of this: his character Mark Studdock in *That Hideous Strength*. The fact that Studdock was a sociologist apparently prevented him from being aware of people. Even when he strolls through a village and observes country folk about their daily round, he fails to see them:

> All this did not in the least influence his sociological convictions. Even if he had been free from Belbury and wholly unambitious, it could not have done so, for his education had had the curious effect of making things that he read and wrote more real to him than things he saw. Statistics about agricultural labourers were the substance; any real ditcher, ploughman, or farmer's boy was the shadow. Though he had never noticed it himself, he had a great reluctance, in his work, ever to use such words as 'man' or 'woman'. He preferred to write about 'vocational groups', 'elements', 'classes', and 'populations': for, in his own way, he believed as firmly as any mystic in the superior reality of the things that are not seen (Lewis 1945: 87).

Of course C. S. Lewis did not go out of his way to compliment sociologists, especially those stolid social statisticians he seems to have encountered. But did he have a valid point? Should the sociologist *as sociologist* be concerned with individual people at all? Christopher Harris, quoted earlier, says that sociology is not intended to help us to meet people in a personal way. It is about social situations and social practices. But is there a limit to this? Can sociology properly be practised obliviously of real live persons?

There *is* something distinctive about the sociological perspective. Let us say that a fictitious character, Ann Wagner, committed suicide on April 15, 1936. A historian may well be interested in the prelude to and consequence of this tragedy, assuming that she was significant to his or her account. After all, she was living in Germany, but recognized the intentions of the Third Reich and tried to resist them. A psychologist might explore her personal background and, from an individual case history, conclude that certain internal tensions, perhaps triggered by the early loss of her mother, had contributed decisively to her suicide. Sociologists working in a Durkheimian mould would take a different tack. Suicide is a *social* act.

Intuitively one might expect suicide to be explicable only on strictly psychological and individual grounds. It seems such a deeply personal choice. No, said Durkheim, if the rate of suicide is examined statistically, it may be demonstrated that a particular kind of society compels a minority of people to kill themselves. One instance might be during some collapse of social organization when individuals experience 'anomie' so acutely that suicide comes to be seen as an option. (The period in Germany preceding World War II could be seen as 'anomic'; the 'normal' rules for everyday life were disappearing so that people were confused and lacking orientation.)

Durkheim argues that real social forces exist which have a collective power over individuals. (This has been dubbed 'methodological holism'.) He is quite explicit: 'Each social group really has a collective inclination for the act, quite its own, and the source of all individual inclination, rather than their result' (Durkheim 1951: 299). He does appear to be suggesting here that the social 'holist' explanation of suicide is more 'ultimate' than any individual psychological explanation.

But what exactly has Durkheim explained? To discuss coroners' reports and official statistics hardly constitutes an explanation of why on April 15, 1936, Ann Wagner 'committed suicide'. To destroy oneself is still an act. Even Durkheim could not argue that the individual would be unaware of the outcome of the act of suicide! Now suicide may surely be the object of sociological investigation, but how may an adequate theory be formed without reference to the self-awareness of the person-in-social-relationships who does the deed? This question along with others related to it have stimulated an industry of sociological debate. One point which has emerged is this. Sociological accounts of suicide differ according to the assumptions about social action and social structure at the base of those theories. How one perceives humanness and person-hood directly affects sociological analysis.

After Durkheim, the next major sociologist to take up his kind of approach was Talcott Parsons. For him it is the notion of 'role' which links individuals to society. Individuals, as he puts it, 'internalize social norms' which means that they as it were play out roles scripted for them by society. So what happens to the father, friend or neighbour that we know so well? They appear to be nothing but a bundle of roles, predictably living up to social expectation. Maybe similar things can be said about my musical preferences, my choice of spouse, even my religious commitment. Are we really just a product of social forces beyond our control? Society in this view appears over against the individual, virtually determining his or her life.

This view is far from dead or dormant. It is revived today by theorists such as French philosopher, Louis Althusser. He and his disciples have brought back the idea that 'hard scientific' analyses of social reality are possible. It is not 'role' so much as 'ideology' which for him provides the 'social cement' integrating individuals into society. He holds that sociology should be concerned with the ways in which structures underlying social relationships actually constrain people to act in particular ways. According to Marxist Althusser, individuals are pawns in the impersonal game of capitalist structures. It would seem from a glance at Durkheim, Parsons and Althusser, that the price paid for the sociological quest of distinctive social explanation is the loss of real living people from the sociologist's range of vision.

The would-be humanizers

Sociological myopia of the sort I have been describing has not suffered from a shortage of critics. The most celebrated warning was issued by Dennis Wrong in his anti-Parsonian article, 'The oversocialized concept of man in modern sociology' (Wrong 1961). Already a small chorus of dissent could be heard responding to Parsonian 'grand theory', but Wrong's critique took a different tack. Though he agreed that Parsons overemphasized social harmony, integration and agreement over shared values, he attacked the 'oversocialized individual' in Parsons. In fact the two things tended to go together: 'when our sociological theory overstresses the stability and integration of society, we will end up imagining that man is the disembodied, conscience-driven, status-seeking phantom of current theory.'

By exposing this aspect of Parson's work, Wrong obviously hoped to exorcize the oversocialized 'phantom' and substitute a fuller view of humanness. But it would seem that the phantom has some resilience and resists repeated efforts at exorcism. It haunts Durkheimian, Parsonian, and now Althusserian sociology. In 1968, Ralf Dahrendorf, worried that 'it is only a step from seeing man as a mere role-player to the alienated world of "1984", where all loving and hating, all dreaming and acting, all individuality beyond the grasp of roles, becomes a crime against society – society in this sense being sociology hypostatized' (Dahrendorf 1968: 86). And yet the phantom grows stronger. As Anthony Giddens has remarked: 'Parsons' actors are cultural dopes, but Althusser's agents are structural dopes of even more stunning mediocrity' (Giddens 1979: 52).

One could call the efforts to bring *people* back into sociology 'humanizing', because they stress one of the unique aspects of humanness: action. And Christian theism, which has a concept of action at its core, is not well served by sociologies which at least imply that action is not very significant. It could be objected of course that Parsons *did* write extensively about action. True enough, but it is a weak view of action in which the bottom line seems to be social influence. As for Althusser, he much more explicitly rejects a Christian notion of action, and proceeds to his social analysis on a militantly anti-theistic base (Althusser and Balibar 1968).

So at the level of sociological world views there is a clash here. We saw earlier that the theistic notion of an active Creator, in whose 'image' humans are made, entails the idea that we too are agents (that is people who act). Human behaviour is not only a passive response to external stimuli. People choose to do one thing rather than something else, intentionally, rationally, morally. A sociology which implies the opposite cannot be acceptable, theistically speaking.

Durkheim was mistaken to imagine that intention, purpose and motive have no place in sociology. He thought that because sociology was about the social aspect that this excluded such individual traits or qualities like *intending* to commit suicide. Yet, as Harris points out, we know about intentions, purposes and so on, not because we can mind-read, but because they are an aspect of social practices in which we also engage (Harris 1980: 25–6). We shall see later that notions of individuality and action are not at all incompatible with ideas like 'society' and 'structure'.

Not all agree with this position, however. An individualistic alternative has some notable defenders. And Christians reared on *The Pilgrim's Progress* may also find the following ideas attractive. For, in reaction against views which seem to reduce human beings to a plastic '*homo sociologicus*', some assert the primacy of the individual. Do not misunderstand me. Bunyan's Christian is graphically portrayed struggling through this earthly life, ever straining towards the celestial city, an example to identify with and emulate. But it is very much the account of an individual, cut off from social reality. If sociology exists at the intersection of biography and history (the contention of Mills 1959), then Bunyan gives us all biography and no history. Christian does not, apparently, even exist in the *social* context of the church, the family of which all 'new-born' believers, biblically speaking, are part. In fact any age which stresses individual responsibility and personal accountability *at the expense of* social and collective responsibility is likely to plump for individualist explanations of social events.

The grandfather of what Steven Lukes calls 'methodological individualism' (Lukes 1970: 76), was seventeenth-century sage Thomas Hobbes. He insisted that 'It is necessary that we should know the things that are to be compounded before we can know the whole compound.' So understanding individuals is prior to understanding society. The name most commonly associated with more recent discussions is philosopher Karl Popper, who asserts that '. . . all social phenomena, and especially the functioning of all social institutions, should always be understood as resulting from the decisions, actions, attitudes, etc., of human individuals, . . . we should never be satisfied by an explanation in terms of so-called "collectives" . . .' (Popper 1966: 98). It seems that Popper is saying that society is nothing but the sum of the individuals who inhabit it. To be fair, he is making the point that sociological discussion of groups and collectivities only refer to 'models' of what is actually happening. One could say that he has a bone to pick with the Durkheims of this world. Why, for example, do all the members of the social group with the supposed 'collective inclination' for suicide not kill themselves? Durkheim's case is incomplete in so far as he fails to acknowledge the role of individual action.

But Popper's work is often used against any attempt at social explanation, as if all social phenomena could be traced back exclusively to individual motivation and intention. Read in this way, Popper appears to be following Hobbes in proposing that society is no more than the sum of the individuals comprising it. This latter view, whether Popper holds it or not, is a popular one today. But in its theoretical form it represents a retreat from anything resembling sociology. And as a view of humanness it is sadly deficient, as we see in the next section.

The reality of the social

I remarked earlier (chapter two) that part of being human, in the Christian account, is being social. It is not good for us to be alone; isolation is unnatural. But our social aspect is more than just being a part of groups and collectivities of other individuals. Sociologists are not simply interested in how individuals 'belong' to families, labour unions, schools or churches, but in the patterns and processes of 'belonging'.

There is no point in pretending that any elaborate sociological imagination gripped the mind of the ancient biblical writers. But it is clear from the creation account that sociality and interdependence are part of being human. That much may be inferred, for instance, from the relationship between Cain and Abel. Part of Cain's life involved being his brother's keeper, though his failure to recognize this ended in tragedy. But the *patterning* of social relationships is recognized elsewhere. Rural radical Amos, for example, impolitely denounces an élite class of female tyrants as the 'cows of Bashan'. Why? Not because they personally supervised or administered harsh treatment to the poverty-stricken landless labourers, but because of their involvement in an unjust pattern of relationships. As a category the powerful rich enjoyed certain privileges which, *because they had them*, were denied to the category which did not, namely landless labour. Of course, Amos was not suggesting that this unjust pattern of relationships was itself 'guilty'. It could not *cause* the suffering and oppression, and neither could it hear his blistering broadside. But he nevertheless recognized the patterning of relationships – the social structuring – by which, in an ongoing manner, the apparently innocent luxury-loving ladies were systematically oppressing the poor (not by *direct* individual action, but through socially structured practices).

By examining social structure in all its complexity sociologists may make a contribution to a fuller understanding of the social aspect of the 'image of God'. A thoroughgoing individualist stance would seem to be uncalled for, though this does *not* mean abandoning interest in the social action of individuals. (For Weber, social action is social 'insofar as its subjective meaning takes account of the behaviour of others and is thereby oriented in its course', Weber 1968: 13. As a sociologist he was not concerned, however, with individual action, or even with 'Mr or Mrs Average'. Rather he believed sociological interpretation had to do with ideal or theoretical *types* of action.) The following example illustrates again the necessity of thinking of structure as well as action in sociology.

An example: racism

The study of social structure is appropriate to sociology; it is indeed 'socio-logic'. First, some notion of structure is required in order to explain social situations and their outcomes. The inadequacy of individualistic accounts is highlighted in David Wellman's study of racism.

Many sociologists would use 'racism' as part of their explanation of why certain minority groups receive discriminatory treatment. Of course numerous analysts have offered a rather individualistic understanding of racism, which in fact depends heavily on psychological studies of attitudes. But David Wellman cuts away at such psychologism in his more sociological assertion that 'prejudiced people are not the only racists in America' (Wellman 1977, chapter one). Individual prejudice is well illustrated by the derogatory comments made by 'working class' T.V. heroes, Alf Garnett (U.K.) or Archie Bunker (U.S.A.). But racism may also be expressed ideologically (for example when biological 'reasons' are given for racial superiority) or institutionally. In the latter case it refers to systematic practices that deny and exclude blacks from access to social resources. Wellman contends that racism includes individual attitudes, but is far more. It is a social process for the defence of (white) privilege. In understanding the position of blacks, then, sociological sophistication demands that they be seen as part of a structure of reward and advantage based on race which includes but transcends the mere prejudice in the *minds* of some white individuals. Wellman's study illustrates well one of the distinctively social patterns of human life, without getting fouled in the holist snare of denying the role of individual action. But he is also stressing that individual action may not be conceived as existing in a social vacuum.

While Wellman's work yields a good instance of the theoretical need for some notion of social structure, it may also be used to illustrate a second reason for rejecting an individualistic stance. That is, social structure is existentially present in the experience of everyday life. Black people are very aware of the structure of privilege which systematically excludes them from full participation in a given, predominantly white society (and, of course, in a predominantly black society like South Africa). They know full well they are up against something very subtle yet very solid when, for instance, they find less qualified whites preferred before them for jobs. Such positions may even be controlled by liberal whites who would openly defend 'equality of opportunity' as a goal. The structure of racist society is certainly an everyday reality to them.

This in turn has implications for sociological analysis, indicating again the need for some notions of *both* action *and* structure. For if social structure is a reality for 'members' of society, then their consciousness of it must be accounted for within a sociological explanation. Social processes and structures do not exist behind people's backs, as the more structural*ist* authors are wont to imply. Rather, commonsense knowledge of how society works is part of how we all make sense of everyday life. We self-consciously (and often habitually) incorporate such knowledge of 'structure' into our reasons for acting.

A third reason for avoiding individualism in sociology is that individual actions, to be meaningful at all, presuppose the existence of social practices and institutions. Some shared meanings (say of 'ethnic', 'discrimination', 'race', 'job-opportunity') have to exist in order for any individual action to make sense. So while any explanation of social structuring must take account of action in some way, it is also the case that individual action may not be understood without reference to the sociality of shared meanings.

A third way

The reader will not have forgotten my earlier comments on the original base from which sociological images of the human have sprung. It was the Enlightenment, with its key notion of human autonomy, which spawned both order and control, action and system views. Within that framework, and at the world view level, there is no special reason for choosing one position or the other. So it should come as no surprise that during sociology's career to date, a flip-flop effect can be discerned. A swing between action and system (or structure) views has occurred. When doing science is the priority, system views tend to dominate the scene, showing the influence (at the second level) of interests and values in a given social milieu. But the resulting social claustrophobia has sparked off trends in the opposite direction, emphasizing action. All right, agreed Wrong, quoting Sigmund Freud, we may be *social* animals, but we are not *entirely socialized.*

The action-orientation also has its dangers. It is often linked with a sort of latter-day Romantic idealism which sees the future as an open door and human beings as having the freedom to walk right in as they choose. If the structural*ist* view miniaturizes persons to ciphers, the action view can magnify personal power out of all proportion. I have already quoted Christopher Harris's view that this is almost tantamount to deifying human beings. Clearly both extremes are to be avoided. At the meta-theoretical level they reflect different but equally secular images of humanness. The appropriate alternative, then, would seem to be a coherent view of humanness which requires both action and structure to be united within one theoretical scheme.

Again we may refer back to the quote from Evans, which nicely encapsulates a biblical view. The human being, he remarks,

> is not only formed by these social relationships; he acts and by
> acting helps to form these roles in turn. He is not only constituted
> by these relationships; he himself constitutes them. He plays a
> role in continuing them, modifying them for better or worse,
> enhancing or degrading their quality and character (Evans 1977:
> 145).

Here is a third way which copes with action and structure. It thus does justice to both aspects of humanness and also the valuing or normative dimension. We may agree with Barry Smart who says that the human sciences are always located between what he calls the dualisms of subject-object and action-structure (Smart 1982). He further claims that to try to transcend them is to go beyond sociology. He is right, of course, if he means that sociology *itself* cannot reveal what is truly human. But Christian commitment does give us a basis for saying that some third way like this is desirable (and emphatically preferable to either of the extremes). Moreover, trying to 'transcend' the dualism may be impossible, but this does not invalidate efforts to show the interdependence of action and structure.

From the angle of Christian guiding beliefs then, those theories which seem to depend on notions of action and structure would comport best. If one accepts that, Marx's own position appears in a favourable light. Early on, Marx evidences an awareness of the dangers of a 'structure-weighted' view: 'It is above all necessary to avoid positing society as a fixed abstraction opposed to the individual' (Marx in McLellan 1977: 91). Later, in his central work, the *Grundrisse*, he attacks the 'insipid illusions of the eighteenth century' such as Robinson Crusoe stories 'which begin their accounts with isolated individuals'. Having already rejected the invention of 'some fixed abstractions', he shrewdly writes of 'social individuals' existing in 'mutual relationships which they reproduce and produce anew' (Marx 1973: 712).

As is frequently the case, Marx shows both his rootedness in the Enlightenment image of humanness *and* his post-Christian desire to overcome the swing between one view and the other. Generations of sociologists have wrestled with the problem since, with more and less illumination resulting. While many, like Peter Berger, clearly wish to maintain a balance, it sometimes appears from their overall stance that in fact one image predominates. Berger assures us that 'unlike the puppets, we have the possibility of stopping in our movements, looking up and perceiving the machinery by which we have been moved. In this act lies the first step towards freedom' (Berger 1963: 176). But some of Berger's other work also gives the impression that the social 'machinery' *is* rather relentless and inescapable.

Other theorists (Christopher Harris and Anthony Giddens are good examples) maintain a proper respect for the limitations of both action and structure approaches, taken on their own, and thus in my view present preferable options. Taking Giddens, as he is rather better known than Harris, we discover that he strives to find a mode of theoretically relating action to structure.

Giddens offers the idea of a 'duality of structure' which is reminiscent of Evans' position, quoted above. He means that 'social structures are both constituted *by* human agency and yet at the same time are the very *medium* of this constitution' (Giddens 1976: 121). This point is best illustrated by reference to social class. Class is not an entity like a church or a business firm. It cannot perceive things in a particular way, or act in some event, despite references in everyday speech which suggest that it can ('the complacent middle classes'). It is even misleading to speak of class membership, as this implies participation in a specific group. Nevertheless, disparities in market capacities which are themselves insignificant somehow become social realities which we readily recognize by the designation, 'class'. A process which Giddens inelegantly dubs 'structuration' takes place. Again harking back to Evans' comments about 'being constituted and constituting', the very existence of class structuration depends upon consciousness of it. Class is in part constituted by humans acting in accordance with will and intention. But it is also the medium of that constitution. Thinking, talking, writing, living 'class' perpetuates it. (As Giddens points out, this is also like language: it is constituted by us, but it is also the medium of its constitution.)

Social sin: sinful structures?

What bearing does our discussion of action and structure have on the question of whether structures are 'good' or 'bad'? In recent years increasing interest has been shown by Christians in social structure. This is related to the awakening of a social conscience in the U.S.A. after Vietnam, and in Britain especially after the 'rediscovery of poverty' in the 1960s. At a wider level, the World Council of Churches has also taken controversially radical stances in relation to social justice. And in Latin America, South-East Asia and Africa new perceptions of social structure have also emerged among Christians of various persuasions. What they have in common is the attempt to marry social analysis and theology by inventing terms like 'social sin' and 'sinful structures' (The American 'Moral Majority', which has some Christian connections, is an exception to this. The 'social sins' they have in mind are frequently personal in character.)

Toronto-based theologian-cum-sociologist Gregory Baum has come up with a term to describe this new movement: 'critical theology'. He chooses to speak of 'social sin' which, he suggests, has four dimensions or levels. First, it is 'made up of the injustices and dehumanizing trends built in the various institutions – social, political, economic, religious and others – which embody people's collective life'. Second are the cultural and religious symbols – 'ideologies' which 'legitimate and reinforce the unjust institutions and thus intensify the harm done . . .' Third is the false consciousness created by the above two in which 'people involve themselves collectively in destruction as if they were doing the right thing'. Fourth, 'collective decisions, generated by the distorted consciousness . . . increase the injustices in society and intensify the power of dehumanizing trends.' At this point also the individual element reappears, as evil intentions and greed can magnify evil done by institutional life (Baum 1975: 201–2). Baum illustrates his thesis by discussing the relationship between the free market economy and world hunger:

> Implicit in the free market for food is an injustice which no amount of personal generosity and goodwill shall be able to overcome (first level of social sin). What will have to change is the system. In the present society, however, the free market is legitimated by cultural and religious symbols (second level). The very raising of the question is regarded as disloyal and subversive. To indict the market system is to question a sacred element in our society. This system, which is the most pervasive in our society, has created a consciousness in us which makes us cooperate with it, look on it as an irreplaceable element of society, and apply its principles to even wider aspects of the social life (third level). . . . The corporate decisions by which the locus of free collective sins – that is, of deliberate acts, committed by people for the sake of greater profit, that increase the injustices in the institution of food (fourth level), . . . for example, the artificial raising of food prices (Baum 1975: 203).

This is a good example which, on a more sophisticated level, has illuminative implications for sociology done in Christian perspective. We shall raise some questions about it in a moment.

Ronald Sider, from an evangelical perspective, alerts us to this phenomenon in a slightly different manner in his well-known study *Rich Christians in an age of hunger*. More carefully, he speaks of structural evil, giving helpful examples:

> There is an important difference between consciously willed, individual acts (like lying to a friend or committing an act of adultery) and participation in evil social structures. Slavery is an example of the latter. So is the Victorian factory system where ten-year-old children worked twelve to sixteen hours a day. Both slavery and child labour were legal. But they destroyed people by the millions. They were institutionalized or structural evils (Sider 1975).

Sider's overriding concern is to show how unjust social structures mean that the affluent 'North' enjoys luxury at the expense of the impoverished 'South'. To Christians, this should be quite intolerable.

A cautionary note must be sounded, however, if our critical integration is to be genuine. Theological as well as sociological confusion arises, especially if the looser terms 'social sin' or 'structural sin' are used. Baum falls foul of this, as do some World Council of Churches' pronouncements. Following the earlier discussion, the first comment is on sociological difficulties.

Sociological questions

Because sin is an intentional category, to do with action, it is misleading to speak of impersonal structures as being 'sinful'. Acts which flout God's directives for fulfilled human life may enter the constitution of structures, but that does not render the *structures* guilty before God. True, in the Old Testament we may find corporate guilt, where a whole group suffered for disobedience. But this punishment came on the group or collectivity, not on the patterns of relationship between the people in the collectivity. Structures themselves can neither act nor be accountable.

But structures (or, better, systems) may be evil, unjust or oppressive. Families, class-divided societies, even churches

135

could be such. In fact some element of imperfection is bound to be present, given that they are in part constituted by the participation of agents who are capable of choice and whose own sin is thus part of the situation. But it is unhelpful only to see structures as evil. All too often structure has a sinister connotation, whether in Christian discourse or not.

Structure as we have discussed it here has no necessarily evil aspect. If structure is the medium of action then it may equally be said to enable as to constrain. A racist social structuring may indeed limit the potential choices of the suffering ethnic minorities. But it may also be said that the market system of social structuring in advanced capitalist societies – amazingly, and specific criticisms notwithstanding – enables people to make certain choices about what they eat, how they dress and where they live. Indeed family patterns are a form of micro-level social structuring. While they can be oppressive and authoritarian inwardly, and help perpetuate particular kinds of unjust society outwardly, few would argue that some kind of family life is *by definition* evil. On the contrary, families enable people to enjoy stable relationships and to raise children until they are ready to cope with the outside world.

The ramifications of this are quite extensive. It is sobering to realize that some of the Christian community's most prized institutions, such as the family, can become thoroughly distorted in terms of the Creator's intentions. We shall refer to this in chapter eight. This demonstrates again the need for sociological awareness among Christians so that, as Barker said, sociology becomes a challenge to Christian practice rather than a supposed threat to Christian faith.

Christian questions

Second, then, let us glance at the theological difficulties with the 'structural sin' concept. The main problem has already been hinted at: because they cannot *act*, structures cannot *sin*. This does have other implications, though, because if structures *can* sin, they may also be redeemed. Knotty biblical problems surround this issue. God's purposes for creation, as we saw early on, are nothing short of cosmic. He has plans to bring everything once more into harmony with his high standards of human justice and welfare. The cross of Christ is the pivotal point of history, which leaves no aspect of creation untouched by the scope of reconciliation.

But, and it is a big 'but', if we confuse on the one hand the personal reconciliation with God of all who acknowledge Christ as Saviour and Lord, and on the other the coming of political justice here or economic welfare there, we simply get in a mess. Salvation words in the Bible point overwhelmingly to a narrow usage, that is, to persons who become the new called-out community of Christ and live in the light of his radical demands. To equate sin with injustice (as some liberation theologians do) or salvation with revolutionary social transformation (which is the logical corollary of the former equation) appears to be unwarranted biblically. The upshot is a limited concept of sin (which seems to let some individuals off the hook), and a misconception of salvation (can the Bolivian miner not be 'saved' *before* the revolution comes, even while in a situation of slave-labour?). Beyond this, the type of political action deemed appropriate becomes circumscribed if one plumps for an exclusively structural approach. As David Kingdon asks in a helpful little article on structural sin,

> If the concept of structural sin appears for some at least to depend upon a Marxist analysis of structures, is it possible to accept the analysis and yet to reject the solution proposed by Marxism? (Kingdon 1980).

In order to see how this question might be tackled, however, we must make a closer examination of Marxism. This the burden of the next chapter.

Part 3

Contemporary challenges

This is a book about doing sociology. The biggest contemporary challenges to the way sociology is done come from Marxism and feminism. The continuing crises of the advanced capitalist societies, the soulless uniformity and unfreedom of many self-proclaimed 'Marxist' societies, and the stark realities of global poverty and inequality all serve to keep the Marxist kettle simmering. At the same time, calls for the abolition of sexual inequality and oppression, and confusion concerning the rapid changes overtaking the family, combine to make feminism the fastest growing movement within social science (though not yet society).

Both these challenges relate at a fundamental level to humanness: Marxism in its preoccupation with work and labour, feminism in its focus on gender division and family. Biblically, being male or female, or transforming nature through labour, are seen as created aspects of being human.

Chapters seven and eight examine Marxism and feminism in a Christian light, commenting briefly on how their insights are appearing today, and how they may be assessed. In both cases a division is discerned within the perspective: there are two Marxisms and two feminisms. This is partly a creative tension, whose open ends leave room for debate. But it also indicates a lack of certainty and direction to which Christian thinking and practice can make valuable contributions.

It will be clear from the rest of this book that sociology is confronted by numerous social and analytical challenges as well as these two. I have alluded in other chapters to race and ethnicity, unemployment, Third World underdevelopment, poverty and urban problems. Nationalism, militarism, medicine, mass media, science and technology, education and welfare are also mentioned but not discussed. All stand in pressing need of Christian social analytical insight, and each may be tackled using a 'human image' framework. I hope that the following discussion of Marxism and feminism will also be useful to those trying to elaborate a Christian perspective in other fields.

7
CRITIQUE AND CRISIS:
MARXISM AND SOCIOLOGY

*But since for socialist man what is called world
history is nothing but the creation of man by human
labour and the development of nature for man, he has
the observable and irrefutable proof of his self-
creation and the process of his origin.*

Karl Marx

Marx has been dead for 100 years. His ideas live on. Historian
Eric Hobsbawm, writing in the centenary issue of *Marxism
Today*, gives three reasons why. One, 'So long as there are good
causes for believing that capitalism has got internal contradictions, people will continue to look to Marxism as a guide to
analysis'. Two, more than one third of the world has been
transformed by Marxism. Such a powerful force demands
attention. Three, an academic reason, 'Marxism is a way of
thinking about the world which has stimulated generations of
people . . .' (Hobsbawm 1983: 7).

Hobsbawm is right. Marxism is attractive to many as a
coherent explanation of current crises of unemployment, world
poverty, and industrial unrest. Marxism has changed the course
of world history (although many Marxists are critical of the
'actually existing' socialist societies). And Marxism does catalyse wide-ranging efforts to grasp what is going on, not only in
social science, but in literature, music, medicine and the mass
media.

Marxism is a social critique of capitalist society. It indicates the inherent contradictions of capitalism which, when they reach crisis point, will lead to the creation of a new form of society. That is not to say that capitalism is all bad. Indeed, the scientific technological productive forces it helps to unleash will be necessary to the human world in the post-capitalist era.

Because Marxism, like sociology, has since its inception aspired to be a science of society, its relationship with sociology has always been uncertain and controversial. As we have seen, it was the *same* capitalist industrial type of society which exercised the intellects of Saint-Simon, Weber, Durkheim and Marx. But is Marxism best seen as a competing theory within the sociological field, or is it an inveterate antagonist of sociology?

For various reasons this question has become more pressing in the last two decades. For one thing it became strikingly clear by the 1960s that Soviet Marxism is not the only available variety. Other equally (if not more) plausible interpretations of Marx and Engels may be produced, based on texts which were only made public in the West long after the Bolshevik Revolution of 1918. Another reason for the urgency of sociology-Marxism discussions is that societies have changed so drastically since Marx and Engels wrote. They saw the oppressive system symbolized by Blake's 'dark satanic mills'. But they did not foresee how, within that system, steps would be taken – the creation of state welfare for instance – to alleviate its worst affects. Neither did they anticipate the massive surge of nationalism in the modern world which simultaneously shattered many hopes of international socialist harmony and also created new problems of its own, especially in the emerging industrial societies.

Our present task, however, is not to survey the relationships between Marxism and sociology, or even Marxism and Christian commitment, in any great depth (on these, see Bottomore 1975, 1978, 1983, Sklair 1981, Miguéz Bonino 1976 and Lyon 1981a). Rather, in line with the general theme of this book, we must raise once more the question of critical integration: how may Marxian and Christian social understanding be related? In particular, how does the question of the human image apply in the case of Marx and Marxism? When it comes to actual analysis what can Marx teach us about the contemporary world of capitalism and socialism, and how might we evaluate his

contribution? These tasks cannot properly be performed, however, without at least a cursory glance at Marx's mission, the
main features of Marxist-sociological discussion and the
varieties of Marxism.

Marx's mission

Marx's work is a major synthesis of nineteenth-century philosophy and political economy, all devoted to the analysis of the
dynamics of capitalist society. Human labour, as Marx asserted
in his early writings, is at the core of human life. The development of interchange between human beings and nature is, for
Marx, the foundation of all social life. This economic twist in
Marx's understanding of labour is what sets him apart from the
abstractions of his mentor, Hegel, and also makes his sociology –
if that is the right word – distinctive.

Unlike Hegel, who saw 'alienation' in spiritual terms, Marx
brought it down to earth. 'Alienated labour' is what happens
when some coerce others to work in a particular manner. It may
be seen in concrete terms as the result of some social-economic
decisions in a specific factory or wherever, but Marx wished to
show that alienated labour was part of the *system* of capitalism.
This was the way in which labour, the relationship between
people and nature, had developed in the nineteenth century.
Politics and government, he believed, came to reflect this relationship. So in *Capital* he could write:

> It is always the direct relation between the masters of the condi-
> tions of production and the direct producers which reveals the
> innermost secret, the hidden foundation of the entire social
> edifice, and therefore also . . . the particular form of the state. The
> form of this relation between masters and producers always
> necessarily corresponds to a definite stage in the development of
> the methods of work . . . (Marx in Bottomore and Rubel 1963:
> 112–3).

The capitalist 'mode of production', according to Marx, contains
within it contradictions, one of which is the conflict between
different social classes (the 'masters and producers' in the above
quotation). This conflict would escalate, he believed, as the
interests of the profit-seeking capitalist class clash more and

143

more with the interests of the 'real producers', the proletariat, and thus a social revolutionary period would ensue. That, at least, is the theory.

In his later writings Marx turned more to an empirical analysis of the actual workings of a capitalist society as a phase of human social development. The *Grundrisse*, an outline of his intended studies (only a fraction of which actually appeared in *Capital*) contains some important continuities and some new directions in his thought. Having once argued that money should be seen as the social bond of capitalist society, he now stresses capital accumulation as the key area to watch. He also makes the category of 'labour' more sophisticated by speaking of 'labour-power' as that which the worker sells to the employer. Because the worker sells this labour-power for less than it is worth in terms of energy put in, he is creating 'surplus-value' which the capitalist creams off as profit.

Capitalism's glory would also be its Achille's heel, however. Marx argues that capitalists, ever seeking profit and accumulating capital, would over-produce. At the same time this would widen the gap between the haves and have-nots which, other things being equal, would lead to capitalism's breakdown. Not that industrialism would die, of course. Within capitalist society technological progress would reach a stage where less labour would be needed for production and could in fact supervise the productive process. Socialism would grow in the womb of the old society.

This then is what Marx called the 'materialist conception of history'. It is 'materialist' because it centres on human labour and the productive process. Marx speaks both of economic activity – man versus nature – and of *praxis*, the way people make and remake human life. But all manner of renderings of Marx are possible, as the twentieth century has shown. Some Marxisms have concentrated on the active side of social practice in Marx's conception of labour. Such are often dubbed 'humanist Marxisms'. Others, usually referred to as 'scientific maixisms' focus on the primacy of the 'economic factor' in producing change. These two views give rise to radically divergent Marxisms and thus different debates with sociology.

A question common to both, of course, is that of class; is the history of all hitherto existing societies *really* the history of class struggle? which is not a merely abstract intellectual query.

Marxism makes an intimate connection between social analysis and political activity which cannot be overlooked. This also challenges sociology which, as we have seen, has often desired the public image of detached analysis. In this chapter we shall make some comments on class analysis, reserving remarks on the 'theory and practice' question for the final chapter.

Marxisms and sociologies

Leslie Sklair rightly describes the multifarious liaisons between Marxisms and sociologies as 'odd couples'. As we have noted, sociology has moved through various phases, from nineteenth-century encyclopaedic efforts at evolutionary schemes of world history to micro-level, empirical studies of everyday life situations. Marxism also comes in different packages, and, as I note below, the different brand-names do indicate substantial differences. Although in sociology's classical phase theorists such as Weber, Durkheim and Tönnies felt bound at least to mention, if not to make a thoroughgoing analysis of, Marx, until the 1960s there was little direct debate between sociologies and Marxisms. Sociology tended to be written off by orthodox Marxists as a 'bourgeois science' (and it *does* of course have links with the less critical theory of industrial society), and sociologists returned the compliment by virtually ignoring developments in Marxism.

Orthodox Marxism, the scientific materialism of Soviet ideology, was for many years the major representative of Marxism after Marx. As David McLellan points out, with the success of Marxism in the Soviet Union, his ideas were

> simplified, rigidified, ossified. Marxism became a matter of simple faith for its millions of adherents, to whom it gave the certainty of final victory. But this entailed an ever-growing distance from the original ideas of Marx and their transformation into a dogmatic ideology with the correlative concept of heresy – or revisionism, as it was often called (McLellan 1979: 2).

As a science of society it accepted only one version of events, one view of reality. The same still tends to happen today. At the World Congress of the International Sociological Association in Mexico, 1982, three Soviet sociologists stood to complain vigorously that a careful empirical study of the Polish 'Solidarity' movement was 'unscientific'! What would have rendered it 'science', no doubt, would be its congruence with Marxist-Leninism.

In the 1960s, amid widespread student and worker unrest, and in the U.S.A. the civil rights movement, a different, humanist Marxism began to blossom again. The Frankfurt Institute for Social Research, founded in the 1920s to search for an alternative to Soviet Marxism, found its moment. It also found its spokesman in Herbert Marcuse whose writings were to become symbolic of a new Marxist image. Marcuse exposed the dark side of *industrial*, and not only capitalist society: alienation might still exist in state socialist societies! He also resonated with a more general counter-cultural quest for an alternative to the artificiality of modern 'civilization'. And he no longer placed all revolutionary potential in the hands of the toiling labourer; other oppressed peoples, such as students, blacks and women, could join or take over the proletariat's historical role.

This period also saw the greatest expansion ever of social science in higher education. Fuelled on the one hand by the turmoil of protest and discontent ('The times, they are a-changin' ') and on the other by the publication of 'new' Marxist texts, Marx was once more a name on numerous lips. Students now had access to Marx's early writings and also, by the mid 1970s, to the highly important *Grundrisse*. At last an alternative to the tired old tunes of establishment sociology *and* establishment Marxism had arrived.

The streams of Marxism flowed on, now in slightly different directions, each having close connections with sociology. The 'humanistic' stream, associated especially with the Frankfurt School, is connected with 'critical theory'. This is a neo-Marxism which takes Marx's Hegelian legacy very seriously, stressing the active side of *praxis*. But this tendency is also seen in the ill-fated Yugoslav *Praxis* group, who attempted to forge an alternative to stultifying state socialism in the 1970s. This stream is committed to a humanistic, liberative and democratic reading of Marx. Some would say, however, that in forsaking the proletariat as *the* agent of historical destiny, and abandoning practical political involvement for critical analysis, groups such as the Frankfurt School have forfeited their position in the

Marxist tradition. Neverthless it is impossible to understand today's most significant guru of critical theory, Jürgen Habermas, without understanding Marx.

The other, 'scientific' stream, which again has ideas in common with sociology, is structural Marxism. This stream stresses the scientific nature of Marxism as a means of accurately determining the forces at work in present society. Its leading light is Louis Althusser. Equally disenamoured with crude economistic interpretations *and* humanistic Hegelian readings of Marx, Althusser confronted the passive industrial societies with a new theory, which could help explain why both bourgeoisie and proletariat had gone flabby and lost their fizz. Forget the conscious activity of *praxis*, suggests Althusser; the determining factor is the unconscious structures underlying social practice. Althusser himself succeeded in irritating large numbers of humanistic Marxists as well as sociologists. But he undeniably opened the door for a series of studies which reflect his impact, studies of class and the state, the city, culture and race. No one today thinks of separating such studies into sealed 'Marxist' compartments. They are simply part of contemporary social scientific debate.

How many Marxisms?

By this time the reader may have a strong and not unjustified sense of *déjà vu*. Does not the distinction between what Tom Bottomore calls 'humanist' and 'scientific' Marxism (Bottomore 1981: 2) echo the distinction between 'action' and 'system' sociology? Right, and the reasons for this division are arguably quite similar; the swing between the two poles is a recurrent theme of post-Enlightenment thought. Needless to say it complicates any would-be evaluation of Marxism in social science today.

Alvin Gouldner goes so far as to say that the internal contradictions which have always been within Marxism mean that Marxism is in a state of crisis. Swedish Marxist Göran Therborn realistically recognizes Marxism's shortcomings, noting that

> Fundamental aspects of Marxist theory have been called into
> question both by its historic defeats, so far, in North America and

147

Western Europe, and by the aftermath of its successes – Stalin-
ism, the Sino-Soviet split, the present social and political condition of that third of the world claiming to be governed by Marxist
theory. These and other contradictory and often unexpected
developments of the union of Marxist theory and practice make it
possible to speak also of a crisis of Marxism (Therborn 1976: 38).

So, not only does the West have its contradictions, and capitalism its conflicts, Marxism also is in disarray. As Gouldner says,
at a profound level, there are 'two Marxisms'.

Gouldner proposes that the tension in Marx is most clearly
visible in the famous eleventh Thesis on Feuerbach, which
states that 'the philosophers have only interpreted the world in
various ways; the point is to change it'. Marx was at great pains
to show that capitalism is governed by lawful regularities, such
that a *science* of society is possible. He scornfully dismisses all
idealism as redundant in an age of science. Yet he urges people
to change the world, which one would normally do in the name
of some ideal, some purpose. This is hardly compatible with the
'impersonal laws' view, which implies that class conflict will
erupt into revolution anyway. Here is the nub of Marx's contradiction; he was

a paradoxically idealistic materialist who suppressed his own
idealism, declaring that he was not really pursuing an ideal but
(like Socrates) was only a midwife delivering what had been
prepared in the womb of history, and calling upon others to do
likewise (Gouldner 1980: 33).

The ethical deficiency of Marx is perhaps the most abiding
problem in contemporary Marxisms. Having eschewed
idealism, and therefore supposedly rejected all normative
schemes, utopias and visions of the good life, Marx gave no
reason *why* the world should be turned in the direction he
proposed. The critical and constructive social analysis proposed by this book attempts to display its 'reasons', its emancipatory and normative direction. It is thus not out of place for
Christians to articulate at least short-term views of the 'good
society', relating on the one hand to the 'future hope' and on the
other to empirical social realities (see Lyon, forthcoming).

It is convenient to group Marxisms in two major categories as long as these are seen as helpful pigeon-holes, not strait-jackets. What I have referred to as 'humanist' Marxism (following Bottomore's usage) Gouldner calls 'critical' Marxism. The terms matter little: the point is that this view stresses the significance of human decision and action, and is concerned to intervene in society, at least as social critique. In this view, society is more likely to be seen as totality, exhibiting features of a specific historical phase. Overcoming alienation and bringing about a truly human society is of the essence. Scientific Marxism, on the other hand, is well represented by Althusser, who sees a break between the 'young' (Hegelian) and mature (scientific) Marx. The impersonal structures of socio-economic institutions are the real historical actors in this view, and they tend to limit and constrict human potential. The objective forms of exploitation, rooted in capitalism, are what has to be overcome by the socialization of the means of production.

Why, then, did two Marxisms develop? As with the 'two sociologies', it will hardly do to see this process in merely intellectual terms. Gouldner, rightly in my view, locates the social origins of the two Marxisms in the secularization of Europe. With Christianity on the wane as a legitimating and culturally potent force, Marxism grew up with its obvious alternative: science. The certainties of Christianity were apparently being eroded; scientific Marxism provided some guarantees of a better future. At the same time, though, Marxism incorporated some old millenarianism from Christianity, giving it a critical edge. Here was comfort in and revolt against suffering, which, as Marx himself observed, is precisely what religion offers.

But Christians have no right to crow at this point. The fact that Marxism may be seen to have a religious dimension (or to perform some religious functions) is an indictment of Christianity. Why have committed Christians not been even more prominent in the struggle to understand and cope with industrial capitalism in the last 150 years? Of course this Janus-faced creature is a threat: Marxism's gaps have been great enough to let the Gulag through. But it is also a challenge both to analyse the world of capitalist and socialist industrialism in the light of the biblical drama and to recover the critical cutting edge of Christian commitment (Lyon 1981b).

Human images in Marx

It has often been scornfully said that Marx had no concept of human nature. Only concrete individuals – the perspiring peasant or the prosperous plutocrat – exist. But Yugoslav philosopher Gajo Petrović makes nonsense of this view (Petrović 1967, see also Geras 1983). Of course Marx was concerned with the concrete, but he also saw human beings as a distinct species with their special characteristics. As Marx says in the *Economic and Philosophical Manuscripts* of 1844, unlike animals 'Man . . . has a conscious life activity'. This , writes Petrović, is *praxis*, the activity by which people create the world and themselves. Naturally Marx does not complete the definition of humanness, because history is open. Humanity has still to make itself. Alienation is yet to be overcome. Clearly the human image here is that of man as his own sun, around which he revolves.

That, however, is a position clearly rooted in critical or humanist Marxism (and linked to the Enlightenment notion of limitless human potential). The better known, and more widely applied, Marxism is the 'scientific' variety, which takes Marx's comments about humanity to refer more narrowly to the economic process of labour. Despite what Petrović says, Marx did spend a lot of energy showing the centrality of labour (Ben Franklin's 'man as a tool-making animal') to the process of history. The result is a Marxian social analysis which is obsessed by class, and oblivious to many other features of the world which capitalism has created.

> Expressed bluntly . . . Marx was wrong to regard human beings as above all tool-making and using animals, and to treat this as the single most important criterion distinguishing the 'species-being' of humanity from that of the animals (Giddens 1981: 155–6).

Giddens goes on, interestingly, to comment that seeing human life as a 'search for meaning' is nearer the mark.

From a Christian angle, what has happened here is a classic case of a single aspect of created life being blown up out of proportion and made the 'guiding thread' for all human (social) understanding. Against this, we may say that life is far more than labour. And labour is not limited to economic activity. An alternative view is required which transcends both the open-ended humanism which makes human autonomy absolute ('doing what is right in our own eyes') and the narrower view that human life really boils down to one essential aspect, which then governs all else. This view must still see the labour process as being highly significant in social change, but it will not focus exclusively on that. At the risk of sounding trite, I cannot but express my conviction that Christian commitment fits the bill. But I quickly add that the best evidence for this is not to be found in aping a grand scheme like Marxism. We must look at some concrete case studies in order to show how a different image of humanness does throw light on the issues urgently exposed by Marxian analysis.

Class: illusion or illumination?

One has to be a rather convinced and committed Marxist to persist in proclaiming Marx's message that all history is about class struggle. But at the same time one would be pretty blind to reject the view that class is a crucially important phenomenon in the modern world, particularly in the West. Although he acknowledged that the idea of class conflict came to him from other sources, Marx still provided future generations of social analysts with a more detailed exposition of the class-dominated nature of capitalist society than anyone else. He alerts us to features of the modern capitalist world which ought not to be ignored or minimized. The class concept and its application to modern life can become an obsession of misplaced faith. But to discard it is equally dangerous. Class is an inherent and distinctive feature of capitalist society, as opposed to the kinds of social divisions which exist in other places and have existed in other times. Here is one of the abiding contributions of Marx to our understanding of the dynamics of capitalist society.

Let me make a few connected observations about Marxism and class in order to suggest how a Marxian concept might be evaluated. Marx, as we have seen, showed how labour-power becomes a commodity within capitalism. Workers sell their labour-power on a market, thus making property the source of class division. At the same time property, via capital, is also the organizing principle of production. Marx and Marxists believe that a fundamental contradiction lies here, though there is disagreement as to exactly what that contradiction is (Young

1976). The point nevertheless remains that unique to capitalism is a contradiction between structural components which coincides with class conflict.

It will not do to protest from a North American vantage point that class is really a British phenomenon, embedded in British history and exhibited in posh drawing-room accents or plebian public house patronage. Neither is it satisfactory to say that because we may not be acutely conscious of class, therefore it does not exist. It is true that the common language of class (which often suggests that class conflict will eventually be swallowed up by a growing middle class) obscures the central features of class. As Marxist sociologists Westergaard and Resler put it, perhaps over-starkly, it is 'the concentration of power and property in a very small section of the population on which the whole ramified structure of class inequality turns' (Westergaard and Resler 1976: 29). There is, in other words, empirical evidence for this aspect of Marxist theory. And to a greater or lesser extent, and in various ways, all capitalist societies are class societies.

Again, it must be stressed that to accept the key Marxian insight about the relationship between labour-power as a commodity and the development of classes in capitalist society in no way commits one to the rest of Marx's analysis. In any case, what exactly constitutes 'the rest of Marx's analysis' is open both to internal dispute and to charges of overall inadequacy. The main point is that the concept of class, whose importance was demonstrated (but insufficiently elaborated) by Marx, helps us to make sense of the pervasive and enduring inequalities which exist in capitalism from generation to generation.

To appreciate the pervasive social influence of capitalism at the class level is vitally important from a Christian angle. Local churches must grasp the significance of class difference, which has also been negatively linked with church-adherence (Wickham 1957), in order to enter into the mind-set of the indifferent unchurched urban worker (Joslin 1982, Sheppard 1974), especially in Europe. More generally, the mobilization of Christian minds and Christian practice within capitalist societies can only be hampered by lack of attention to the specific class configurations of societies in different parts of the world.

But what of the 'internal dispute' mentioned above? In Christian or in Marxist circles there is room for discussion about class. The main division among Marxists is between those who see class as a *category*, designating particular places in relation to the means of production (Erik Wright leans this way in his analysis of American class structure), and on the other hand those who see class as a social *force* which makes history (English historian E. P. Thompson focuses on this aspect). This division will come as no surprise after our comments on the 'two Marxisms'. The one relates to structural and scientific accounts, the other to active and critical accounts. It is a source of considerable difficulty, even embarrassment. For those defined as 'proletariat' sometimes appear to be stodgy, private and passive, while others, who don't seem to fit the Marxian scheme at all, *do* try to catalyse change. As American Marxist, Burawoy, picturesquely says,

> Marxists find themselves embracing one notion of class or the other – hanging from one pole while stretching for the other as it recedes into the distance. Those who have vacillated have dropped into the gorge between the two (Burawoy 1978: 55).

Similar comments to those made with reference to 'action' and 'structure' in the previous chapters may be applied here. But this particular paradox is also symptomatic of a Marxist myopia which focuses all attention on the analysis of class (for unremarkable political reasons). Thus at least four factors remain obscure or insufficiently noted: changes which have occurred in capitalism since Marx, other profound social effects of capitalism, specific circumstances of a given society, and the actual actions and aspirations of groups within that society.

With regard to the last, irritation with the rather rigid framework of the more structurally inclined authors has sparked off efforts to find suitable alternatives in the work of other theorists. Max Weber, for example, often misinterpreted as being concerned only with 'status', not class, is a case in point. Weber certainly held that it is one's class situation which is the predominant factor in the system of relationships generated by modern capitalism. Frank Parkin has revived Weber's notion of 'social closure' in a way which complements a possible Marxian understanding of class.

Parkin's strategy is first to show how Marxists may get very confused over the boundary question: where is the *line* to be drawn between different social classes? Having shown that several Marxian explanations are deficient, he goes on to argue that class is better conceived of in terms of closure. This is a *process* in which 'collectivities seek to maximize rewards by restricting access to rewards and opportunities to a limited circle of eligibles'. Access is thus 'closed' to others. Social groups may form – maybe around property – in order to exclude others from getting at what they control. Others in turn, being excluded and thus hostile to the first group, will attempt to usurp their position (Parkin 1979). This analysis puts the spotlight on *action*. Such correctives to the more orthodox and static Marxist views may be elaborated with a Christian commentary, which brings out the ethical dimension so sadly lacking in Marx.

The desire to monopolize rewards and opportunities is seen in this light as being a feature of the 'usurping' as well as the 'excluding' collectivities. A blow is thus immediately struck against the idealizing of the suffering 'working class' so common in certain Marxist writings. Alan Storkey has emphasized this side of class analysis from the standpoint of a 'Christian perspective which recognizes that all systems grow out of the motives and actions of men . . .' (Storkey 1979: 178). In a brief historical look at class relationships in Britain he highlights the note of fear, social distance and guilt in the responses of the propertied classes of the nineteenth century. Because this group was afraid of those they exploited they created means of keeping social distance, as symbolized by the isolated country home, but also expressed more subtly. They also tried to alleviate fear and guilt by providing welfare. At the back of all this, however, Storkey detects self-interest and coveting – on both sides. This kind of analysis, while it has to be complemented by social structural accounts, which show how capitalism is conducive to particular kinds of exploitation, helpfully reflects the realism of the second aspect of the biblical drama.

One further extension of class studies deserves mention. Marxism, as we noted in the introduction, currently offers some striking insights into the workings of the *world* economic system. More general exposure of the relative poverty of the 'South' of the globe in contrast with the 'North' suggests to many that there is now a *world* system of social stratification. This represents another crucially important area for Christian analysis and action. The God of the Bible is vitally concerned about poverty and international justice (see for example the condemnation of transnational injustice in Amos 1: 1–2: 5). While Marxism may stimulate investigation (and thus also dialogue with Christians) along these lines, many difficulties remain. Not least is the embarrassing situation of the advanced societies' proletariat, which now appears to be as much exploiter as exploited! For those in the 'North' are exploiting both resources and artificially created consumer markets in the 'South' to the detriment of the latter.

Margins of Marxism

Marxism has its limitations. Both inside and outside its fuzzy margins there is considerable room for debate. Contrary to the comrades' insistence it does not have all the answers. Ironically some of Marxism's strength is also its weakness. For Marx emphasized that capitalism is not only an economic system; one may speak of capitalist *society*. Some neo-Marxists who have revived the idea of a society 'totality' are following an important Marxian clue here. For capitalism has a pervasive effect, creeping into every sphere of life, reducing everything to commodities.

As we saw, Marx made the seminal observation that under capitalism labour-power becomes a commodity. Unfortunately, rather than analysing in detail how this process is repeated elsewhere in the system, he gives the impression that everything hinges on this. From this the erroneous conclusion follows that the forces of production have primacy in the organization of and changes in a given society.

In recent years, however, it has been precisely those who maintain the 'primacy of the mode of production' view who have catalysed new developments in social analysis and theory – Marxist and non-Marxist. Two prominent examples are Nicos Poulantzas in class and political sociology, and Manuel Castells and his colleagues in urban sociology. The latter, who has acquired an international following, sees the city as having a central role in today's capitalist 'crisis'. One does not have to adopt Castells' Althusserian position in order to see the importance of this development of an old Marxian theme. The 'urban question' is both urgent and profoundly linked with the

155

development of capitalism. The crucial insight is that capitalist urbanism turns space into a commodity. (Similarly, time is commodified in the capitalist workplace with the introduction of clock-regulated labour discipline. 'Time is money' is a phrase exuding the inescapable scent of capitalist civilization.)

At the same time as acknowledging the salience of these novel explorations into industrial capitalism, it must be admitted that some Marxist analyses do more to pose a challenge than to present palatable theories. For while someone like Castells has done urban sociology a favour by getting it out of a rut, if one is unwilling to view the city's crises as a kind of knee-jerk reflex of capitalism's structural contradictions, then the 'Marxist' component of one's studies will become increasingly diluted.

Indeed some intriguing insights presented by theorists such as Richard Sennett and Anthony Giddens open up lines of urban inquiry which are as fruitful for general social analysis as they are uncongenial to Marxist orthodoxy. As Giddens says, 'Capitalist cities are almost wholly manufactured environments, in which an architectural functionalism produces the prosaic surroundings that become the settings in which the bulk of urban life is carried on' (Giddens 1981: 153). By sucking urban space and time into the commodity market, capitalism systematically strips everyday life of its moral and rational content. Capitalist industrialism contributes to the meaninglessness of life in mass society. It is the novelist Honoré de Balzac who for Richard Sennett most evocatively captures the impact of industrial capitalism (along with a 'secular faith in personality') on nineteenth-century Paris:

> To Balzac, the modern city with its culture of voracious mobility was really a revelation of the human psyche fully emancipated from stable obligations, feudal contracts, traditional ties. In the city, petty corruptions, little mindless cruelties, seemingly insignificant slights became inflated to moral absolutes: there was no longer any transcendent principle of king or God to oppose these cruelties (Sennett 1978: 155).

Marxism points the way to this kind of analysis – Sennett makes reference to Marx on 'commodity fetishism' – but the analysis steadily leads us beyond Marxism.

Evolution and revolution

Marx's scenario for the transformation of capitalism into socialist and eventually 'human' society is firmly set on the stage of evolution. Of course this has been a major bone of contention among Marxists, and it is also another locus of the Marxism-sociology debate. The question is, can history be conceived in terms of evolutionary laws of development – dialectical or other – or is the future really open?

The dispute is best seen in Italian Antonio Gramsci's critique of early Soviet theoretician Nikolai Bukharin. In his *Prison Notebooks* Gramsci sets out his theory of the philosophy of praxis (Marxism) over against Bukharin's *Theory of Historical Materialism: A popular manual of Marxist sociology*. Marxism is not sociology, Gramsci points out, for sociology is based on a 'pre-elaborated philosophical system . . . evolutionist positivism.' The natural science model leads to an inappropriate

> attempt to define 'experimentally' the laws of evolution of human society in such a way as to 'predict' that the oak tree will develop out of the acorn. Vulgar evolution is at the root of sociology . . . (Gramsci quoted in Joll 1977: 78).

Now while this description of sociology may be appropriate to Comte and Spencer, and while evolutionism is clearly also a feature of Durkheimian and Parsonian studies, Gramsci was also arguing against Marx's Marxism in order to defend his own philosophy of praxis.

For crucial aspects of Marx's theory of capitalism do depend on an evolutionary view, his own sporadic emphasis on praxis notwithstanding. Capitalism's contradictions were to resolve themselves in a higher form, in which eventually exploitation, classes and the state would all disappear. Because it *will* happen, according to this scheme, we need no interim ethic to guide us in the present. Neither do we need to go beyond the dialectics of labour – that is where the action is. Marx was confident, on the grounds of the laws of capitalist development discovered by him, that capitalist societies would experience some sort of revolution (he was never dogmatic about whether it would be cataclysmic or gradual) culminating in socialism.

But what if the evolutionist philosophy turns out to be false?

Could not a terrible situation occur where, say, revolution did take place, where a socialism was created in Marx's name, but where exploitation and the state did not wither away? Again, might it not be possible for exploitation to take other forms apart from the domination of a bourgeoisie over a proletariat? What if the nationalism already brewing in Marx's Germany led to the exploitation, in conjunction with capitalist development, of ethnic groups along racial lines? Or could it be that age-old conflicts between the sexes might be fuelled by capitalist separation of home and workplace, producing novel forms of exploitation of women? Marx, wearing his evolutionary blinkers, and clinging to a human image of 'tool-making animal', did not consider these possibilities.

Revolutions have taken place, of course, though most have flagrantly defied Marx's predictions by bursting forth in situations where capitalism is not advanced. Political movements of various kinds use Marx's ideas (modifying them as convenient) to spark off coups and power transfers. In Latin America, where there was once a 'religious monopoly', there is an ever present attraction of a 'secular monopoly' take-over in the name of Marx (see Martin 1978: 44). But in the West chances of a Marxist revolution are slim, if not non-existent, given the power of the controlling establishments. Which is not to say that Marxist slogans will not be seized upon by sectional interest-groups from time to time. Perhaps the bigger danger of the present is from right-wing authoritarianism; another potential development unforeseen by the prophet Marx.

Thus in the end a critical integration approach draws very similar conclusions for Marx as for other major social scientists. We find our ambiguous human image in the Marxist legacy, which is capable of interpretation in two very unchristian directions. In particular the primacy of labour-relations in human life produces a social theory obsessed with class difference and blind to other manifestations of contradictory and exploitative human experience since the fall. Some of Marx's emphases are invaluable, such as seeing society as a totality, linking theory and practice, and, more specifically, indicating the commodification of all life under capitalism. Thus his work and that of his followers deserve utmost respect. But even those categories which might be acceptable from a Christian stance may not help to explain specific social situations. Is the notion of 'proletariat', deriving its content from Dickensian English cities, appropriate in the Third World, for instance? (see *e.g.* Lloyd 1982). As usual, both kinds of questions must be addressed for social analysis to be done with Christian integrity and insight: one, is the theory or concept acceptable in a Christian social perspective (Marx's evolutionism must be jettisoned for example), and two, does the theory help us interpret social situations and discern the signs of the times?

8

NO WOMAN'S LAND:
FEMINISM AND SOCIOLOGY

*Give her the reward she has earned, and let her
works bring her praise at the city gate.*

Biblical proverb

Feminism is not a fleeting fad. The question of 'women's place'
is perennially pertinent to any society, but in the late twentieth
century it is especially urgent. Half the human race, frequently
obscured from sight in sociology as in society, is becoming
visible in a new way. The article from which I filched the above
chapter title is about women in British sociology of education,
or rather about their conspicuous absence. But the point can be
made about each area of social analysis and of society: women
frequently have an inferior and subordinate place.

Feminism: challenge and response

As with Marxism, feminism thrusts a challenge before society
and sociology. It also similarly challenges Christian commitment, the axis on which this book turns. So once again we must
explore not only the social and sociological but also the Christian meaning of feminism(s). With the flood of feminist files on
the market, now making complete lists and even bookshops
dedicated to 'women's studies', it is impossible to touch on all
the terrain. In this brief chapter, I only hope that my glossing of

complexity will simplify and not trivialize or misconstrue the issues. I am aware of the grave dangers of writing as a male on this topic: its challenge is rightly directed at men.

That feminism has forced itself into the foreground in the present era is not the only reason for discussing the issue. The 'woman question' is inextricably part of the 'human image' debate which runs through this book. It also stands in close connection with the world of work and the issues of household and family. In responding the dangers for Christian people are two-fold. One is that of wheeling out some tired traditional notions which cannot survive scrutiny in the light of biblical illumination. The other is that of over-hasty acceptance of some feminist stance without first exploring its underlying assumptions.

So critical integration once more involves the ticklish task of discernment and debate. Because we are discussing social analysis, it should also generate discovery. For while feminist sociology again exposes the interpenetration of analysis and action, it is the former which is of primary concern here. Thus little attention is paid to the (equally pressing) policy problems associated with the women's movement (particularly those of marriage and welfare legislation, abortion, and so on).

Many feminists would claim today that the sociology of women has become a perspective in its own right (thus generating distinct methodologies, see e.g. Roberts 1981, Oakley 1982: 317–334). It focuses on the activities, life-styles and interests of women in sexually unequal society. Items including housework, child-rearing, health care and inequality of employment form the staple diet. For example, the great influx of women into the labour market since the Second War has caused many to experience the tension between domestic and paid labour. Women begin to ask themselves why they should be obliged to do *two* jobs? The problem is that work done in the home is not counted as work. As Hilary Wainwright puts it:

> In an economy in which a person's capacity to work is bought and sold in exchange for a wage, labour which is performed on the basis of personal relations rather than on the basis of monetary exchange is not recognized as labour. Consequently women's work in caring for children and husbands does not

> appear as necessary labour; it appears as a natural part of family
> life . . . (Wainwright in Abrams 1978: 160).

Such issues precisely indicate the need for sociological analysis, and the pressure to explore new theoretical approaches which might account for this.

Needless to say, the women's perspective does not stop there. Accounting for the social position of women is not the goal of feminist sociology. Awareness of inequality is joined to a sense of injustice that women should receive such systematically different treatment from men. The analysis which shows how women are chained to the kitchen sink cannot finally be separated (though it may be distinguished) from the effort to break the chains. An explicit commitment is present among those working in this area to the abolition of oppressive sex-differences which constitute a socially-constructed inequality. The women's movement is not concerned for mere equality (as the suffragettes once were). Feminists do not simply ask to be treated 'the same as men' (by being granted the vote for example). Rather, the call is for a human world, where women as well as men are treated as full persons. Feminist sociology analyses the reality but questions the justice of 'a man's world'.

Of all the areas of contemporary sociological concern this calls forth Christian comment. Church teachings are frequently at the receiving end of vitriolic verbal attacks in feminist literature. All too often the churches do seem to 'put down' women, so the feminist attack is not surprising. The gauntlet having thus been thrown down, Christian honour is risked if no one will pick it up. Sadly, responses range from a defensive denial of either the validity of the feminist charges ('we don't oppress women') to a denial of the need to take them seriously ('women *should* be subordinate'). What is required is sensitive dialogue in which the real positions (and maybe disagreements) are made clear. Christian humility demands that the churches as well as the world be subjected to critique – not partisan but biblical critique.

Two Adams: two feminisms

A creative tension exists within feminism today, a tension between two (sometimes contrasting) accounts of how woman's place came to be what it is. Margaret Stacey speaks about the problem of 'overcoming the two Adams' (Stacey in Abrams 1981). On the one hand is an explanation relating to the division of labour within capitalism, of which Adam Smith was the analyst and ideologue. This would locate the problem in the area of production and control of workers. But on the other hand is a more ancient explanation, having to do with the social meaning of the biological difference between Adam and Eve. The focus thus shifts to domestic gender relations and the social control of women. Put another way, there are two main approaches to the sociology of women: a Marxist and a (radical) feminist.

Both views are presented in contradistinction to those popular in the hey-day of functionalist sociology. This is perhaps especially true in the U.S.A. While acknowledging that a social institution such as the family may be seen as performing certain functions within a given social system – cushioning its members from external shocks and preparing them for involvement in the wider systems – feminists reject the unqualified approval often given to such arrangements. That is, while the analysis may be fruitful, implications drawn from it lead to a perpetuation rather than a change in the system. Talcott Parsons especially is often singled out as the *bête noire* in this respect. This is due largely to his consistent assumption that the status quo of women's major task as nurturing the male members of the labour force is appropriate and necessary.

In North America the interactionist perspective is also fairly important in this area, concentrating on the micro-sociological aspects of gender-roles and the socialization of children. Traditional roles are certainly not taken as given in this view. Much interest is directed to processes such as that connecting 'boys' and 'girls' toys and books to conceptions of 'men's roles' and 'women's roles'. Also there is often a link between the micro-level sex role definition kind of analysis and feminist therapy and counselling. This smacks of a somewhat individualized approach to an issue which most feminists believe requires more substantial analysis and action.

As I say, however, a gap yawns between two versions of what this more substantial analysis might be. Although the more insightful social researchers struggle to reconcile the two positions (recognizing that each has strengths and weaknesses), a division yet remains.

The radical feminist, well represented by Shulamith Firestone, maintains that the enemy is patriarchy. That is, the historical dominance of men over women in family and society is universal, and may well outlive the capitalist industrial society we know today. In *The Dialectic of Sex* Firestone insists that the basis of female oppression is sexual; women's natural reproductive destiny means that, as a sex, women occupy a protected and subordinate (and therefore inferior) place. Her answer is to dissociate child-bearing and -rearing from womanhood. How? By using the technological potential for abortion and test-tube babies and by organizing child-rearing on a communal basis. Only then will women be able to control their own bodies, and thus their own destinies (Firestone 1970).

Marxist feminists disagree. The problem they insist is a social one, not merely biological. The issue is one of gender, not just sex. Marxists argue that the way a society organizes its productive potential is crucial. Women have dual roles. They are in a 'double-bind'. At home they work as wageless housewives, but in so doing contribute to the productive process by nurturing those in employment. But in the labour force they are exploited, through pay discrimination, even though they work alongside men. Within Marxist feminism, as one might expect, there are disputes but a bottom line of agreement would be that 'pink-collar workers' form at least an 'under class' in contemporary capitalist societies. As a group they hold a position in the labour market characterized by low pay, lack of tenure and little unionization or chance of promotion. The abolition of such inequalities is, for the Marxist feminist, closely bound up with the abolition of capitalism itself.

But there are problems. Marxist feminists have yet to come up with an answer to the riddle posed by Leon Trotsky: 'the boldest revolution . . . cannot convert a woman into a man – or rather, cannot divide equally between them the burden of pregnancy, birth, nursing and the rearing of children' (quoted in Hamilton 1978: 80). What about the deep-seated inequality seemingly built into the human biological constitution? And what of the sexism which seems to be more closely connected to this than to some aspects of capitalist society?

This seems to direct us back to the radical feminist position which tries to examine precisely these issues. But then they underestimate the impact of the division of labour in a capitalist society, and lack a historical perspective which would reveal that patriarchy has not always exhibited the same features. And despite my promise not to make much comment on it, the radical feminist policy options have some sinister undertones. Not only are fetal lives threatened by the logic of using abortion to 'control one's fertility', but the frightening totalitarian potential of test-tube babies is offered as a solution to women's exploitation.

What then are the assumptions underlying these competing feminist analyses? The crucial unresolved issue is that of the fundamental cause of inequality between men and women. Once that is uncovered, appropriate analysis and action may take place. The language of sex roles and patriarchy betrays a biological explanation, in which the sex differentiation within the human species is taken to be the root of the trouble. The solution is understood to be a denial, or a transcending of that biology. Women may be (technologically) enabled to possess themselves. The language of gender, however, refers more to the socially defined differences of interest and opportunity accorded to men and women. This the Marxist's stress, pointing in particular to the ways in which capitalism accentuates the antagonism between men and women. The whole complex apparatus of capitalism, in which sexism plays an intrinsic role, must be dismantled for such antagonisms finally to be dissolved. As Ann Oakley demonstrates in her *The Sociology of Housework*, feminist sociology must involve a thoroughgoing critique of society itself (Oakley 1974).

Puritanism manqué

The best way to approach the vexed issue of women's place is via historical analysis. This helps to disclose not only the roots of contemporary inequality but also to discern the role played by the church in this process. Only then may a proper appraisal be made of the feminist debate, and of how Christians might contribute to it.

Roberta Hamilton's *The Liberation of Women* provides a significant starting-point (Hamilton 1978). The value of her study lies exactly in its historical emphasis, and its exploration of the interplay between capitalist captivity of women on the one hand and the influence of Protestantism on patriarchical ideology on the other.

Most people have some inkling that a separation of home and workplace occurred with the development of industrial capitalism. Although this has been a commonplace observation, its implications for social understanding are being radically reworked in the light of today's sociology of women. One does not have to adopt a rigid mode of production outlook to appreciate the impact of capitalism on the internal structure of households. Men began to go 'out to work', leaving women 'at home'. Of course, what women *did* at home had a lot to do with which class they happened to be born in. Women in Jane Austen's novels had plenty of time to take tea and visit friends, ever waited on by faithful men and maidservants. But those in Emile Zola's novels struggled to make ends meet, to retain their toil-weary husbands and their sanity.

Hamilton casts her net back to the seventeenth century in search of data which might link the two feminisms. She shows how the novel teachings of Protestantism led to an embrace of life in this world. God was interested in the ongoing life of the creation; humans were responsible to God for the way they opened up its possibilities. This included the (biblical) rejection of celibacy as an ideal, and thus a reappraisal of the Christian meaning of the family. A new image of *proper* family relationships emerged. A big step was taken in restoring women's dignity; wives and husbands were regarded more as *partners*. This was by no means a reflex of capitalism, for, as historian A. G. Dickens points out, the Puritans distrusted modern capitalist trends. The Puritans, he says, 'were more outspoken than any group in their denunciation of usury, economic greed, and social injustice' (Dickens 1964: 317). What happened, says Hamilton, was this:

> An army of modest, hardworking, loyal and godly wives became the fond dream of the preachers. But their dream did not come true. Through no fault of theirs it was aborted as Protestantism crossed historical paths and became entwined with capitalism (Hamilton 1978: 95).

The Puritan ideas were adopted, and adapted, becoming in time the ideological basis for the bourgeois family.

Thus the Puritan elevation of the family *coincided* with the new role for the home as the place of consumption rather than production. So with 'a stroke of historical irony', observes Hamilton, 'when the world was divided in two, not only women but religion itself was relegated to the home' (p. 96). From then on predominant churchly concern was to be with the world of consumption, the home, and not with production. As Max Weber observed,

> Wealth [became] bad ethically only insofar as it [was] a temptation to idleness and sinful enjoyment of life, and its acquisition is bad only when it is the purpose of later living merrily and without care (Weber 1958: 163).

Unanticipated by the Puritans, home became not a centre of morality *and* industry, but a retreat, a shelter from the world. So the Protestant view of women failed to take root, as women were now isolated from production and economically dependent on their husbands.

The Protestant image changed under capitalism in a manner which, as Hamilton points out, the Puritans would not have recognized at all. The idea of marriage as an economic and spiritual partnership, sweetened by love, bit the dust. The 'love' part alone remained, and became the fragile romantic ideal prized by later centuries as the supposed basis of marriage. Women's place had become firmly established. Puritanism thus had some quite unintended consequences in the domestic as well as the public sphere. The gains it achieved in upsetting patriarchal privilege – especially through an erosion of the medieval idea that women were 'less spiritual' than men – were short-lived. It was a puritanism manqué: unsuccessful through no fault of its own.

Christian feminism?

A brief historical glance at some of the interrelations between Puritanism, capitalist industrialism and the position of women should stimulate further questions and study. Some feminists and some Christians have been much too quick to draw conclusions without examining historical evidence and without hearing what the other is really saying. Christians, often on traditional rather than biblical grounds, may be heard to talk of 'chains of command' in the family, or that feminism is 'breaking up' stable marital relationships. Feminists, on the other hand, quickly fall back on to some anti-Christian rhetoric about the churches' sexism, Paul's misogyny and the centrality of a *male* Saviour.

Sadly, these charges have not appeared out of thin air. Some virulently anti-male or anti-family feminists have probably had a detrimental effect on some marriages. And some churches do promote attitudes which perpetuate male domination and female subservience. Christians, while regretfully acknowledging the latter, have a duty to make clear a biblical position. An honest examination of the documents – in a properly sociological manner which bears in mind the historical circumstances and thus eschews anachronism – is the only way to get an accurate picture.

Feminists have argued for a long time over the *origins* of inequality. While historical and anthropological data can throw some light on different *forms* of patriarchy, the question is ultimately unanswerable in empirical terms. In the framework of the biblical drama, however, sexual inequality is seen as part of the pattern of asymmetrical power relationships stemming from the fall.

Humans were created, in God's image, as male and female. The only differentiation of tasks resides in the actual reproduction of the race: begetting children. Coping with this difference has led to a major proportion of the man-woman discord of a fallen world. This is because men have used it as an opportunity to hold women down, taking advantage of their vulnerability during the child-bearing and -raising process. But this is a deviation from the divine intention. For the tasks given to God's representatives (humans: the image of God) are given to *male and female*. These tasks are the stewardship of creation's resources and the opening up of the possibilities of the creation (Genesis 1: 27–30). Such mutuality is also clearly written into the child-raising process: it is the responsibility of mothers and fathers together (Exodus 20: 12; Ephesians 6: 1–4).

The dislocation of creature and creature is a fault line which also tore open the togetherness of man-woman relationships. The result was a breakdown of trust, horizontally as well as vertically. The consequent curse gave the whole picture a new twist. Biblical scholars disagree over the exact meaning of the 'curse' in Genesis 3: 16; 'your desire will be for your husband, and he will rule over you.' One view would be that the husband's 'rule' is part of the curse which is to be reversed in Christ, just as we combat the curse by struggling to tame the earth. Another view is that women would try to compensate for their child-bearing vulnerability by manipulating or dominating their husbands, but that husbands would in the end retain their proper position.[1]

Even those who take the latter view would not necessarily insist that the 'proper position' of men is at the head of a chain of command. It seems to me that the *overall* biblical picture is one which overwhelmingly stresses mutuality and complementarity. (Equality may not be the best word because it is quite clear that an inequality *is* inherent in the reproductive sphere.) When the Bible speaks of 'headship' then, this should not be sidestepped. But if the overall picture is one of complementarity, then the meaning of headship would seem to be that, in God's order for marriage, men take responsibility for caring for their wives and wives nurture husbands in return. Paul puts the Christian ideal clearly in 1 Corinthians 11: 11–12:

> . . . woman is not independent of man, nor is man independent of woman. For as woman came from man, so also man is born of woman. But everything comes from God.

There is, however, no substitute for careful biblical homework at this point. Christian opinion varies, but no one may dispute the view that the Bible affirms women as being as fully human as men, right from the beginning.

Difference, then, certainly does not equal deficit. Radical feminists sometimes seem to miss this crucial point. Trying to eliminate all difference is not the answer. Anthropology has yet to show us some society where difference has been abolished. Even the relatively undifferentiated pygmies have some role-distinctions. The following Eskimo saying is in tune with the

---

[1]The former view is taken by Jewett 1975, and Scanzoni and Hardesty 1974. Their willingness to doubt the correctness of biblical teaching at some points is criticized by Foh 1979. Loyalty to what the Scriptures actually teach is a matter of importance here (although Foh, while making many good points, does gratuitously imply that all who take a different line (e.g. of women's ordination) have a low view of the Bible). Helpful guides for biblical exegesis are found in Cook 1978 and Hurley 1981.

mood of the Scriptures at this point. These people, whose survival depends on adequate clothing, know that 'a man is only as good a hunter as his wife is a seamstress' (Van Leeuwen 1978, see also Hunt 1972). This kind of attitude is also reflected in Jesus' teaching and practice.

Jesus and Jewish patriarchy

Against the rampant Jewish patriarchalism of his day, Christianity's founding father was a sexual radical. Jesus struck deeply into the social and cultural subordination of women. As Dorothy Sayers comments, women had

> never known a man like this man – there never has been such another. A prophet and teacher who never nagged at them, never flattered or coaxed or patronized; who never made arch jokes about them, never treated them either as 'the women, God help us!' or 'the ladies, God bless them!'; who rebuked without querulousness and praised without condescension, who took their questions and arguments seriously; who never mapped out their sphere for them, never urged them to be feminine or jeered at them for being female; who had no axe to grind and no uneasy male dignity to defend . . . (Sayers 1971: 47).

The title, 'no woman's land' certainly cannot be applied to Jesus' attitude. As James Hurley says, 'the most striking thing about the role of women in the life and teaching of Jesus is the simple fact that they are there' (Hurley 1981: 82). In first-century Palestine, men, especially rabbis, did not even speak to women in public. Jesus spoke, healed, taught and discussed with them. He supported but did not sentimentalize motherhood. He broke the rules about allowing women a religious education, even arguing against a woman who was over-concerned with home-making to spend time learning from him.

One does not have to deny the Jewishness of Jesus to see that he rejected patriarchal prejudice as being an authentic aspect of Judaism. It was one of his many refusals to accept the status quo which, from a human viewpoint, eventually culminated in the cross. Likewise, Christians are not obliged to accept the cultural blinkers worn by some church-people who have allowed tradition precedent over text. We would all do well to listen carefully to the feminist cases, evaluating each in the light of the teaching of the whole Bible.

Contemporary Christians are already rediscovering what their ancestors realized in times past: we do not have to be squeezed into a cultural mould. Nineteenth-century evangelical leaders in the U.S.A., following the anti-slavery campaign, were ready to view other texts in an emancipatory light. John Blanchard of Wheaton College opposed the sexism of his day by locating himself in the tradition begun by Christ: 'the first alteration which Christianity made in the polity of Judaism was to abrogate this oppressive distinction of sexes' in which, he went on, 'women had almost no rights; they were menials to their husbands and parents' (quoted by Dayton 1976: 92). Similarly Free Methodist W. A. Sellew saw that women's rights had 'been taken from her by force' and advocated laws

permitting her to earn and own property and manage her personal business affairs untramelled by a class of men who think they possess superior knowledge on how a woman's money should be spent (Dayton 1976: 92; see also Olive Banks' discussion of the nineteenth-century evangelical contribution to feminism, in Banks 1981).

This is fully in line with the epigram quoted at the beginning of this chapter. The wise wife of Proverbs 31 is patently not an oppressed or subservient woman. Her earnings should be reckoned as a man's. Respect and dignity should be accorded her in the fundamental structuring of social arrangements, as symbolized by 'praise at the city gate'. (The 'city gate' in ancient times was the centre of public, legal and commercial life.) As I said earlier, the 'woman question' is equally the 'man question'. The biblical stress, unlike today's, is not on self-liberation. It is on the quest for all-round justice in which God's ways are found to liberate. This calls more for repentance and change in the 'man's world' than for militant feminist struggle.

At the same time, much work remains to be done. Distinctions and clarifications have to be made in the feminist and the biblical claims. No one may take the title 'Christian feminist' who merely wishes to impose a secular agenda on the biblical documents. The language of 'fertility-control' for instance has strong overtones of the possessive individualism of those claiming their 'rights' in capitalist societies. It reflects the fallen human desire to autonomy, not the restored aspiration to find and implement God's ways for the world. At all times Christian arguments must also be biblical ones. It will not do to argue that because women should have social and economic equality in the occupational structure that this applies to particular roles within the church. Without prejudice to the question of 'ordained women elders', arguments should be derived from Scripture, which does seem to make distinctions between church, family and other institutional areas.

Feminism and families

Feminist social analysis upsets the staple diet of traditional sociology texts. Not only do 'invisible' women come into view, along with the newly-discovered significance of their roles and work, but this also has implications for the rest of sociology, content and practice. In the U.S.A. especially it has led to a re-evaluation of men's roles. This is enormously important, if the man-woman issue is seen in a human context. But equally, the sociology of marriage and the family cannot remain the same after encounter with the feminist critique.

Jack Balswick, an American sociologist of the family, argues for a constructive Christian attitude to the contemporary re-evaluation of the place of men and women, marriage and family, in today's society. 'Rather than reacting against such changes,' he insists, 'we must be actively involved in examining the legitimacy of such change in the light of Scripture' (Balswick in De Santo 1980: 327). So often, calls for the abolition of the nuclear family or of the oppressive institution of marriage are taken to be a threat to Christian teaching. Let us examine this a little further.

The critique fuelling current sociological analysis highlights the privatized nature of the family under capitalism. It has developed into an institution geared to the nurture and care of its members, where the main burden of labour falls on the woman. This labour is not remunerated or even recognized as 'work', is seldom shared by husbands, and yet is patently necessary. If women 'escape' into paid employment, the contradiction is heightened because they have to enter the lower-paid, less interesting kinds of occupations. The home, which supposedly is the cosy nest of comfort and opportunity to 'be ourselves' (see Walter 1980), is in fact the locus of severe tensions. These are perpetuated by cultural ('boy's work/girl's work'), economic (housework is necessary) and political (legally protected patriarchy) processes.

In the 1960s, the functionalists assured us that, despite the rising divorce rate, marriage itself was still as popular as ever. Why? Many more divorced people re-marry. Apart from the obvious dysjunction between the Christian notion of *lifelong* monogamy and mere 'serial monogamy' in the definitions of marriage, this functionalist argument fails to account for the fact that marriages are made by men *and* women. In fact, marriage and remarriage (at least in Britain) is more popular among men (Burkitt and Rose 1981). This is hardly surprising, given that the current terms for marriage are so unequal: men stand to gain much more, at least economically.

When put thus, doubtless many Christians would agree that they do not wish to support *those* kinds of families and marriages. What so often happens is that the cultural norms (revealed by social analysis) are confused with a Christian ideal (shown in the Bible). It indicates that our task of relating biblical ways and sociological inquiry is still urgently required. Paradoxically, Christians may well find themselves in agreement with those Marxist feminists who are not out to destroy the family as such. Sharon Mayes, for instance, fully recognizes human need for nurturance, support and affection. She sees the growth of the 1960s commune movement partly as a response to privatized family crisis, but argues that a more realistic solution is to 'open up the privatized family'. She confidently states that

> New forms for the family can be developed that provide personal attachments, warmth and security, but not at the expense of women. It is the social relations of capitalism and the kind of family it fosters that hinders the meeting of these needs in the current social milieu. Women, men and children all share an interest in creating social relations that fulfill personal and social needs (Mayes in McNall 1981: 383; see also Clark 1981 for Christian comment).

One does not have to be a Marxist to utilize the insight that capitalism has shaped the family in an unhealthy way. But the resources of Marxist feminism itself are inadequate to indicate those truly human ways of 'opening up the privatized family'.

Some critical sociological thinking must be done by Christians in order to help the churches decide what kind of family we do want. At a moment in history when the family is an arena of battle, between some feminists and others who wish to abolish it, and politicians and churches who hope to revive and support it, time is ripe for saying what 'it' might be. Some of the ills blamed on the family, such as neuroses or child-abuse, may justly be related to the *forms* which pass as 'family' today. Society has changed immeasurably with the advent of capitalist and socialist industrialism. But are some well-meaning Christians still unwittingly colluding to support the kind of institution whose underlying ideology was unintentionally fashioned by Christians many generations before?

Before Christians embark on further militant displays of what might turn out to be a thoroughly misplaced familism, some serious social analysis is called for. The feminist challenge in social analysis is a challenge to the whole social order, from the micro-level, day to day routines of domestic life, through to an examination of the family's wider dependence upon, and shaping by, social institutions of welfare (see e.g. Wilson 1977, Bernard 1975), education and the media. Christian people who wish to take the family seriously, seeing it in the light of divine directives for human welfare, have to seek a proper means of analysing it in the modern world. Mark Poster's 'critical theory of the family' begins with the notion that the family is 'its own center of intelligibility' (Poster 1978; see also Davis 1982). That is, it may not be reduced to a reflex of welfare-capitalism *or* inflated to the status of society's most fundamental unit. The notion of critical integration demands that we pay particular attention to theories such as this, precisely because it seems to comport well with Christian commitment.

Salt and savour

The challenge of feminism is as profound in sociology and Christian commitment as it is in society. Some suggest that the feminist critique is more radical than that of Marxism in terms of its potential impact on social analysis and theory. It also confronts Christian commitment in a unique way, offering a new kind of opportunity for Christian involvement in sociology. The potential pitfalls, needless to say, are equally singular. The chief danger is of Christians jumping on some feminist or anti-feminist bandwagon. The effect of that is that both options miss the opportunity to be sociological salt, providing a contrasting and constructive perspective through contact with actual social situations. Salt which has lost its distinctive flavour, Jesus bluntly observed, is fit for nothing but trampling underfoot.

Without elaborating upon them, let me list some of the conclusions and inferences which may be drawn from this chapter.

First, feminisms are frequently encountered with some explicit stance in relation to Christian faith already incorporated in their accounts. One text, for example, states that the Genesis passage about husband's rule is regarded by sociologists as 'a mythological justification for the position of women in society' (Haralambos 1980: 369). The significance of commentaries such as Roberta Hamilton's study of puritanism, capitalism and the bourgeois family is thus immediately apparent. Christians are, as it were, invited to the debate.

Second, and following from this, the two-way traffic implied by critical integration is shown to be essential. For while, from a Christian stance, questions must be raised about the mode of theorizing gender and family relationships, the obverse also holds. The view the other way shows Christian pronouncements and practice in poor shape in terms of their relevance to the real social world. No sell-out to contemporary cultural patterns is involved in the insistence that Christian theory must be equal to current domestic practice. The lessons of history are salutary at this point.

Third, the need for an approach which locates humanness in the biblical drama becomes strikingly apparent. Anyone can produce a repressive sexist ideology or an emancipatory battle-cry from isolated biblical texts. A systematic survey of the actual data supports no such unqualified simplism. The picture emerging from detailed studies is still depressingly opaque at crucial points. The only promising approach lies in finding a wide measure of agreement on the complementary sexual significance of different moments in the biblical drama.

Fourth, feminist-inspired sociology is a fertile field for applying various Christian criteria in theory-assessment and

175

choice. As I suggested in chapter seven, Marxism is simply not adequate for understanding sexual inequality, although it supplies some significant signposts. And although radical feminism will not do, either, the force of its analysis, based on biological difference, may not biblically be evaded. Christians, it seems to me, would want to be among those searching for a third way between these two positions, each of which offers essential but limited insights. If Christians really believe in male-female *partnership* in marriage (and other spheres) this will be reflected in their analysis and action. Similarly the conviction that the identity and dignity of men *and* women is discovered only in being human – the image of God – has practical as well as analytical implications.

Again, with respect to other perspectives, Christian guiding beliefs direct us away from narrow exclusiveness. Parsons and Marx, each in their way, rightly stress the links between family and other social institutions in the wider society. But it is left to others to focus on the examination of everyday life at the household level. If we are to avoid the reductionism which sees the position of women and households as mere echoes of the clattering capitalist machine, this is essential. At each level the chance is presented of articulating a Christian view of men, women and family relationships, which stimulate and aid theory-choice.

Let me insert one example here. Sheila Kitzinger's study of *Women as Mothers* embraces these two levels, and thus takes a stand with which Christians may be comfortable. She draws attention both to the impact of other institutions on the task of mothering, and to the everyday life identity erosion which afflicts modern mothers:

> We have organized a society in which responsibility for healing, education and birthing has been handed over to the professions. As a result the motherhood role has become impoverished. All too often the only personal satisfaction and social recognition that a woman can find is in a job outside the home. We have lost something precious. For being a mother is one of the most important jobs anyone can do (Kitzinger 1978: 274).

At the same time, such sentiments should not be permitted to reintroduce totally 'separate spheres' of activity for men and women. Kitzinger is rescuing motherhood from second class status, not giving an excuse to men to evade their fathering responsibilities.

My fifth and last comment is that feminist social science is closely bound in with social and political practice. It will be evident by now that I see no problem with this: analysis and action are inseparable though distinguishable. The virtues of scientific rigour, when yoked to emancipatory aims like 'opening up the privatized family' or giving motherhood the respect and rewards it deserves, add up to a powerful tool for the cause of Christian commonwealth. Such future hopes may only be forged in the heat of debate and decision, of strategic alliances on one hand, but of refusal to be seduced by unscriptural slogans on the other. The contemporary challenge of feminist sociology will not be met without pain. The promise, however, is worth it.

Part 4

A different drummer

Amid the hubbub of crisis and confusion in society (and sociology) is a distinct sound of distant drums. Their rhythm is at once familiar yet strange. Familiar because it is the call of our Creator. Strange because our ears have grown accustomed to the cacophony of a fallen world. I hope you have heard the drums as you have read thus far.

Some sociological implications of the different drumbeat are suggested in the two final chapters. First, in chapter nine, we explore the idea of 'Christian sociology', discover that it is not such a novel notion after all, defend it against certain objections, but finally reject it in favour of a 'Christian perspective in sociology'. The latter term makes more sense in relation to the 'human image' framework and the 'critical integration' method. Practical comments on how such a perspective might be fostered are also offered. But it is also made quite clear that there are no easy answers: the debate between sociology and Christianity is indeed a complex conversation.

Lastly, in chapter ten, we glance at how the different drummer affects our thinking about how social science relates to socio-political action. The biblical quality of 'wisdom' is introduced as a proper basis for relating theory and practice. If that sounds abstract, however (and it really is not), I also add yet another sober reminder of the contemporary social and sociological babel. In the midst of this Christians *are* in a position to nurture a realistic sense of priorities for analysis and action. The distant drums send a message from outside the human situation, yet one which makes sense of it. Tentatively and self-critically, we can move forward to propose an agenda.

9

CHRISTIAN SOCIOLOGY:
PROS AND CONS

'Socialist sociology' is as much a contradictio in adiecto as 'sociological Americanism', as are 'black sociology', 'feminist sociology', 'Christian sociology' and so on.

Peter Berger

A clear and explicit avowal of the implicit metaphysical presuppositions which underlie and make possible empirical knowledge will do more for the clarification and advancement of research than a verbal denial of the existence of these presuppositions accompanied by their surreptitious admission through the back door.

Karl Mannheim

It must be clear by now that sociology and Christian faith cannot be seen as separate, sealed compartments of life. Sociology rests upon certain crucial but ultimately 'unprovable' assumptions which are rooted in world views (such as the place of humans in the natural world). At the same time, Christian faith has a strong bearing both on how and what we know of social relationships. The question is, when seen together, out of compartments, does the amalgam equal 'Christian sociology', 'a Christian perspective in sociology', or what?

The aim of this chapter is to explore these questions. They are

181

approached in three ways. First, historically, by looking at some previous attempts to make a Christian sociology, we may see the benefits and limitations of such a project. Second, apologetically, by assessing some contemporary criticisms of this and other efforts at linking social analysis and world-view. Third, programmatically, I start to spell out some dimensions of a Christian perspective in sociology.

A hidden heritage

Given the contemporary feeling among many sociologists that Christian believing is irrelevant to sociological studies, it comes as a surprise to discover that Christian sociology is not a new idea. In the U.S.A. a Society of Christian Sociologists was set up in 1889, and in inter-war Britain a journal of Christian sociology was regularly published. Christian sociology in the U.S.A. formed a bridge between the social gospel movement and the establishment of American sociology as a university discipline. Christian sociology in Britain was intellectually influential in the creation of the Welfare State.

Scott Matheson, a Victorian free churchman, saw the need for Christian thinking in social science. He recognized the importance of early efforts at doing sociology as a means of getting a more accurate understanding of social problems. But he was also acutely aware that sociology would attempt to exclude Christian assumptions. He saw sociology as the new 'science of the reading public, as theology was in Puritan times' (Matheson 1893: 16), but objected to its late-nineteenth-century secularism. His alternative was that the ethics of Jesus should guide such sociological analysis. At that time, especially in the London School of Economics where British sociology first had a home, ethics and sociology were seen to be clearly linked. While some early sociologists optimistically believed that they could construct an ethic from sociology, others felt that ethics should guide sociological development. Christian sociologists on both sides of the Atlantic engaged themselves in the latter activity.

The American social gospel movement had a significant influence on the founding of American sociology. Social gospellers aimed to 'Christianize society' partly through social reform. As with any movement it had good and bad points; but some Christians remember it better for the bad! In so far as the social gospel substituted social action for the good news of God's grace in Jesus Christ, it could clearly not be applauded by biblical people. But the aim of many was to show the relevance of Christian social thought to contemporary social issues and thus bring more, rather than less, credit to Christ. And many early American sociologists were connected in some way with the social gospel. This fact in many cases lent greater legitimacy to their sociological activity and aided the acceptance of sociology in American universities (Morgan 1969). An example of the importance of Christian sociology is seen in its being discussed by Albion Small in the editorial of the first issue of the *American Journal of Sociology* in 1895:

> To many readers the most important question about the conduct of the *Journal* will be with reference to its attitude to 'Christian sociology'.

Once established, however, American sociology tended to cut itself loose from the social gospel. Its practitioners tried rather to strengthen it as a 'scientific' discipline, which on Kantian terms came to be seen as incompatible with 'religion'. This also ties in with the shifting understanding of the term 'sociology'. 'Christian sociology', in Small's editorial, could mean Christian social philosophy or social theology. And while Small himself insisted that the motivation for and research priorities in sociology should be directed by such principles, he did not carry this over into the way sociology was actually done. Thus, rather like a discarded rocket which has assisted a spacecraft into orbit, the Christian prefix fell away from sociology.

In Britain things were worked out somewhat differently but the end result was the same. While evangelicals such as Scott Matheson were prominent early on, the most important impetus for Christian sociology was Christian socialist and Anglo-Catholic. Again, however, the term really meant Christian social thought, and this seldom spilled over into actual analysis. And if analysis took place, as in the monumental study of unemployment carried out by the Pilgrim Trust during the Depression (Temple 1938), Christian ideas were important only on the motivational sidelines, not on the analytical field.

No close relationship existed between Christian and university sociology in Britain, although some who were to participate in the post-war boom had been influenced by Christian sociology. Certain Christian ideals embodied in the Christian sociology movement were enshrined in the state welfare principles of the 1940s, especially those articulated by 'the people's bishop', William Temple. But although some sincere and insightful attempts had been made to justify the idea of Christian sociology, it was social philosophizing and practical social reform which in fact engaged its advocates.

The same crises and contradictions of industrial capitalism which provided the topics for other sociological analysis and theory had also inspired efforts at doing Christian sociology. People such as Vigo Demant, a member of the British Christian Sociology movement, had clearly understood the need for a structural analysis of social relationships to precede and inform any political activity. Demant, with his colleagues, was seeking alternative social-economic arrangements than those which seemed to have no 'human' side during the years of massive inter-war unemployment. Although some in Christian sociology dreamed of recreating a version of medieval paternalism, Demant believed that this was inappropriate. Contemporary social analysis, guided by Christian belief about labour, wages and employment, was a better way to revive what he saw as the human *spirit* of medieval catholic doctrines. But even though he (uniquely, I believe) got as far as making a plausible agenda for such study, actual analysis never got off the ground (Lyon 1983a). Within a few years, however, studies in academic sociology which were to set the tone of British sociology for over a decade were well under way. And this 'most secularized discipline', as Karl Mannheim called it, tended to turn only sceptical and cynical eyes towards Christian faith.

In concentrating on England and the United States, of course, I could be said to be neglecting important work which has been done in continental Europe and elsewhere. Ernst Troeltsch, for example, who was a friend and colleague of Max Weber, struggled with the sociology and Christianity issue. This German scholar produced an influential work on *The social teaching of the Christian Churches* (Troeltsch 1931). Another continental, Hermann Dooyeweerd from the Netherlands, is held in high esteem by a number of Christian social scientists for his contribution to formal or philosophical sociology. His work in fact combines some overly negative comments about the 'menace' of modern (secular) sociology with some interesting insights about the possibilities of sociological analysis. His comments are largely relevant to the sociological world view, though some of his ideas may fruitfully be applied at the level of intellectual practice (Dooyeweerd 1958; see also Storkey 1979).

Rejection and rejoinder

(The reader may wish to skip this section, which is a discussion of why the idea of Christian sociology is not as invalid as some suggest. The next section, 'A Christian perspective in sociology', picks up the threads.)

What then are the specific objections to the idea of a Christian sociology? In fact the objections most commonly rehearsed are ones which apply to other world view linked sociologies. They tend to attract charges of social sectarianism and intellectual closed-mindedness. The attempt to make a Christian sociology is not, in this sense, a special case. A consideration both of some analogues to Christian sociology, and also of objections to them, is a necessary prelude to any conclusions we may come to on whether or not to speak of 'Christian sociology'.

Recall, however, the distinction made between three different levels of sociology. It may be thought of as an overarching perspective, or world view, in terms of its disciplinary or institutional base, and as a set of intellectual practices. We have been concerned especially with the impact of world view on intellectual practice. Is it a *contradictio in adiecto* (contradiction in terms) to have a sociology linked to a world view, or not? If it is not, then in what ways might world view affect analysis? Let us glance at some examples; Islamic and Buddhist sociology are less well-known, Marxism quite the opposite.

A leading ideologue of the Iranian revolution of 1978, Ali Shari'ati, produced what he believed was a distinctive Islamic sociology (Shari'ati 1979). The *Qur'an* became his source-book for concepts. Thus for example the distinction between Cain and Abel is for him the fundamental source of all social distinction. They represent ruler and ruled, whether in an economic relationship (as Marx's class theory would have it) or not. However, while Shari'ati's work certainly did have the catalysing effect of inspiring Iranian students and intellectuals, and laid the basis for an Islamic critique of Western social thinking, his work does not yet seem actually to have generated any empirical research.

Another route has been taken by those influenced by Buddhist teaching. But although Alan Watts and others have done much to popularize Eastern teachings, Buddhist sociology has not (as yet) made any impact either. Inge Powell Bell, who discusses its possibilities (Bell, in McNall 1979), fails to demonstrate any analytical potential which Buddhist sociology might possess. It may provide, she argues, new insights on the individual-and-society issue, a way of overcoming self-interested bias in research, and a new understanding of sociological practice. In particular she wants to restore teaching as a central value of sociology, so that people learn *from* sociology rather than just 'doing' it or 'learning' it. Such comments should not be lightly dismissed. They indicate a quest for a different kind of sociology from what we now know. Analytical advantages have yet to be demonstrated.

If other world views have failed to generate empirical research or theories of social relations, the same cannot be said for Marxism. Tom Bottomore, in his sympathetic critique of the notion of Marxist sociology, has put a sensitive finger on the crucial issues. He discusses distinctive features of the putative Marxist sociology. In Karl Korsch's terms there are 'the primacy of economic structure, the placing of social phenomena in a historical context, the setting of empirical studies in a historical-economic context, and the recognition of revolutionary as well as evolutionary change' (Bottomore 1975: 67–8). But he charges Marxist sociology with over-boldness of claims and a failure to see the limitations of all sociological thought in the face of the vast complexity of social interaction. And why is it bold? Because, as he says, it must also be committed to the ideal of socialism as a future form of society.

Bottomore is arguing that a distinctive Marxist sociology cannot ultimately be distinguished from Marxism as a world view. In any case difficulties arise because 'Marxism' is a many-headed animal, as is sociology, and also because sociology and Marxism are already interrelated. Similar comments could be made with regard to the possibility of a Christian sociology. All kinds of Christian groups (Evangelicals, Episcopalians, Anglo- and Roman Catholics) have mooted the Christian sociology idea, and their different theological emphases are reflected in their varying sociological interests. Again, as we have seen, sociology and Christianity are already interrelated, enjoying a complex relationship which may be illustrated with reference to the impact of certain Christianly-derived ideas on sociology. So does 'Christian sociology' stand any more chance of an independent existence than 'Marxist sociology'? Bottomore's objections would suggest not.

Bottomore makes further points on sociology and world view, however, which are worth quoting:

> . . . a distinctive theory of society might be conceived as being strictly dependent upon the world-view – upon its ontology, theory of knowledge, and ethics – so that one could define a 'Marxist Sociology' in the same way as a 'Christian Sociology', a 'Hindu Sociology', or perhaps a 'Humanist Sociology' might be defined (Bottomore 1975: 65).

Yet he believes that this is neither plausible nor fruitful. He freely admits that sociological theory raises philosophical questions, but says that

> It is not the case at all that the construction and development of sociological theories has depended upon, or does depend upon, the prior elaboration of, and continual reference to, a total world-view (Bottomore 1975: 66).

This comment requires disentangling. As we have argued, while the construction of sociological theories may not have depended upon the *elaboration* of a world view, some particles of world views or incoherent world views may be traced within sociology as an intellectual practice. Moreover, Bottomore comments only on what is or has been the case, not on what should be. Surely intellectual honesty demands that our academic endeavours be as closely related to our world view as possible? This, in any event, is what I have maintained. As far as Christian faith is concerned, the basic Christian confession of 'Jesus Christ is Lord' involves the attempt to see every area of human activity in the light of that 'lordship'.

Nevertheless, Bottomore's hesitations about world view related sociologies are to be taken seriously. As far as Marxism goes, he points to the relative lack of empirical studies within this tradition (although, as we have seen, this situation has been changing), and to its dogmatism and blindness to other schools or approaches. One would add to this list the complaint made by Berger, and which lies behind the latter's rejection of world view related sociologies (quoted at the beginning of the chapter): such efforts are soon revealed in their true colours of 'sectarian or tribal particularisms' (Berger and Kellner 1981: 212).

With a few exceptions[1] there is as yet little evidence of attempts at self-consciously Christian sociological analysis at the present. Often such attempts ultimately fail to transcend mere social philosophizing, and thus fail to get a footing within the general sociological field. There are undoubtedly a number of studies by Christian authors who have attempted to integrate their faith with their learning, but in a less overt manner (Moberg 1967, 1978). Nevertheless, there is no *a priori* reason why Christian commitment should not generate distinctive forms of social analysis and theory. Indeed, I hope that this work might stimulate precisely that.

What of dogmatism and closed-mindedness? The thrust of this book is that neither is justified within sociology. Christians dare not close their eyes to sociological data, or foreclose empirically open questions. Certainly I have suggested that Christians ought self-consciously to decide between different kinds of explanation, on Christian grounds. But this is an alternative, not to doing 'better science' but, as our Mannheim epigram has it, to denying the existence of presuppositions and then surreptitiously admitting them through the back door. Certain items informing Christian sociological reflection cannot be negotiable. Like consistent Marxists, Christians have specific expectations (for example that sin will continue to have a pervasive effect in the social realm) and hopes (for example of the new heaven and earth, where sin will be abolished for ever). But it does not follow that the presence of such non-negotiable pre-theoretical beliefs produces a 'dogmatic' social analysis.

The clearest reason for this is that there is no Christian justification for such dogmatism: quite the reverse. A biblical understanding of sin is aware of the intellectual ramifications of our estrangement from the God of truth. All people, Christian or not, have to some extent a distorted view of reality. This is a

---

[1]One could mention Storkey 1979, Walter 1980, some contributions to De Santo 1980 and Grunlan and Reimer 1982, Poloma 1982 and Heddendorf 1972. Such a list encompasses great diversity, however. See Davis *et al.* 1980 for a brief discussion of different approaches.

handicap over and above our creaturely limitations, and means that scholarly work is always tentative and provisional. At the same time, the belief that humankind as such is the image of God entails a realization that all, whatever their specific religious outlook, have some knowledge of God and his world. Closed-mindedness is therefore not a Christian stance. As Paul the apostle puts it, Christians are committed to openness as we 'test everything and hold to the good'. However distasteful certain Christians may find some ideas of a Karl Marx, a Talcott Parsons or a Harold Garfinkel, we dare not foreclose the possibility that such theorists have made contributions compatible with Christian sociological reflection.

What should we make of Berger's worry about the sectarian or tribal spirit of something like 'Christian sociology'? His concern is two-fold. One, that a sociologist with an 'exclusionary program will logically have to excommunicate from sociology (or from its "true" segment that he alone represents) all those who do not agree . . .' (Berger and Kellner 1981: 120). Two, that the political usefulness of such a sociology is also nil: '. . . It can no longer represent itself as *anything but* an ideological legitimation of these particularistic interests' (Berger and Kellner 1981: 121).

I have already made exactly the same kind of complaint about 'absolutized' perspectives in sociology (or the 'only one sociology' variety), and pleaded for an integration of a modest and guided pragmatic position on the one hand, and the attempt to forge new concepts and explanations, on the other. Any exclusion which takes place will be of the same type that Berger himself practises; the rejection of certain kinds of explanation on grounds other than strict empirical constraint. As for the fear that any political usefulness is evacuated from such a sociology, Berger's argument is not necessarily right. True, efforts such as the French *sociologie religieuse* have given the appearance of a sociology committed only to 'particularistic interests'. Under the leadership of Gabriel Le Bras, this (Catholic) movement has been involved in the mapping of religious commitment by geographical region. Despite the sociological and pastoral benefits which might accrue to such an enterprise, sociology has been seen in this case more as a technical skill at the service of the church, that is, serving its interests. But my argument here is precisely that Christian faith provides a basis for a *human* sociology, universal in scope, and rooted in a commitment to the Originator of our sociality. In no way should this be confused with a tribal or churchly narrowness.

Despite various objections which may be raised, the notion of sociology as an intellectual practice linked to a world view is not a non-starter. True, Marxist sociology is the only distinctive case so far, but one could argue that eclectic humanism is the incoherent world view underlying most sociological accomplishments. Islamic and – more likely – Buddhist sociology may have important corrective insights to other Western humanistic sociology but they clearly do not pose a substantial threat right now. Neither, for that matter, does Christian sociology. But such an admission is not defeatist. Christians have a responsibility to work out the implications of their position within sociology, whether or not the product is labelled 'Christian sociology' (and I would not so label it). The pitfalls (such as merely engaging in social reform, social philosophizing, or turning sociology into an arm of the church) must be avoided at all costs. But the potential, Bottomore and Berger notwithstanding, remains.

A Christian perspective in sociology

Sociology presents us with a perplexing plethora of perspectives, a fuzzy focus and dubious direct relevance. Often this is combined with an unsettling cynicism. Each perspective within sociology depends upon a commitment to a particular view of social reality, but such 'domain assumptions' are not always spelt out. Deciding between them is an apparently arbitrary and pragmatic business. Choice of research fields often seems to be determined more by 'who pays?' than by ethical considerations of justice or welfare.

My contention is simply that sociology need not be adrift on a sea of relativism, driven by winds of convenience, comfort or caprice to unknown or undesirable destinations. Christian commitment offers the unique potential to cut through some of the contradictions, provide direction and aid decision, not from a purely human-centred perspective but from a God-centred one. In fact, as we have argued, such a perspective is the only one which can ultimately claim to be fully or truly human, based as it is on the assumption that humans are the image of God.

This 'Christian perspective' is by no means oblivious to

sociologies not rooted in Christian commitment. Rather it develops its distinctive assumptions, using them as a base from which to criticize, modify, or, sometimes, supersede other sociological work, at an analytical level.

Even the possible alternative concepts must not, however, be thought of as somehow 'separate' from other sociologies. The academic world is inevitably a meeting-place for different perspectives and theories. I have advocated 'critical integration' as a working ideal, where sociology and Christian faith inform each other. Of course, if the dominant sociologies were monolithically deterministic or state-controlled, a case might be made for a more radical withdrawal from the mainstream, but in most societies open enough to admit the somewhat sceptical presence of sociology, no party line exists.

In fact, Jesus himself once made use of two kinds of images for involvement during the same discourse. We may think of sociology done in a Christian manner as part of the 'salt of the earth', making its presence felt by contact. And at the same time we may think of it as a city on a hill, shedding light by virtue of its distinctiveness and separation. The images should not be set one against each other, but seen as complementary.

In all this we are increasingly able to make important distinctions. The confusion surrounding earlier historical usage of the term 'Christian sociology' stemmed from the implications that it was a distinct body of knowledge or that it was an instrument of the church. That is not the claim here. On the contrary, the present focus is upon Christian ways of doing sociology: assumptions, approaches, concepts and methods. The outcome may, if you wish, be labelled 'Christain sociology', but my fear would be that this is counter-productive; it is likely to mislead or alienate one's audience. Better, perhaps, to speak of a *Christian perspective in sociology*. The Christian sociologist, like any other worth his or her salt, will use logical argument, deduction, evidence and parsimony. But as we have seen, decisions in social science go beyond this. Choice of research priorities, concepts and methods may be made in an authentically Christian manner.

Mention of audience introduces another important point. Within the Christian community, explicit references to God in sociological writing may be quite natural, as it is, for example, in history (Bebbington 1979: 187). If the object of the exercise is to persuade folk of the truth of Christian faith, then historical (or sociological) evidence may be used as part of the argument. For example, sociological writings may furnish evidence which accords with the notion that God intends humans to live within some kind of family unit. Policies designed to destroy all parent/child or husband/wife relationships seem everywhere to founder before long. But the research article or undergraduate term paper do not have to contain explicit references to God, and it may be quite wrong to include them. One is not obliged to mention that the cooling off of an inner city riot is evidence of divine restraint, or that the establishment of new civil liberties shows God's intervention, even though belief in a justice and peace-loving God may well involve such possible inferences. It is pointless alienating one's audience unnecessarily.

Is this therefore to back away from the implications of doing sociology Christianly? By no means. The fact that I do not pepper every utterance with references to divine direction does not mean that I have ceased to believe in a sovereign God or ceased to shape my life by his ways. A Christian social perspective is still present in a piece of work consciously forged in line with it, even if the word 'Christian' does not appear. If others so wish to label it, so be it. The earliest use of the very word 'Christian' (in ancient Antioch) was as a label attached to Christ-followers. Brand names do not have to be used for the origin of the product to be clear.

One further point, which may be a tip for undergraduate students. The arguments one makes in an essay may often be made by quoting sociologists who make no Christian profession at all. For example, without necessarily agreeing with either of them in other substantive areas, it is instructive to note that Dennis Wrong uses Sigmund Freud against some functionalist assumptions in sociology. Remember that in his famous article on 'The oversocialized conception of man in modern sociology', he neatly encapsulates what is equally a Christian comment: 'To Freud man is a *social* animal without being entirely a *socialized* animal'. This process of appropriating for Christian use the arguments of others is sometimes referred to for reasons which should not be obscure as 'plundering Egypt'!

A complex conversation

Far from proposing a quiescent integration of faith and learning, in which Christian faith accommodates itself to superior sociological reason, I am suggesting that Christian faith demands that sociology be done in a distinctive way. This critical integration of religious belief and intellectual endeavour calls for sociological engagement. This discipline is worthwhile and should receive Christian support. It has Christian justification as a human science. But it also requires serious Christian conversation with sociology. As Ecclesiastes says, there is 'a time to be silent and a time to speak' (Ecclesiastes 3: 7). We must listen to and speak to sociology. The traffic may be two-way without sacrificing either sociological or Christian integrity. Yet I speak of *critical* integration because the *intellectual* pursuit of sociology is seen in a perspective derived from *religious* faith in Christ. Dialogue partners do not have to be equals in every sense for the dialogue to be fruitful.

More specifically, a Christian perspective in sociology is founded upon a biblical understanding of human sociality. The key assumption is that, because our Maker has told us about himself and ourselves, disclosing his mind to us through a book, that here is the basis for a truly human outlook on the world. As the image of God, people are social creatures, and what the Scriptures tell us about this aspect of our lives pertains directly to the kinds of issues raised in sociological discourse. Our sense of history is profoundly bound up with the *direction* of human history, understood in a biblical light, and this has deep sociological implications. The biblical drama of creation, fall, redemption and the new age locates us not only within a historical flow, but also in terms of our relationship with God. Sociology may sometimes be seen transgressing the bounds of its competence (for example in hinting that it has uncovered the *ultimate* origins of some conflict or injustice). But Christian faith not only puts proper limits on sociological inquiry, it may also suggest directions for that inquiry (as, for example, in the case of the explanation of sexism). We may also see our own task as one of recalling sociology to creation priorities, through the renewing work of Christ, aware of the distorting effects of the fall but spurred on by the hope of the coming kingdom of God.

This general biblical understanding, along with specific

193

insights into human social situations, may be woven into a coherent Christian perspective which yields specific 'guiding beliefs'. These in turn assist us in making judgments both as to the kinds of sociological explanation which are appropriate and also a proper assessment of the purposes of sociology. Examples of the former include the requirement that both human action and the structuring of social relationships be taken into account in any adequate social explanation. As to the latter item, sociological purposes, I have endeavoured to hint at a critical *and* a constructive role for sociology, a third way between the sociological poles of libertarian emancipation and technocratic control. These kinds of guiding beliefs are yet at a general level, and further work must be done in specific areas.

The kind of critical integration proposed may open the door for 'alternative' types of sociological theorizing, but more likely is a continuation of the complex conversation with existing sociology. In fact, in some areas the work done by Christians is indistinguishable from that done by others. By 'common grace' there is considerable overlap in sociology as in many other realms. But the conversation is also likely to force Christians to construct distinctive explanations and to follow different directions from others. A Christian perspective is rather like the feminist, in that its assumptions pervade the whole field of sociological studies. While there may be concerted efforts to develop a feminist perspective, it does not have to turn into an exclusivist and sectarian force. Exactly the same can be said for a Christian perspective. And to take the notion of a 'complex conversation' a little further, Christian sociologists have much to learn from colleagues attempting to work out a Christian perspective in history (e.g. Bebbington 1979, MacIntire 1974, Marsden and Roberts 1975). It could be argued that relationships between history and sociology will, in any case, grow closer as sociologists increasingly take the time-dimension into account, and as historians look to sociology for explanatory concepts. What has been said of history is also true of the study of sociology:

> History is eminently suited, given its assignment to draw the whole of human life within its purview, to do three things: to remind us of the intricate texture of social reality; to show the importance of the time-dimension to human life; and to reveal the

formative power of tradition in our personal and communal lives
(Van Dyke 1981).

One might wish to add the 'space dimension' and also the
formative power of interests. But there is an intimate relationship between sociology and history which means that attempts
to work out a Christian perspective in one discipline are ger-
mane to the other.

Reference to history, however, leads to another point. With
Inge Powell Bell, and her comments on Buddhist sociology,
Christians may share the concern to learn *from* sociology. Despite the comments made above, about sociology not being
reduced to an instrument of the church, it is nevertheless true
that there may be spin-offs for the Christian community. This
happens in at least two important ways. First, the church may
gain a heightened awareness about her place in the modern
world and also about the implications of a significant perspective on that world. Sociology teaches us much about the discontents and directions of our social milieu. Second, an awareness
of sociology itself makes Christians grappling with sociological
analysis more reflexive. Christian sociologists may have as an
aim to be as conscious as possible of their own context and the
potential consequences of their work.

Vocation and vulnerability

Christians have no excuse for falling into the trap of being *only*
socially reflexive. Our social self-awareness is constantly en-
riched by our being part of a new community of God's people,
identifying no temporary human institution as being a fulfilment of God's purposes, but rather being intent on seeking the
'city with foundations, whose architect and builder is God'. This
constitutes a call, not only for a new sociology, but for new
sociologists. Such are marked by humility and by confidence.
Humility born of an encounter with the living God, who in
Christ liberates us from misdirected thoughts and ways, and
which in turn gives birth to an academic modesty and careful-
ness. And confidence (not arrogance rooted in scientific
rationality) rooted in the reality and relevance of God's self-
disclosure in the Bible and in Jesus. Here is an alternative
vocation in sociology.

A different drummer

This is a way of doing sociology profoundly at variance with the relativism, rationalism and unchristian humanism which so frequently characterizes all its major schools. Christians are to be found among the sociological ranks, but marching to a different drummer. It provides a coherent justification for sociology, a way of choosing appropriate kinds of explanations and concepts, as well as a wider normative context for the discipline itself. To attempt to do sociology Christianly may court the impatience, scepticism and opposition of colleagues. This is Christian vulnerability. It is to be expected; it is a conscious risk taken by radical disciples of Jesus. But if our work is characterized by reflexive biblical social understanding and by critical attention to the important canons of social scientific discourse, then our work will stand or fall on its own merits. The remaining offence will be the scandal of the cross. The world may well object to God's wisdom articulated in the social realm. But Christians are called to faithfulness, not necessarily to ride the crest of academic acclaim. Our doing sociology Christianly interacts with our prayer that God's 'will be done on earth as it is in heaven'. Together, these two constitute an authentically Christian sociological praxis.

10
ANALYSIS, PRAXIS AND
THE REAL WORLD

*The social problem of the twentieth century is
whether the civilized nations can restore themselves
to sanity after the nineteenth century
aberrations of individualism and capitalism.*

Albion Small

When Albion Small wrote these words in 1914 the civilized
nations were about to tear each other apart in a terrifying new
aberration called world war. Soon after, another aberration,
called totalitarianism, began to rear its fascist and communist
heads. Meanwhile capitalism and individualism rode on into
the present, apparently unimpeded by nationalist, socialist,
democratic and anarchist efforts to destroy them. As for sanity,
it seems as remote as ever. This chapter, after the final comment
of the previous one about sociological praxis, concerns the
relationship between social analysis and practical life in the real
world. I begin with some comments on reason, wisdom and
praxis.

Rational or wise?

Small, along with other founding fathers of sociology, sought
solutions to the social dislocations and discontents of capitalist
industrial society. Social science was seen as a means of sus-
taining sanity in the new urban industrial milieu. But, not

surprisingly, sanity means different things to different people. The appeal to reason does not necessarily produce intellectual agreement and social harmony. While consensus might be obtainable on forms of logical discourse, we soon discover that what is accepted as 'reasonable' depends partly on one's world view.

Of course talk of world views can become an intellectual pastime, unrelated to social reality. For while in the real world some people do hold to coherent world views (such as existentialism), many accept a much vaguer 'spirit of the age', which is a rag-bag of world view fragments (Sire 1976 helpfully discusses world-views, though with little reference to the social context question). Some argue that because of this 'spirit' in the modern world many Christian beliefs are simply unintelligible. The view that wives might be submissive to husbands, for example, does not 'make sense' in contemporary terms and should therefore be rejected. So it is said.

I am not appealing to reason as a touchstone in this book (though I am not lapsing into irrationalism either!). The point is that reason on its own cannot answer our quest. Reason exists within world views, or, sociologically, within social 'norms of intelligibility' (MacIntire, quoted in Hudson 1980). Because the rationality of this book grows out of a Christian world view, it seems more appropriate to focus on 'wisdom' than on reason.

Wisdom, biblically, is that quality which enables one to see that while life 'under the sun' *is* vain and meaningless, meaning and purpose derived from 'beyond the sun' make sense of our human situation. The Old Testament sage, Ecclesiastes, saw clearly the futility and absurdity of life if nothing exists beyond the horizon of time and space. Business enterprise, technological endeavour, art and science – all are pointless unless there is a Creator who gave humans the world for our enjoyment and care, and to whom we are accountable.

Wisdom includes reason but transcends it. Wisdom relates human purpose to divine intention; its source is respect for and reliance on God. Biblically, wisdom is intensely practical. It values knowledge and technical skill, but this is ever related to social, political, economic or other purposes in the real world. But it may not be acceptable to others. That the crown of wisdom, Christ's crucifixion, is also a major stumbling-block (why should the just die for the unjust?) should prepare us for some hard work in convincing others of the wider relevance of Christian wisdom.

On the other hand, aspects of Christian social wisdom do speak strikingly to current concerns. I have tried to demonstrate the appropriateness of a Christian view both to theoretical questions such as action and structure, and to practical problems such as poverty and sexual oppression. I firmly believe that a Christian perspective refuses to squeeze social analysis into a clinical compartment, isolated from the 'contaminations' of social context and political struggle. It is simultaneously relevant to social understanding and social change.

Do not misunderstand me. I am not inviting social scientists to turn into grass roots politicians or become banner-waving members of protest movements. Rather, I am reiterating what I believe to be the thrust of biblical wisdom – that knowledge be geared into practical purposes in the real world. Praxis is another word for essentially the same thing. Not even 'religious knowledge' should be cut off from life. The Old Testament speaks of knowing God as 'doing justice', the New of 'true religion' being care for the vulnerable and powerless (Jeremiah 22: 16; James 1: 27). 'Knowing God' and 'religion' are emasculated if they are *reduced* to praxis. But if praxis is not present, we may safely assume that true religion is also absent.

Trouble at t'mill

Ideas are potent forces for good or ill. But if sociology teaches us nothing else, we should be aware that ideas do not stalk the world on their own. Remember the fate of Puritan ideas about the family! Those wishing to infiltrate the social scientific ranks with a Christian perspective must do so with eyes open. Sociology is not practised by some cultured savants, insulated from the pressures and pains of the struggle for survival. Far from it! In fact, as we say in Yorkshire, there's trouble at t'mill.

In most societies where sociology is pursued it is part of a liberal academic establishment. This means that Christian views, though they may be tolerated (sometimes!), are unlikely to be welcomed. Worse, social science is under threat, at least in Europe and North America, due to economic recession. Being recipients of public funds, which are drying up as fast as public sympathy, social scientists are entrenching themselves – ideologically as well as occupationally.

It is of course no accident that it is usually conservative governments which restrict money flowing into sociological coffers, given the image of social science as a radical threat to social stability. But the irony is profound. The same groups who wish to constrain sociological activity also call for explanations of social malaise. Is inner-urban unrest connected with unemployment? Why is the legitimacy of governments so fragile and the creditability of politicians so minimal? Such ironies are part of everyday life in social science today. The very validity and worthwhileness of sociology is in question. This is the context of a would-be Christian contribution.

Our anxious age is after answers. Debate and hesitation are seldom seen as virtues. So an intellectual area which seems uncertain of its identity (is it an art or a science? social emancipation or social engineering?) tends to be discounted as a source of illumination or guidance. Having attracted attacks varying from 'pseudo-science' to 'sorcery' to 'subversion', it is not surprising that internal uncertainty is almost as rampant as external dismissal.

Even if sociology can survive, and with an intact identity at that, will it be seen to be relevant? The grand theory of a Talcott Parsons and the statistical head-counting of the empiricists seemed massive irrelevancies to the radicals of the 1960s. They caustically complained that such high-flown concerns coincided with, but never grappled with the struggle for civil rights, worker alienation at many levels, industrial strife, and the birthpangs of newly independent territories. But why were the shouts of protest short-lived? Much American sociology never raised its eyes above empirical fact-grubbing. Many Europeans continue cosily to cocoon themselves in philosophical fantasy. The demand for relevance frequently fell on deaf ears, it seems.

To be realistic, then, this is the world of social science today: publicly beleaguered, fuzzy in focus, of doubtful relevance and lacking direction. That, at least, is the bad news. (Good news includes the emergence of some very fertile thinkers, whose work is discussed elsewhere, who are continuing the classical quest for a social analysis and theory related to the real world.) No different perspectives will make any headway in social science which fail to see the situation as it is.

Pressures and priorities

What then should we make of the principle of praxis and the call for relevance? Our era is one in which secularization has eroded the vocabulary with which we may speak of certain virtues and values. Capitalism has also reduced so much to 'commodity' level that it is difficult to conceive of 'value' which does not carry economic connotation. Hardly surprising then that Richard Fenn should remark on the lack of sense of direction and priority in sociology today: social science is a child of our age.

Two dangers are apparent in the assessment of priorities. One is that of traditionalism. Clinging to time-honoured beliefs and codes of conduct may well be an honourable stance. In the modern world it has become devastatingly obvious that not all that is new and up to date is good – think of the ecological disaster of the wasteful sixties. But tradition is not always a good guide. Traditional modes and manners may become counterproductive or irrelevant. They may also have unintended consequences which annul their value. But the other danger is 'bandwagonism'. Those addicted to this vice are quick to abandon old ways, seeing instant advantage and benefit in novelty. Now being aware of historical movement and social transformation is one thing. Cataclysmic conversion to voguish causes is another, be it urban renewal, anti-nuclear protest, save the otter, sport for all, abortion on demand, or Scottish or Québecois separatism.

Treading the knife-edge between these two extremes is not easy. I propose that the way to achieve it is via a conversation, involving the biblical drama on the one hand and existing social analysis on the other. The sociological imagination must in part emerge out of current analyses; critique and re-study is essential to the advancement of our social understanding. It must be informed by criteria, which in Christian terms are derived from the biblical drama. This yields insight on human identity and purpose, our frailty and our fallenness.

One staunch opponent of trendy fads is Bordeaux sociologist Jacques Ellul. Although some of what is said here is at odds with his viewpoint he does represent one important example of a credible attempt to allow Christian belief to shape his sociological research at the level of priorities (Temple 1980). He sees Christian faith as providing the place to stand which is lacking in a society dominated by technique. As he says 'Man in our society has no intellectual, moral, or spiritual reference point from which he could judge and make a critique of technique' (quoted in Temple 1980: 247). He believes that modernity means obsession with technique – it has been turned into a modern 'sacred' – and that we tend to make all our choices *within* the bounds of technique (means) rather than ends.

An illustration would be from the (increasingly significant) area of critical media studies. Ellul discusses modern media as a prime instance of direction by technique, that unrelenting quest for efficiency. From the days of early printing presses onward, the expansion of capacity and its organizational refinement, technique seems to have taken over. Today's multi-channel T.V. networks have simply become agents of propaganda, obeying the imperative of technique, blind to moral and critical reason. The media orchestrates establishment conformism in a subtle and sinister manner (Christians and Read 1979).

In this and other ways, Ellul pleads that people step back and view modern trends from a social and ethical vantage-point and not merely in a monochrome means-centred manner. Neither the establishment orthodoxies nor radical panaceas are acceptable to him. He argues that sociological priorities may only be derived from moral vision. The moral vision which he espouses is derived, in turn, from Christian commitment. (Ellul's position is influenced by Karl Barth, see Gill 1981.)

Sociological intervention: sleepers awake!

Despite Ellul's Weberian distinction between fact and value, he follows Weber in believing that sociology should be highly value-relevant. He insists that sociology should, in a sense, intervene in society. It is a call for sleepers to awake. By describing and analysing social situations with utmost clarity, Ellul believes we may resist the tide of totalitarianism, of being swamped by the state in the name of technical efficiency.

What a contrast with the desired sociological intervention of a Saint-Simon or an Auguste Comte! Far from visualizing sociology as a barricade against technical control, they predicted a time when it would be an instrument of social engineering. It would be superfluous to point out that some social science has become, in the modern era, a means of legitimating social control of one sort or another. It is unlikely, for example, that ideas of 'scientific management', or 'community policing' would have emerged without the assistance of a social scientific outlook.

Ellul's views not only differ from those of the social engineers, they also stand opposed to radical sociological interventionist ideas such as those of Frenchman Alain Touraine. From his studies of social movements – he is best known for his interpretations of the Paris student-worker revolts of May 1968 – he concludes that this is what sociology should be all about. Society *is* social movement, according to him; anything purported to be a 'structure' is very much a product of active people, shaping their own destinies.

In *The Voice and the Eye* social analysis is seen as a form of and aid to group self-consciousness in which people come to perceive more sharply their needs, aspirations and constraints. He maintains that it is high time social science exchanged its outworn nineteenth-century spectacles for a new way of seeing, which is simultaneously a way of speaking out:

> After so many years dominated by the modernizing optimism of the technocrats and by discussion of the laws of capitalism, the social movements which are making their new voices heard are calling for a new type of analysis, a sociology of action, and a new method of study – sociological intervention (Touraine 1981: 222).

So there is a veritable spectrum of positions which may be taken! From our earlier discussion it should be evident that I regard at least a strong Weberian sense of value-relevance to be vital for responsible social analysis. And if one is in accord with some version of post-empiricism, and sees the biblical link between knowledge and action in 'mission', this may be taken further (though maybe not as far as Touraine!).

For if it is the case that social science is not a neutral instrument, then it is in some ways already linked to practice in the real world. Recall the arguments that its very models, concepts and explanations are value-laden, and that there is a genuine potential social impact as people begin to recognize themselves in the (fuzzy) mirror of social science and act partly in response to what they see. If this is the case then sociology is already a form of social intervention. The question then arises, what kind of social intervention is involved? Of course this differs immensely with the kind of study being pursued. But recognizing the potential social impact of social science is the least a reflexive researcher ought to do.

Beyond that, it seems to me that a Christian approach would raise questions about the views of humanness embedded in theory, and the relationship of some aspect of Christian conceptions of the social good to the situation in question. Critical theorists often focus on the *felt* needs and desires of populations under study (Fay 1975). While no one wishes to foist some social-political doctrine on unwilling subjects, it is doubtful whether social analysts could leave *all* their normative baggage behind when doing research. The point is to be aware of such baggage and to evaluate it in a Christian manner.

An example might be taken from so-called 'consciousness-raising', an idea popularized especially in Latin America by Paulo Freire (Freire 1972). Social theory has an educative function in alerting people (in his case peasants and the urban poor) to their condition of oppression so that they can take steps to throw off their yoke. While the emancipatory dimension to this may be laudable in certain respects, a Christian understanding of emancipation has ethical limits. It is all too easy to engender unnecessary discontent through consciousness-raising. It impugns the principle of contentment. Even child-sponsorship schemes, in which westerners 'aid' a third world child, tend to fuel aspirations which can never be met. How much more, then, might a socially educating policy directed at whole groups and collectivities have this potential effect? Christian realism demands the building in to theory (and practice!) of some ethically-informed ideas of 'need' (Taylor 1975). Biblically, the artificial creation of 'needs' (by socialist consciousness-raisers as much as by capitalist advertising) is as deplorable as political tyranny.

If Christians do have emancipatory concerns in social science they are not necessarily the same as those of other liberationists. The emancipation for which Christians strive is the freedom to live as God intended. True humanness may be realized only *in certain ways.* Understanding of these ways begins and continues with a reversal of our 'unnatural' thinking, distorted by the fall. It begins with a self-sacrificial death through which new life is obtained. This stresses our utter God-dependence as humans.

In our endeavours to open up the social world to God's ways there is another reversal. Rather than calling upon the oppressed and exploited to unite and promote their self-liberation, the biblical emphasis is rather on the need for the oppressors to change. Male mistreatment of women, the rich and powerful who crush the poor, the majority population who oppress the alien minority – the Bible condemns all these without arousing discontent among the victims.

This is not the place to develop these ideas. But they must be mentioned, because once the idea is accepted that social science means social critique (and intervention), some understanding of social ethics and political practice becomes essential. Once again the point about images of humanness comes into its own. For the political questions of justice and welfare also hinge in part on views of humanness. As Graham Room demonstrates in *The Sociology of Welfare*, the liberal philosophical anthropology of humans as individual self-interested atoms is at variance with Marxist views of 'man as historical and social, creating himself and his world through cooperation with his fellows in the productive process' (Room 1979: 109). The third, social democratic option, still sees the human as a social being, but sociality is not in this case 'narrowly rooted in the production system' as in Marxism. Particular sociological models and specific political philosophies and practices have in common a relation with images of humanness. There thus exists a requirement for all to be sure that their political practice as well as their sociological theory accords with their view of humanness. A growing number of books on the market should aid Christians in their search for consistency in practically bringing together sociological with social involvement in the real world of today (e.g. Sider 1975, Goudzwaard 1979, Sugden 1981, Mouw 1976, Joslin 1982).

Agenda for social analysis

It would be presumptuous for me to suggest some universal agenda for Christianly directed social analysis. I entertain no such ambitions. Nonetheless, this book would be lacking (at least in this respect) if some tentative suggestions were not made. Naturally the agendas will differ depending on social and political context, the intended level of research and the interests of the individual. As I have attempted to write this book in a Christian manner, however, two further points may be made.

The first, I hope, has been sufficiently presented by now: the requirement to operate out of a Christian world view. This carries with it, I have argued, a balance derived from the biblical drama (which makes it natural that Christians frequently seek third ways between differing images of humanness and social theories and models). The second point is that forming agendas for analysis is best done within a community of like-minded persons. I am indebted to two or three groups in which I participate for the shared burden of scholarship and social responsibility.[1] Such fellowships are an extremely valuable aspect of Christian discipleship today, without which Christian social involvement in analysis and action would be the poorer.

I hope that this book serves to stimulate Christian reflection on appropriate agendas. Renewed interest in the family, for example, invites critical thinking which is in tune with the social realities of the late twentieth century. And although we would not place the productive process at the pivot of our analyses, the work world also cries out for Christian contribution, especially in view of unemployment, underemployment and the impact of micro-electronics. Poverty and dependence, with their allied policy-analysis, represent other areas of urgent significance in which a Christian voice could be articulated.

Although I have endeavoured to highlight the potential for applying a Christian approach to the whole field of sociological study, and have therefore not focused heavily on the sociology of religion, the latter is nevertheless a crucially important area. Religion goes through phases of popularity and neglect in sociology. Central to classical sociology, virtually ignored by the mainstream in the 1960s, religion now seems to be staging a comeback as a sociological topic.

[1]In Britain I belong to the London-based Ilkley Group of Christians in sociology. Information from Mill Grove, Crescent Road, South Woodford, London E18. In the USA the Christian Sociological Society has broad aims, though some of its members are devoted to developing a Christian perspective. Information from George Hillery, Virginia Polytechnic Institute and State University, Blacksburg, VA24061. A much smaller group is Sociology Teachers in Christian Colleges, but it is more committed to Christian perspective development. Information from Harriet Parsons, Grove City College, Grove City, PA 16127.

Understanding the place, shaping, role, impact and trends of churches, religion and the sacred today is vital not only for Christian believers but for general socio-cultural understanding. Jonestown, Solidarity, the New Right, Latin American liberation movements, popular music, the American Constitution, legitimation crises – none of these phenomena are properly comprehended without reference to social analysis of religion and the sacred. A concept like secularization, with its corollary, sacralization, helps us to grasp the huge transformations that churches and their public acceptance have undergone in the past two hundred years, and the surrogates for faith which have emerged.

Canadian Harold Fallding makes some further suggestions for agenda-items. One important area is analysing the influence of good and evil in social life. Although he too (like Ellul) prefers to distinguish between facts and values ('characterizing and appraising value-judgments' to be exact) he says that ' "good" and "evil" influences have their objective character in their socially and personally damaging effects, and they are to be defined (and therefore also identified) by that' (Fallding 1982: 21). Not only may the power of evil be documented in oppression, greed, waste and so on, but also its reversal through individual and group resistance. Such a 'sociology of unpopularity' may not go down too well in the sceptical halls of Academe, but as Fallding points out, this may be precisely because it points to the 'way of the cross'. But those who discern the significance of a prophet-stoning or a crucifixion in causes of truth, justice and forgiveness may wish to direct attention to contemporary manifestations of actions which promote them. Fallding's conclusion, however much it contrasts with other views, is palpably Christian: 'when service is given through initiative and responsibility . . . no room is left for the tyrant.'

In this and other ways, Christians will want to march – or dance – to a different drummer. At many points a Christian perspective in sociology has congruence and analogue in the theories and concepts of others. But occasion will also demand alternatives and a radically different stance. This applies especially in relation to the biblical drama. Christian commitment is uncompromising when it comes to human creaturehood, the dislocation and contradiction which stem from the alienation of Creator from creature, the possibility of renewal

207

and restoration and the future hope of a better day. 'Rather than leaving aside problems of what the "good society" might look like,' writes Giddens, 'it is today more necessary than ever to confront them directly.' As he adds, there is no need for such thought to 'relapse into utopianism if it is related to analyses of the "actually existing" . . . societies' (Giddens 1981: 248). But at this point also Christian views sit uneasily with others. The 'good society' of critical theorists (and others) frequently depends upon some idealizations of reason, or on the realization of material benefit. While a Christian view is inauthentic which has no concern for material life, it is equally false if this world is its only horizon. Christians in sociology above all others should care that bread be available for all: this is the Father's will. But Christians in sociology are also acutely aware, and their social analysis should reflect this, that humans made in his image do not live by bread alone.

BIBLIOGRAPHY

Abrams, Philip (1968) *The origins of British sociology* (Chicago: University of Chicago Press).
  (1978) (*et al.* eds.) *Work, urbanism and inequality* (London: Weidenfeld and Nicolson).
  (1981) (*et al.* eds.) *Practice and progress: British sociology 1950–1980* (London: Allen and Unwin).
Althusser, Louis and Balibar, Etienne (1968) *Reading Capital* (New York: Shocken Books; London: New Left Books).
Balswick, Jack (1980) 'Changing male-female roles in Christian perspective' in De Santo (1980).
Banks, Olive (1981) *Faces of Feminism* (Oxford: Martin Robertson).
Barker, Eileen (1980) 'The limits of displacement' in Martin (1980).
Barrs, Jerram and Macaulay, Ranald (1978) *Christianity with a human face* (Leicester: Inter-Varsity Press; U.S.A. *Being human*, Downers Grove: Inter-Varsity Press).
Baum, Gregory (1975) *Religion and alienation: a theological reading of sociology* (New York: Paulist Press).
Bebbington, David (1979) *Patterns in history* (Leicester and Downers Grove: Inter-Varsity Press).
  (1982) *The nonconformist conscience: chapel and politics 1870–1914* (London and Boston: Allen and Unwin).
Bell, Daniel (1982) *The social sciences since the second world war* (New Brunswick and London: Transaction Books).
Bellah, Robert (1970) *Beyond belief* (New York: Harper and Row).

Bibliography

Bernard, Jessie (1975) *Women, wives, and mothers* (Chicago: Aldine).

Berger, Peter (1963) *Invitation to sociology: a humanistic perspective* (Harmondsworth: Penguin; New York: Anchor-Doubleday).

(1967) *The social reality of religion* (Harmondsworth: Penguin; U.S.A. *The sacred canopy*, New York: Anchor-Doubleday).

(1970) *A rumour of angels* (Harmondsworth: Penguin; New York: Anchor-Doubleday).

Berger, Peter and Kellner, Hansfried (1981) *Sociology reinterpreted: an essay in method and vocation* (Harmondsworth: Penguin; New York: Anchor-Doubleday).

Bernstein, Richard (1976) *The restructuring of social and political theory* (Philadelphia: University of Pennsylvania Press).

Berry, David (1974) *Central ideas in sociology* (London: Constable; New York: Peacock).

Blamires, Harry (1963) *The Christian mind* (London: S.P.C.K.; Ann Arbor: Servant Publications).

Bocock, Robert (1980) (*et al.* eds.) *Introduction to sociology* (London: Fontana).

Bottomore, T. B. and Rubel, Maximilien (1963) *Karl Marx: selected writings in sociology and social philosophy* (Harmondsworth: Penguin).

Bottomore, Tom and Nisbet, Robert (1978) (eds.) *A history of sociological analysis* (London: Heinemann; New York: Basic Books).

Bottomore, Tom (1975) *Marxist sociology* (London: MacMillan).

(1978) 'Marxism and sociology' in Bottomore and Nisbet (1978).

(1981) *Modern interpretations of Marx* (Oxford: Blackwell).

(1982) (*et al.* eds.) *Sociology: the state of the art* (London and Beverley Hills: Sage Publications).

(1983) 'Sociology' in McLellan (1983).

Brown, Colin (1969) *Philosophy and the Christian Faith* (Leicester and Downers Grove: Inter-Varsity Press).

Burawoy, Michael (1978) 'Contemporary currents in Marxist theory' *The American Sociologist* 13, pp. 50–64.

Burkitt, Brian and Rose, Hilary (1981) 'Why be a wife?' *Sociological Review* 29, 1, pp. 67–76.

Burrow, John (1966) *Evolution and society* (London and New York: Cambridge University Press).

Campbell, Tom (1981) *Seven theories of human society* (Oxford and New York: Oxford University Press).

Cavanaugh, Michael (1982) 'Pagan and Christian: sociological euhemerism versus American sociology of religion' *Sociological Analysis* 43, 2, pp. 109–129.

Christians, Clifford and Read, Michael R. (1979) 'Jacques Ellul's contribution to critical media theory' *Journal of Communications* Winter, pp. 83–93.

Clark, Stephen B. (1981) *Man and woman in Christ* (Ann Arbor: Servant Publications).

Clements, Kevin (1971) 'The religious variable: dependent, independent or interdependent?' in Hill (1971).

Cohn, Norman (1965) *The pursuit of the millennium* (London: Paladin).

Cook, David (1978) *Are women people too?* (Nottingham: Grove Books).

Coser, Lewis (1977) *Masters of sociological thought* (New York: Holt, Rinehart and Winston).

Cuzzort, R. P. (1969) *Humanity and modern social thought* (Hinsdale: Dryden Press).

Dahrendorf, Ralf (1968) *Essays in the theory of society* (Stanford: University of California Press).

Daines, Brian (1975) 'Functionalism and the organismic model' Ilkley Group occasional papers, *Christian commitment and the study of sociology.*

Davis, Howard, Lyon, David and Walter, Tony (1980) 'A pocket guide to sociology' *Third Way* June, pp. 11–13 (expanded version as *Introduction to Sociology and Christianity,* an annotated bibliography published by U.C.C.F.A., 38 De Montfort Street, Leicester, England).
(1982) 'Current trends in the sociology of marriage and family' Ilkley Group paper (available from Mill Grove, Crescent Road, London, E.18)

Davis, Kingsley (1948) *Human Society* (New York: Macmillan).

Dawe, Alan (1978) 'Theories of social action' in Bottomore and Nisbet (1978).

Dayton, Donald (1976) *Discovering an evangelical heritage* (New York: Harper and Row).

De Coppens, Peter Roche (1976) *Ideal man in classical sociology* (Philadelphia: Pennsylvania State University Press).

Dekker, Gerrard (1978) 'Cooperation between sociologists and theologians' Paper read at Oxford symposium on sociology and theology.

De Santo, Charles (1980) (*et al.* eds.) *A reader in sociology: Christian perspectives* (Scottsdale: Herald).

Dickens, A. G. (1964) *The English reformation* (London: Batsford).

Dooyeweerd, Hermann (1953 – 1958) *A new critique of theoretical thought*, 4 vols. (Philadelphia: Presbyterian and Reformed).

Durkheim, Emile (1933) *The division of labour in society* (New York: The Free Press; London: Collier-Macmillan).

(1950) *The rules of the sociological method* (New York: The Free Press).

(1952) *Suicide: a study in sociology* (New York: The Free Press).

Eldridge, John (1983) *C. Wright Mills* (London and New York: Ellis Horwood and Tavistock Publications).

Emmet, Dorothy and MacIntyre, Alasdair (1970) *Sociological theory and philosophical analysis* (London: Macmillan).

Evans, C. Stephen (1977) *Preserving the person: a look at the human sciences* (Downers Grove and Leicester: Inter-Varsity Press).

Fallding, Harold (1982) 'How Christian can sociology be?' Paper presented at Xth world congress of the International Sociological Association, Mexico City.

Fay, Brian (1975) *Social theory and political practice* (London and Boston: Allen and Unwin).

Fenn, Richard (1982) 'The sociology of religion' in Tom Bottomore (1982).

Firestone, Shulamith (1970) *The dialectics of sex* (New York: Morrow; London: Cape).

Foh, Susan (1979) *Women and the Word of God* (Grand Rapids: Baker Book House).

Freire, Paulo (1972) *Pedagogy of the oppressed* (London: Sheed and Ward; New York: Continuum).

Friedrichs, Robert (1970) *A sociology of sociology* (New York: The Free Press; London: Collier–Macmillan).

Geras, Norman (1983) *Marx and human nature* (London: Verso).

Gerth, Hans and Mills, C. Wright (1958) *From Max Weber* (New York: Oxford University Press; London: Routledge and Kegan Paul).

Giddens, Anthony (1971) *Capitalism and modern social theory*

(London and New York: Cambridge University Press).

(1976) *New rules of sociological method* (New York: Basic Books; London: Hutchinson).

(1977) *Studies in social and political theory* (London: Hutchinson; New York: Basic Books).

(1979) *Central problems in social theory* (London: Macmillan; Berkeley: University of California Press).

(1981) *A contemporary critique of historical materialism* (London: Macmillan; Berkeley: University of California Press).

Gill, David W. (1981) 'Jacques Ellul: the prophet as theologian' *Themelios* 7, 1.

Glasgow Media Group (1976) *Bad news* (London and Boston: Routledge and Kegan Paul).

Goodwin, Barbara (1978) *Social science and utopia* (Brighton: Harvester).

Goudzwaard, Bob (1979) *Capitalism and progress: a diagnosis of western society* (Grand Rapids: Eerdmans).

Gouldner, Alvin (1980) *The two marxisms* (New York: Seabury Press; London: Macmillan).

(1970) *The coming crisis of Western sociology* (London: Heinemann; New York: Basic Books).

Graham, Fred (1975) *John Calvin: constructive revolutionary* (Grand Rapids: Eerdmans).

Gramsci, Antonio (1971) (ed. Quintin Hoare and Geoffrey Norwell Smith) *Selections from the prison notebooks* (London: Lawrence and Wishart).

Grunlan, Stephen and Reimer, Milton (1982) (eds.) *Christian perspective on sociology* (Grand Rapids: Zondervan).

Habermas, Jürgen (1971) *Knowledge and human interests* (Boston: Beacon Press; London: Heinemann).

Hamilton, Roberta (1978) *The Liberation of women* (London and Boston: Allen and Unwin).

Haralambos, Michael (1980) *Sociology: themes and perspectives* (Slough: University Tutorial Press).

Harrington, Michael (1962) *The other America* (Harmondsworth: Penguin; New York: Macmillan).

Harris, C. C. (1980) *Fundamental concepts and the sociological enterprise* (London: Croom–Helm; U.S.A. *The sociological enterprise*, New York: St. Martin's Press).

Harvey, Lee (1982) 'Use and abuse of Kuhnian paradigms in the sociology of knowledge' *Sociology* 16, 1, pp. 85–101.

Hawthorn, Geoffrey (1976) *Enlightenment and despair: a*

history of sociology (London and New York: Cambridge University Press).

Heddendorf, Russell (1972) 'Some presuppositions of a Christian sociology' *Journal of the American Scientific Affiliation* September, pp. 110–117.

Hesse, Mary (1978) 'Theory and value in the social sciences' in Hookway and Petitt (1978), reprinted in Mary Hesse (1980) *Revolutions and Reconstructions in the Philosophy of Science* (Notre Dame: Notre Dame University Press).

Hill, Michael (1971) (ed.) *A sociological yearbook of religion in England* (London: S.C.M. Press).

Hobsbawm, Eric (1983) 'Karl Marx: 100 not out' *Marxism Today* March, 27, 3.

Holman, Robert (1978) *Poverty: Explanations of social deprivation* (London: Martin Robertson).

Holmes, Arthur (1979) *All truth is God's truth* (Leicester and Downers Grove: Inter-Varsity Press).

Hookway, Christopher and Petitt, Philip (1978) (eds.) *Interpretation and Human Action* (London and New York: Cambridge University Press).

Hudson, Donald (1980) 'The rational system of belief' in Martin (1980).

Hunt, Gladys (1972) *Ms means myself* (Grand Rapids: Zondervan).

Hurley, James (1981) *Man and woman in biblical perspective* (Leicester: Inter-Varsity Press; Grands Rapids: Zondervan).

Illich, Ivan (1975) *Medical nemesis: the expropriation of health* (London: Calder and Boyars).

Isbister, J. N. (1978) 'The basis of human nature: a critical analysis of the new science of sociobiology' *Third Way* 2, 4, pp. 3–6.

Jewett, Paul K. (1975) *Man as male and female* (Grand Rapids: Eerdmans).

Johnson, Benton (1977) 'Sociological theory and religious truth' *Sociological Analysis* 38:4, pp. 268–288.

Joll, James (1977) *Gramsci* (London: Fontana; New York: Penguin).

Joslin, Roy (1982) *Urban harvest* (Welwyn: Evangelical Press).

Kingdon, David (1980) 'Some questions about structural sin' *Christian Graduate* 33, 2, pp. 10–13.

Kirk, J. Andrew (1979) *Liberation theology: an evangelical perspective from the third world* (London: Marshall, Morgan and Scott; Atlanta: John Knox Press).

Kitzinger, Sheila (1978) *Women as mothers* (London: Fontana).

Kolb, William (1961) 'Images of man and the sociology of religion' *Journal for the scientific study of religion* 1, 1, pp. 6–22.

Kuhn, Thomas (1962) *The structure of scientific revolutions* (Chicago and London: University of Chicago Press).

Kumar, Krishan (1978) *Prophecy and progress: the sociology of industrial and postindustrial society* (Harmondsworth: Penguin).

Lakatos, Imre and Musgrave, Alan (1970) *Criticism and the growth of knowledge* (London and New York: Cambridge University Press).

Lemert, Charles (1978) *Sociology and the twilight of man* (Carbondale: University of Southern Illinois Press).

Lewis, C. S. (1945) *That hideous strength* (London: Bodley Head; New York: Collier-Macmillan).

(1970) *Undeceptions* (London: Bles; U.S.A. *God in the dock*, Grand Rapids: Eerdmans).

Lewis, Oscar (1949) *Life in a Mexican Village* (Urbana: University of Illinois Press).

Lloyd, Peter (1982) *A third world proletariat?* (London and Boston: Allen and Unwin).

Louch, A. R. (1966) *Explanation and human action* (Oxford: Blackwell; Stanford: University of California Press).

Lukes, Steven (1970) 'Methodological individualism reconsidered' in Emmet and MacIntyre (1970).

(1973) *Emile Durkheim: His life and thought* (Harmondsworth: Penguin Books; New York: Harper and Row).

(1977) *Essays in social theory* (London: Macmillan; New York: Columbia University Press).

(1982) 'Of gods and demons: Habermas and practical reason' in Thompson and Held (1982).

Lyman, Stanford (1978) *The seven deadly sins* (New York: St Martin's Press).

Lyon, David (1975) *Christians and sociology* (London and Downers Grove: Inter-Varsity Press).

(1979) *Karl Marx: an assessment of his life and thought* (Tring: Lion Publishing and Leicester and Downers Grove: Inter-Varsity Press)

(1980) 'Utopia and social change' in De Santo (*et al.* eds.) 1980.

(1981a) 'Christianity and Marxism: the aftermath of dialogue' *Faith and Thought* 108, 1/2, pp. 28–38.

(1981b) 'The challenge of Marxism' in Wright (1981).

(1983a) 'The idea of a Christian sociology: some historical precedents and current concerns' *Sociological Analysis* 44, 3.

(1983b) 'Valuing in social theory: postempiricism and Christian responses' *Christian Scholars' Review* XII, 4.

(forthcoming) *Future society* (Tring: Lion Publishing).

MacIntire, C. T. (1974) *The ongoing task of Christian historiography* (Toronto: Wedge).

MacKay, Donald (1974) *The clockwork image* (Leicester and Downers Grove: Inter-Varsity Press).

Mannheim, Karl (1943) *Diagnosis of our time* (London and Boston: Routledge and Kegan Paul).

Marsden, George and Roberts, Frank (1975) (eds.) *A Christian view of history?* (Grand Rapids: Eerdmans).

Martin, David (1978) *A general theory of secularization* (Oxford: Basil Blackwell; New York: Harper and Row).

(1978a) *The dilemmas of contemporary religion* (Oxford: Basil Blackwell).

(1980) (*et al.* eds.) *Sociology and theology: alliance and conflict* (Brighton: Harvester Press; New York: St Martin's Press).

Marx, Karl (1848) *The communist manifesto* in McLellan (1977).

(1973) *Grundrisse* (Harmondsworth and Baltimore: Penguin).

Masterman, Margaret (1970) 'The nature of a paradigm' in Lakatos and Musgrave (1970).

Matheson, Scott (1893) *The church and social problems* (Edinburgh: Oliphant, Anderson and Ferrier).

Mayes, Sharon (1981) 'The political economy of women's liberation' in McNall (1981).

McLellan, David (1977) (ed.) *Karl Marx: selected writings* (London and New York: Oxford University Press).

(1979) *Marxism after Marx* (London: Macmillan; New York: Harper and Row).

(1983) (ed.) *Marx: the first 100 years* (London: Fontana).

McNall, Scott (1979) (ed.) *Theoretical perspectives in sociology* (New York: St Martin's Press).

(1981) (ed.) *Political economy: a critique of American society* (Glenview: Scott, Foresman and Company).

Menzies, Ken (1977) *Talcott Parsons and the social image of man* (London and Boston: Routledge and Kegan Paul).

Miguéz Bonino, José (1976) *Christians and Marxists: the mutual challenge to revolution* (London: Hodder and Stoughton; Grand Rapids: Eerdmans).

Mills, C. Wright (1959) *The sociological imagination* (Harmondsworth: Penguin; New York: Oxford University Press).

Moberg, David (1962) *The church as a social institution* (Englewood Cliffs: Prentice–Hall).

(1967) 'Science and the spiritual nature of man' *Journal of the American Scientific Affiliation* 19, pp. 12–17.

(1978) 'Presidential address: virtues for the sociology of religion' *Sociological Analysis* 39, pp. 1–18.

Morgan, J. Graham (1969) 'The development of sociology and the social gospel in America' *Sociological Analysis* 30, 1, pp. 42–53.

Mouw, Richard (1976) *Politics and the biblical drama* (Grand Rapids: Eerdmans).

(1981) 'Explaining social reality' *Themelios* 6, 2, pp. 7–12.

Oakley, Ann (1974) *The sociology of housework* (London: Martin Robertson).

(1982) *Subject Women* (London: Fontana).

O'Neill, John (1972) *Sociology as a skin trade* (London: Heinemann).

Outhwaite, William (1975) *Understanding social life: the method called verstehen* (London and Boston: Allen and Unwin).

Packer, James (1980) *For Man's sake* (Exeter: Paternoster Press; U.S.A. *Knowing Man*, Westchester: Cornerstone).

Parkin, Frank (1979) *Marxism and class theory: a bourgeois critique* (London: Tavistock; New York: Methuen).

Parsons, Talcott and Shils, Edward (1951) *Towards a general theory of action* (Cambridge: Harvard University Press).

(1961) 'Comment', *Journal for the scientific study of Religion* 1, 1, pp. 22–29.

Petrović, Gajo (1967) *Marx in the mid-twentieth century* (New York: Doubleday).

Poloma, Margaret (1979) *Contemporary sociological theory* (New York: Macmillan; London: Collier-Macmillan).

(1982) 'Toward a Christian sociological perspective: religious values, theory, and methodology' *Sociological Analysis* 43, 2, pp. 95–108.

Popper, Karl (1966) *The open society and its enemies* (London and Boston: Routledge and Kegan Paul).

Poster, Mark (1978) *Critical theory of the family* (New York: Seabury Press; London: Pluto Press).

Bibliography

Powell Bell, Inge (1979) 'Buddhist sociology: some thoughts on the convergence of sociology and Eastern paths of liberation' in McNall (1979).

Redfield, Robert (1947) 'The folk society' *American Journal of Sociology* 52, 3, pp. 293–308.

Rex, John and Tomlinson, Sally (1980) *Race, Colonialism and the city: a class analysis* (London and Boston: Routledge and Kegan Paul).

Rex, John (1981) *Social conflict* (London and New York: Longman).

Rigby, Andrew (1974) *Alternative realities* (London and Boston: Routledge and Kegan Paul).

Ritzer, George (1975) 'Sociology: a multiple paradigm science' *The American Sociologist* 10, pp. 156–167.

Roberts, Helen (1981) *Doing feminist research* (London and Boston: Routledge and Kegan Paul).

Robertson, Roland (1968) *The sociological interpretation of religion* (Harmondsworth: Penguin; New York: Shocken Books).

(1978) *Meaning and change* (Oxford: Basil Blackwell; New York: St Martin's Press).

Room, Graham (1979) *The sociology of welfare* (Oxford: Basil Blackwell and Martin Robertson).

Ross, Edward (1907) *Sin and society* (Boston: Houghton-Mifflin).

Runciman, Gary (1966) *Relative deprivation and social justice* (Harmondsworth: Penguin).

Sayers, Dorothy (1971) *Are women human?* (Downers Grove: Inter-Varsity Press).

Scanzoni, Letha and Hardesty, Nancy (1974) *All we're meant to be* (Waco: Word).

Schrag, Calvin O. (1980) *Radical reflection: the origins of the human sciences* (Philadelphia: University of Pennsylvania Press).

Sennett, Richard (1978) *The fall of public man: on the social psychology of capitalism* (New York: Vintage Books).

Shari'ati, Ali (1979) *On the sociology of Islam* (Berkeley: Mizan Press).

Sheppard, David (1974) *Built as a city* (London: Hodder and Stoughton).

Sider, Ronald (1975) *Rich Christians in an age of hunger* (Downers Grove: Inter-Varsity Press; London: Hodder and Stoughton).

Sire, James (1976) *The universe next door: a basic worldview catalog* (Downers Grove and Leicester: Inter-Varsity Press).

Sklair, Leslie (1981) 'Sociologies and marxisms: odd couples' in Abrams (1981).

Smart, Barry (1982) 'Foucault, sociology, and the problems of human agency' *Theory and Society* 11, 2, pp. 121–141.

Smart, Ninian (1973) *The science of religion and the sociology of knowledge* (Princeton: Princeton University Press).

Stacey, Margaret (1981) 'The division of labour revisited, or overcoming the two Adams' in Abrams (1981).

Storkey, Alan (1979) *A Christian social perspective* (Leicester: Inter-Varsity Press).

Sugden, Christopher (1981) *Radical Discipleship* (London: Marshall, Morgan and Scott).

Taylor, John V. (1975) *Enough is enough* (London: S.C.M. Press).

Temple, Katharine (1980) 'The sociology of Jacques Ellul' *Research in Philosophy and Technology* 3, pp. 223–261.

Temple, William (1938) (*et al.*) *Men without work* (London: Pilgrim Trust).

Therborn, Göran (1976) *Science, class, and society* (London: New Left Books).

Thomas, David (1979) *Naturalism and social science* (London and New York: Cambridge University Press).

Thomas, W. I. (1923) *The unadjusted girl* (Boston: Little, Brown and Co.)

Thompson, John B. and Held, David (1982) (eds.) *Habermas: Critical Debates* (London: Macmillan).

Tiryakin, Edward (1978) 'Emile Durkheim' in Bottomore and Nisbet (1978).

Touraine, Alain (1981) *The voice and the eye: an analysis of social movements* (London and New York: Cambridge University Press; Paris: Editions de la maison des sciences de l'homme).

Towler, Robert (1974) *Homo religiosus: sociological problems in the study of religion* (London: Constable).

Troeltsch, Ernst (1931) *The social teaching of the Christian churches*, 2 vols. (New York: Macmillan).

Trotsky, Leon (1970) *Women and the family* (New York: Pathfinder Press).

Tudor, Andrew (1982) *Beyond Empiricism* (London and Boston: Routledge and Kegan Paul).

Twaddle, Andrew (1982) 'From medical sociology to the sociology of health' in Bottomore (1982).

Bibliography

Van Dyke, Harry (1981) 'The nature of history and the history teacher's task' *Anakainosis* 3, 4, pp. 2–6.

Van Leeuwen, Mary Stewart (1978) 'A cross-cultural examination of psychological differentiation in males and females' *International Journal of Psychology* 3, 2.

(1982) *The sorcerer's apprentice: a Christian looks at the changing face of psychology* (Downers Grove: Inter-Varsity Press).

Wainwright, Hilary (1978) 'Women and the division of labour' in Abrams (1978).

Walter, J. A. (1979) 'Bad kids and bad homes' *Faith and Thought* 106, 2/3, pp. 169–177.

(1980) *A long way from home* (Exeter: Paternoster Press; U.S.A. *Sacred cows*, Grand Rapids: Zondervan).

Weber, Max (1950) *The methodology of the social sciences* (New York: The Free Press).

(1958) 'Science as a vocation' in Gerth and Mills (1958).

(1958) *The Protestant ethic and the spirit of capitalism* (New York: Scribners).

(1968) *Economy and society* (New York: Bedminster Press).

Wellman, David (1977) *Portraits of white racism* (London and New York: Cambridge University Press).

Westergaard, John and Resler, Henrietta (1976) *Class in a capitalist society* (Harmondsworth: Penguin).

Wickham, E. R. (1957) *Church and people in an industrial city* (London: Lutterworth).

Wilson, Bryan (1982) *Religion in sociological perspective* (London and New York: Oxford University Press).

Wilson, E. O. (1975) *Sociobiology: the new synthesis* (Cambridge: Harvard University Press).

Wilson, Elizabeth (1977) *Women and the welfare state* (London: Tavistock Publications).

Wolfe, David (1982) *Epistemology: the justification of belief* (Downers Grove and Leicester: Inter-Varsity Press).

Wolff, Kurt (1960) *Essays in sociology and philosophy* (New York: Harper and Row).

Wolterstorff, Nicholas (1976) *Reason within the bounds of religion* (Grand Rapids: Eerdmans).

Wright, David (1981) (ed.) *Essays in evangelical social ethics* (Exeter: Paternoster).

Wrong, Dennis (1961) 'The oversocialized concept of man in modern sociology' *American Sociological Review* 26, 2, pp. 183–193.

Young, Gary (1976) 'The fundamental contradiction in capitalist production' *Philosophy and Public Affairs* 5, pp. 196–234.

INDEX

261
L991

74077

LINCOLN CHRISTIAN COLLEGE AND SEMINARY

Index

3 4711 00178 5866